# Between Clouds of Memory

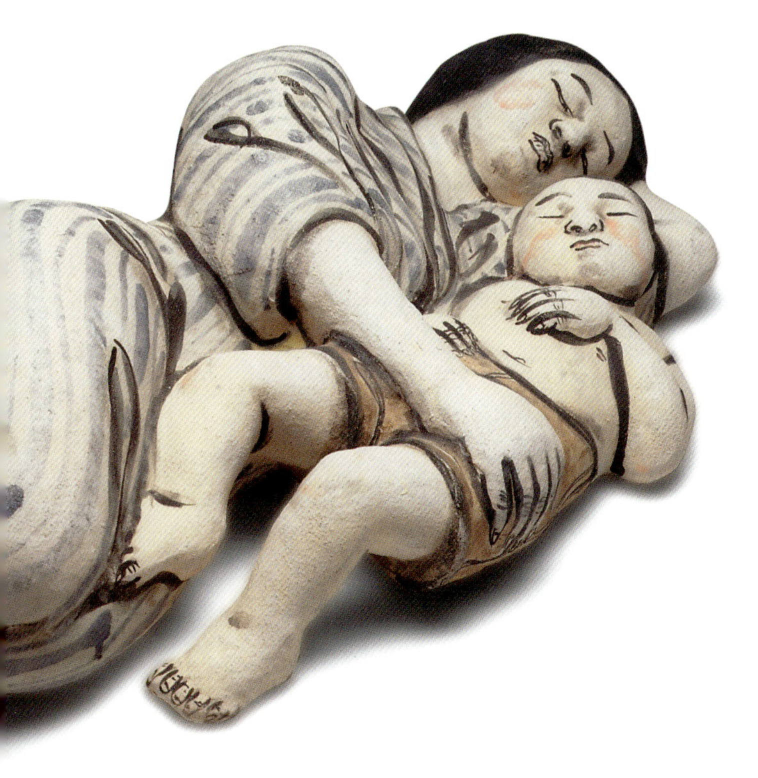

To: Janet & Lorraine
Akio
Dec. 1st 2007

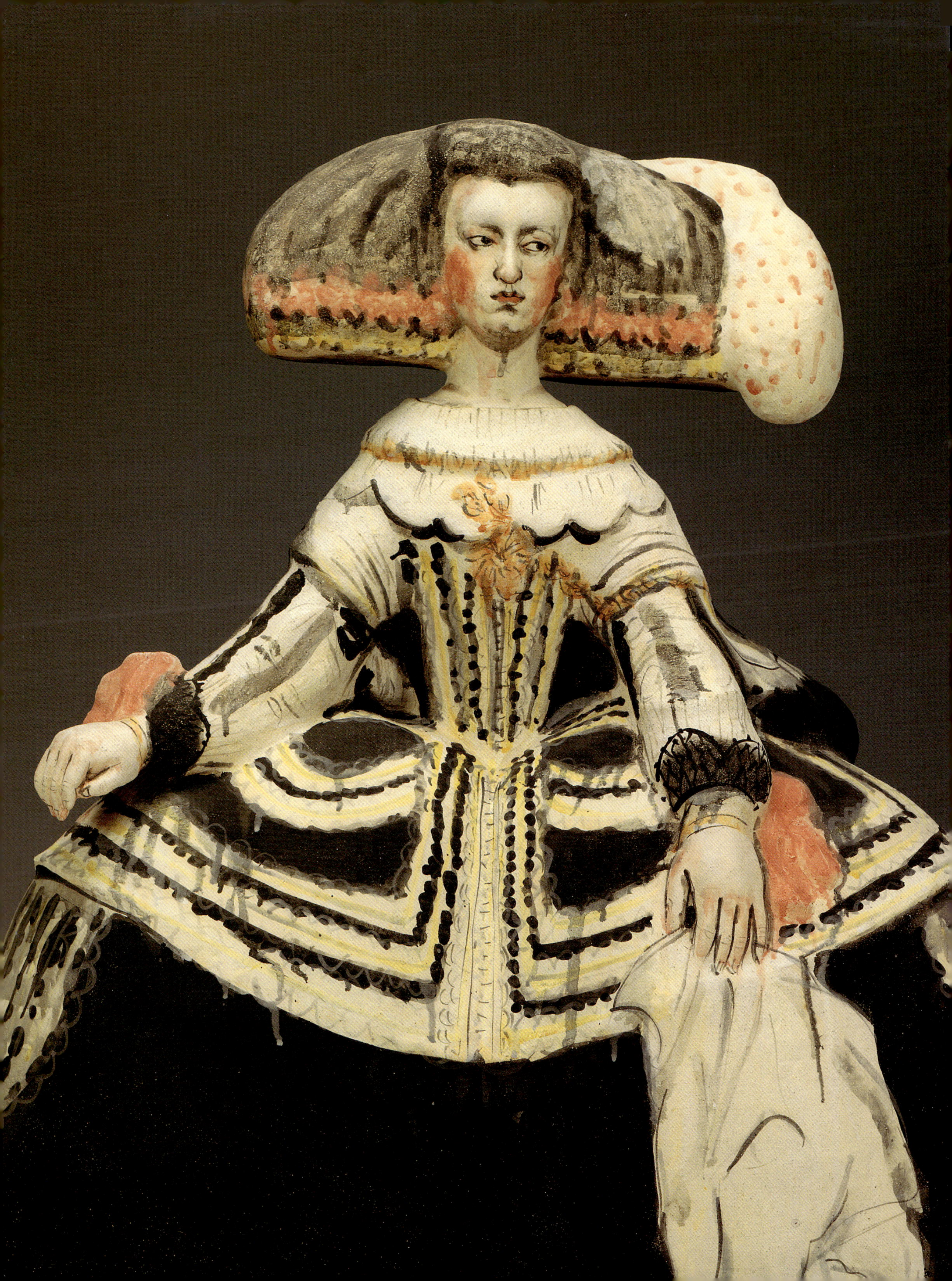

# Between Clouds of Memory

## AKIO TAKAMORI, A MID-CAREER SURVEY

Edited by Peter Held
Essays by Garth Clark, Peter Held, Toyojiro Hida, Edward Lebow

Arizona State University Art Museum
Ceramics Research Center
Tempe

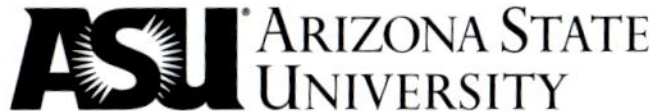


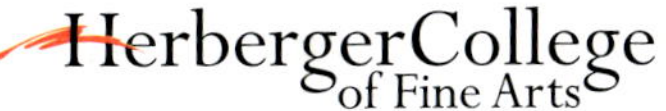

This book is dedicated to the memory of:
Ken Ferguson (1928–2004)
David Shaner (1934–2002)
Peter Voulkos (1924–2002)

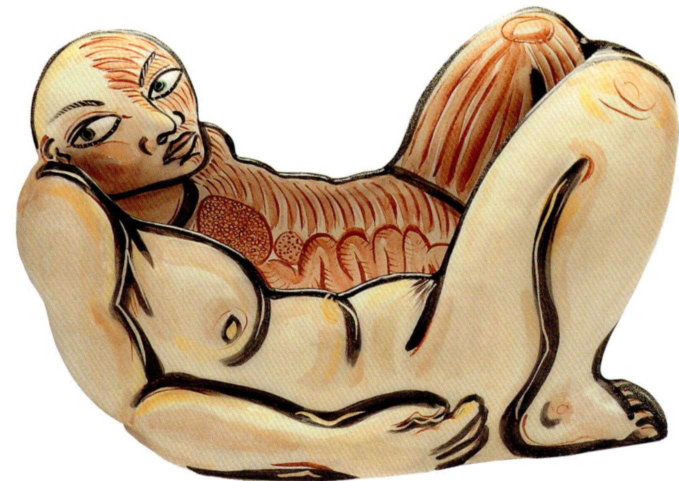

This catalogue was published in conjunction with an exhibition at the Arizona State University Art Museum.

Arizona State University Art Museum
Herberger College of Fine Arts
Tenth Street and Mill Avenue
Tempe, Arizona 85287-2911
tel. 480.965.2787 fax 480.965.5254
http://asuartmuseum.asu.edu

TOURING ITINERARY
Arizona State University Art Museum
Tempe, Arizona
September 9, 2005–January 14, 2006

Marylhurst University, The Art Gym
Portland, Oregon
March 7–May 3, 2006

Tacoma Art Museum
Tacoma, Washington
June 10–October 2, 2006

Racine Art Museum
Racine, Wisconsin
October 29, 2006–March 18, 2007

Catalogue produced by
Arizona State University Art Museum


Distributed by
University of Washington Press
PO Box 50096
Seattle, Washington 98145-5096
www.washington.edu/uwpress

Library of Congress
Cataloging-in-Publication Data
Takamori, Akio.
Between clouds of memory : Akio Takamori, a mid-career survey / edited by Peter Held ; essays by Garth Clark . . . [et al.].
p. cm.
Catalog of an exhibition held at the Arizona State University Art Museum, Sept. 9, 2005–Jan. 14, 2006, and at other museums at later dates.
Includes bibliographical references and index.
ISBN 0-9679547-8-9 (hardcover : alk. paper)
1. Takamori, Akio—Exhibitions. 2. Ceramic sculpture, Japanese—20th century—Exhibitions. I. Title: Akio Takamori. II. Held, Peter. III. Clark, Garth. IV. Arizona State University Art Museum. V. Title.
NK4210.T265A4 2005
730'.92—dc22 2005012659



Page 1: *Sleeping Woman and Child,* 2003 (detail, cat. no. 40)
Frontispiece: *Queen,* 2003 (detail, cat. no. 39)
Page 4: *Human,* 1987 (detail, cat. no. 11)
Page 8: Studio view of *Ensemble,* 2000. Photo: Kate Preftakes
Page 12: *Her Love,* 1987 (detail, cat. no. 10)
Page 20: *Western Paradise,* 1996 (detail, cat. no. 48)
Page 34: *Village,* 1976 (detail, cat. no. 1)
Pages 68–69: *Tree,* 1991 (detail, cat. no. 21)
Page 152: *Sleeping Nude Man,* 2003 (detail), 8 × 15 × 132 in., stoneware with underglaze

Paper: 150gsm Demi Matte
English text: Monotype Bembo by Francesco Griffo, 1495–1501, with refinements by Monotype; and FontFabrik Thesis TheSans by Luc(as) de Groot, 1994–99
Japanese text: IBM Heisei Mincho Standard and IBM Heisei Kaku Gothic, 1995

Photographer: Anthony Cuñha
Catalogue design: John Hubbard
Translator: Keiko Katsuya
Copy editor: Michelle Piranio
Proofreader: Laura Iwasaki
Indexer: Candace Hyatt
Color separator: iocolor, Seattle
Producer: Marquand Books, Inc., Seattle
www.marquand.com
Printing and binding:
C&C Offset Printing Co., Ltd., China

# Contents

# Foreword

THIS PUBLICATION AND THE RETROSPECTIVE EXHIBITION THAT it accompanies constitute the first monographic project, on a major scale, undertaken by the Arizona State University Art Museum Ceramics Research Center. It is made possible through the generosity of many foundations and individuals, and the Museum is grateful for the recognition that this support demonstrates. The project was conceived and brought to life by Peter Held, Curator of Ceramics, and reflects his long association with Akio Takamori. And finally, it is made possible by Akio, who placed his trust in Peter and the Center to present his work in a survey that reveals his evolving content and processes.

This exhibition embodies the mission of the Center as a national and international destination point for the hands-on study and enjoyment of ceramics. The Center combines a gallery space that provides a framework for focused exhibitions; open storage that allows the public access to a large portion of the permanent collection of more than 4,000 objects; and a research archive. It is a teaching and research facility, an educational component of the Herberger College of Fine Arts. The collection focuses on representative works by renowned and emerging artists, and on subject matter that reflects the social, cultural, and historical activities of the world. The international holdings demonstrate the full range of techniques, aesthetic approaches, and material possibilities within the medium. Major artists represented in the collection include Rudy Autio, Hans Coper, Ruth Duckworth, Shoji Hamada, Karen Karnes, Bernard Leach, Maria Martinez, Otto and Gertrud Natzler, Lucie Rie, Edwin and Mary Scheier, Angus Suttie, Akio Takamori, Peter Voulkos, Kurt Weiser, and Betty Woodman, to name just a few.

The Museum's ceramics collection began in the late 1960s, under the leadership of founding director Rudy Turk. The collection has grown through acquisitions and the support of individuals actively collecting and exhibiting ceramics. Gifts came from Jay and Joyce Cooper, Joanne and James Rapp, Astrid Thomas, and many others with a passion for ceramics. In 1998, the Museum was the recipient of the Anne and Sam Davis Collection, consisting of 315 modern and contemporary ceramic works by 120 British and American ceramists, a gift that raised the profile of the collection to one of national importance. When the new Ceramics Research Center facility opened in March 2002, Sara and David Lieberman generously made a promised gift of their impressive collection of international contemporary artists to the Center. Reflecting many of the important artists, movements, and accomplishments in ceramics in the second half of the twentieth century, the Lieberman gift of 350 works established the collection as one of the most extensive in its field. In 2003, Susan Harnly Peterson gave her archive of books, ceramics, and more than fifty years of research, including important documentation on Shoji Hamada and Maria Martinez, steering the Center more clearly toward research. In 2004, Stéphane Janssen donated his collection of 686 ceramic objects, collected with his late partner, Michael Johns, who was himself a talented ceramist. The Janssen gift enriches the collection with works by Michael's teachers and fellow students at the Otis Art Institute in Los Angeles, and it further elevates the collection with outstanding examples by many accomplished artists and large-scale sculptural works by Robert Arneson, Viola Frey, and Jun Kaneko.

Having quickly outgrown its temporary facility of 7,200 square feet, the Ceramics Research Center will move to new quarters within the expanded Museum, projected to open in 2008. The Herberger College of Fine Arts will occupy what has been known as the Tempe Center as part of the new Arts and Business Gateway, a 13-acre project now in the planning stages. The new facility will allow the Center to serve students, artists, scholars, and all those who enjoy ceramics with new and pioneering programming.

Marilyn A. Zeitlin, Director and Chief Curator
Arizona State University Art Museum

# Acknowledgments

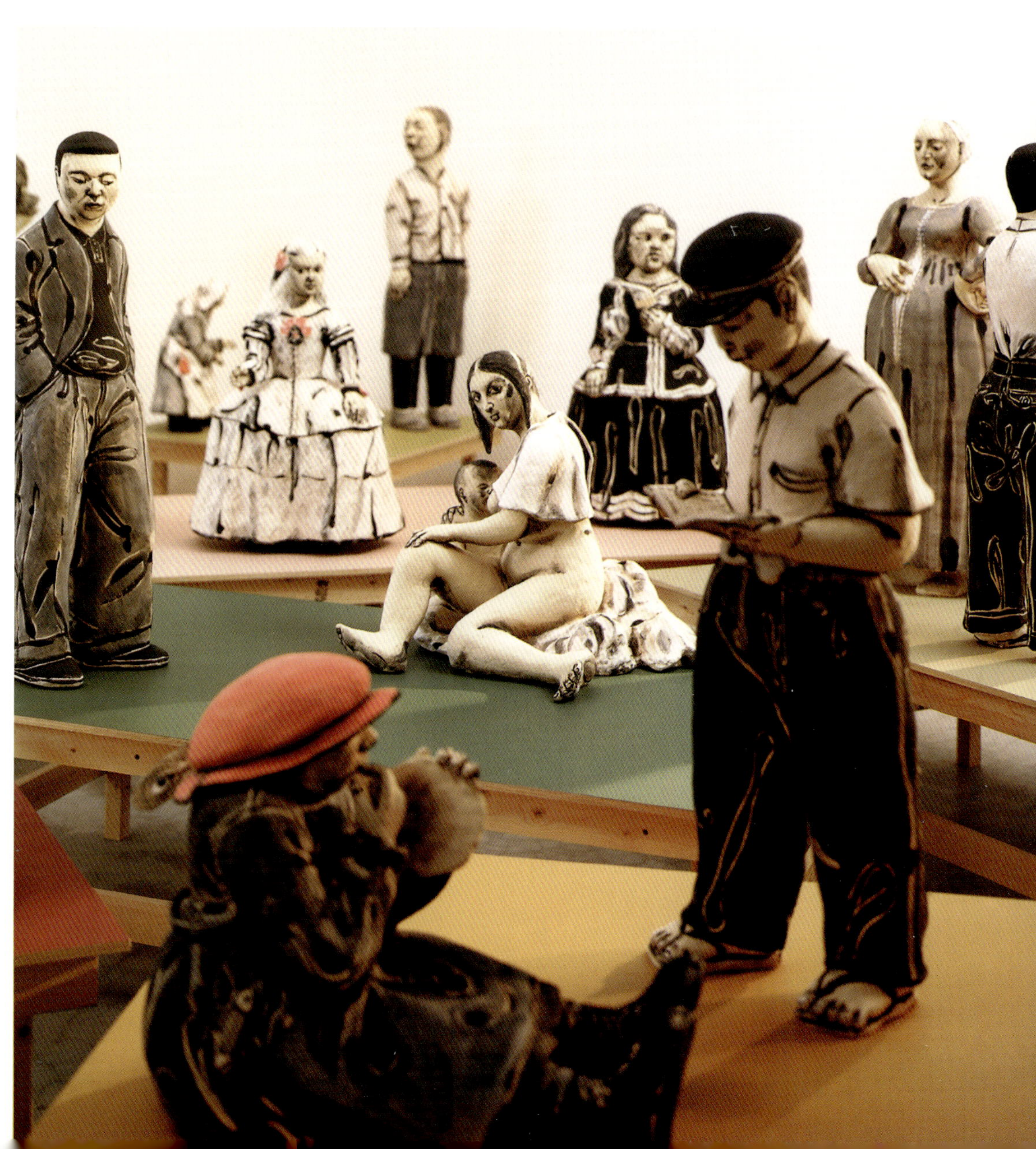

ONE OF THE GREAT SATISFACTIONS IN UNDERTAKING THIS PROJECT has been my close involvement with Akio Takamori, an artist whose work I have admired since our first meeting at the Archie Bray Foundation for the Ceramic Arts in 1978. In the ensuing years, I have been captivated by his work and pleased to have witnessed his career develop and evolve. His contribution to contemporary ceramics, through both his art and his teaching, has had an enormous impact on the field. I extend my deepest appreciation and gratitude to Akio and his wife, Vicky, for their tireless efforts in making this exhibition and publication possible. They have been instrumental in my research efforts, providing necessary documentation at every critical turn. My hope is that, through the works on view and the discussions in these pages, a broader audience will come to recognize Akio Takamori's ingenuity and creativity, which bridge three decades of artistic excellence.

I would also like to thank the contributing essayists for their insightful observations on Takamori's work. I'm especially pleased to have the participation of Toyojiro Hida, Associate Professor at the Kyoto Institute of Technology; it is the first time that a Japanese writer and critic has written on the artist's oeuvre. A former curator of the Crafts Gallery at the National Museum of Modern Art, Tokyo, he brings a wealth of experience and a sharp intellect to this undertaking, providing crucial insights into Japanese cultural and social influences in Takamori's work. Edward Lebow is a leading voice in ceramics criticism and has written a thoughtful and witty analysis of the work included in the exhibition. Garth Clark, a noted ceramics historian, author, and dealer in modern and contemporary ceramics, reflects, in his thoughtful and personal introduction, on his relationship with the artist, now spanning more than twenty years. I am also appreciative of the efforts of Rick Newby in casting a critical eye on my own writing. Thanks also to Bruce Cochrane, Chris Holmquist, Tom Muller, Yuki Nakamura, and Jeanne Quinn for providing me with personal accounts of their relationships with the artist.

I am indebted to the staff at Marquand Books, with whom it has been a pleasure to collaborate on this publication. Long after the exhibition closes, this book will serve as a visual record for many years to come. My thanks go to Ed Marquand,

Marta Vinnedge, and designer John Hubbard, as well as independent copy editor Michelle Piranio.

Los Angeles–based photographer Anthony Cuñha did a splendid job of photographing the majority of the works in the exhibition, presenting them to their best advantage. I would like to thank all the museums and patrons that provided images of artwork from their collections, adding an invaluable historical perspective to Takamori's work.

*Between Clouds of Memory: Akio Takamori, A Mid-Career Survey* will travel to three additional museums on its national tour. I would like to thank my colleagues at the museums for their appreciation and support of the artist's work and acknowledge the gracious efforts of their staff in presenting this exhibition: Patricia McDonnell, Chief Curator, Tacoma Art Museum; Bruce Pepich, Executive Director, and Davira Taragin, Director of Exhibitions and Programs, Racine Art Museum; and Terri Hopkins, Director and Curator, Marylhurst University, The Art Gym. I would also like to thank Ted Vogel and Thomas Orr, on-site liaisons for the 40th Annual Conference, National Council on Education for the Ceramic Arts, for their support in hosting this exhibition at Marylhurst University, and the NCECA Board of Directors for their financial support.

It is an honor and privilege to have the generous financial support of so many foundations, organizations, and individuals, ensuring the success of this project. Early commitments and enthusiastic support from the E. Rhodes and Leona B. Carpenter Foundation and from the Friends of Contemporary Ceramics and Founding Chairperson Linda Schlenger propelled this project from dream to reality. Generous financial support was also received from The Blakemore Foundation, HBB Foundation, Zaltec Familian and Lilian Levinson Family Foundation, the Ceramics Leaders of ASU and the Artists Advisory Committee of the Ceramics Research Center, the Jack and Grace Pruzen Faculty Fellowship, Garth Clark and Mark Del Vecchio at Garth Clark Gallery, New York, Frank Lloyd at Frank Lloyd Gallery, Santa Monica, Dale & Doug Anderson, Sandy Besser, Marc and Diane Grainer, Joanne and James Rapp, Roger and Janet Robinson, and Kurt Weiser. Support in underwriting the fund-raising dinner hosted at Arizona State University came from Sid and Elaine Cohen, Midge and Jerry Golner, Wendy Haas, owner of the Cervini Haas Gallery/Gallery Materia, Scottsdale, and the many people who attended the event. A special note of thanks goes to John Armstrong, of Armstrong-Prior, Inc., for the splendid framing of the prints in this exhibition.

This project would not have been fully realized without the heroic support and assistance of the following individuals: Garth Clark, President and Director, Mark Del Vecchio, Vice President and Director, and Osvaldo Da Silva, Associate Director, Garth Clark Gallery, New York; Frank Lloyd, Frank Lloyd Gallery, Santa Monica, California; and Susan Grover at the Grover/Thurston Gallery in Seattle. All have been staunch advocates in supporting Takamori's career for many years and have assisted in fielding a multitude of questions, locating critical works, and facilitating their transportation.

Many private collectors and institutions have graciously loaned works for the exhibition. It has been a pleasure becoming acquainted with those who share an equal passion for the artist's work. It is difficult to part with beloved objects for more than two years, and I extend my thanks to all the lenders listed on page 142.

This exhibition and attendant publication would not have been possible without the institutional support of Arizona State University. My heartfelt appreciation goes to J. Robert Wills, Dean of the Herberger College of Fine Arts; Marilyn A. Zeitlin, Director and Chief Curator of the ASU Art Museum; and Senior Curator Heather Sealy Lineberry. Tiffany A. Fairall, Curatorial Assistant/ Assistant Registrar, supervised the photographic requirements of this publication and along with Anne Sullivan, Registrar, managed loan forms, packing, and transportation of works. In the Development and Business Office, I wish to thank Ted Decker, Manager of Special Museum Initiatives, Kathleen T. Wacker, Business Manager, and Dawne Walczak, Office Specialist, for their support in facilitating special events and overseeing fund-raising efforts. Laura Stewart, Curator of Education, was especially helpful in the coordination of educational programming related to the exhibition. Thanks also to Stephen Johnson, Chief Preparator, and Exhibition Specialists Theodore Troxel and Fausto Fernandez for their sensitive and handsome installation of the exhibition. I feel fortunate to serve with such professional colleagues.

Lastly, I would like to acknowledge the support of my wife, Terri, and our children, Sarah, Daniel, and Matthew, for their continuing encouragement throughout the duration of this project. Their love and friendship never fail to provide the necessary perspective.

Peter Held, Curator of Ceramics
Ceramics Research Center
Arizona State University Art Museum

# Memories in Lieu of an Introduction *by Garth Clark*

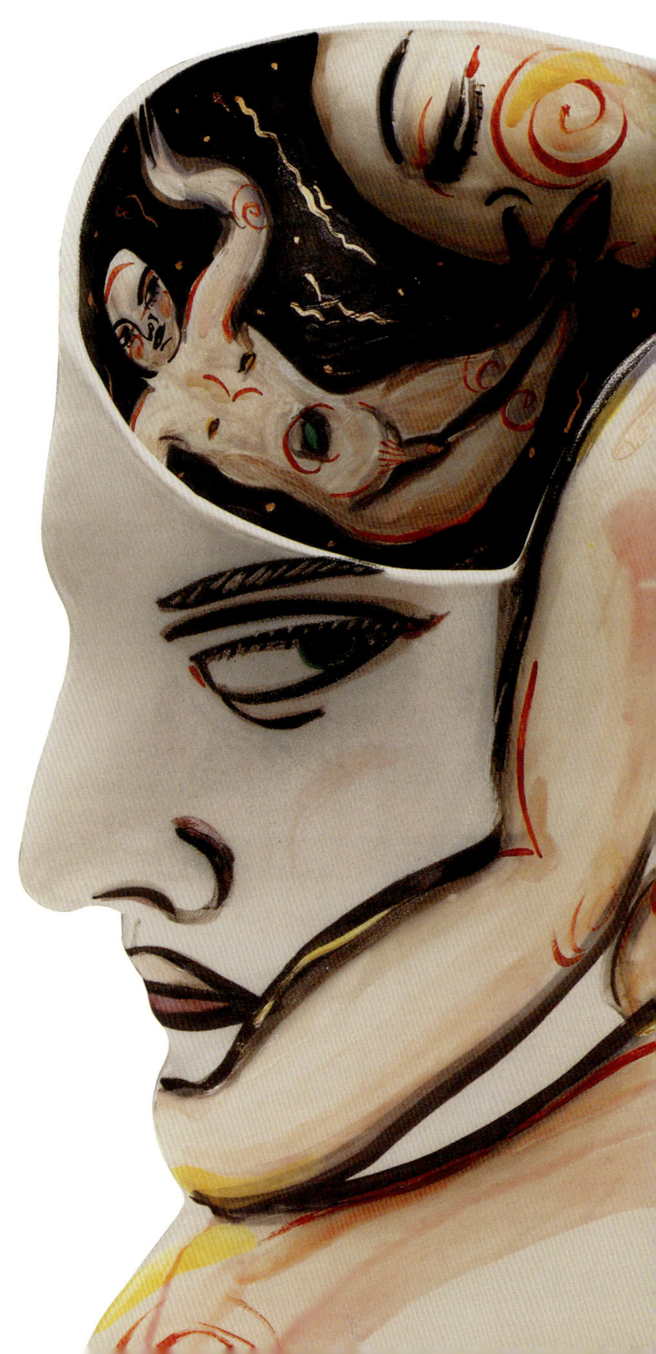

MEMORY IS THE LEITMOTIF OF THIS EXHIBITION, BOTH IN THE retrospective character of the exhibition and in the nature of Akio Takamori's evocative art. So I will draw from this theme to look briefly at more than twenty years of working as a dealer with one of the most exciting and imaginative artists to emerge from the halcyon years of ceramics in the 1980s. I will extend this license to write personally, and not formally, about an artist I respect deeply and for whom I feel immense affection.

The relationship between artist and dealer is a complex one. If it is a good relationship, the dealer will be part confessor, part analyst, part critic, part friend, part goad, and full-time booster. If it is a great relationship, the artist will in turn give back to his dealer, inspiring him to continue in what can be an exhausting field, recharging him with each new body of work, giving him the security of that artist's loyalty, patience, and understanding during difficult market periods. By those standards, I can look back on an exceptional period of collaboration with Akio.

I have always known that this is a wonderful partnership, but in preparing notes for this essay, I have come to appreciate more fully the richness of the gifts that have been exchanged over more than two decades. I have come to appreciate anew what a source of energy the art and the support of this artist have been to our enterprise. They have benefited not just my partner, Mark Del Vecchio, and me but all of the artists who have worked with us.

But let me be clear. I am speaking not of sales and the normal currencies of the art market but of the kind of richness that derives from interlocking passions. As both Akio and I can attest, ceramics is not an easy path to wealth, at least not of the more conventional kind. One of my great rewards stems from having been able to provide a stage for Akio's emergence as a renowned leader in contemporary ceramic art, admired throughout the field for his energy, facility, vigor, and creative resilience.

We met before I knew we had met, as I will explain later. But my first conscious recognition of Akio's art came in 1981 when I was visiting the Canadian potter Bruce Cochrane, who was a friend of Akio's from Alfred University in New York. After an enjoyable dinner, I was getting ready to leave when a small vessel in Cochrane's living room transfixed me (fig. 1). It turned out to be one

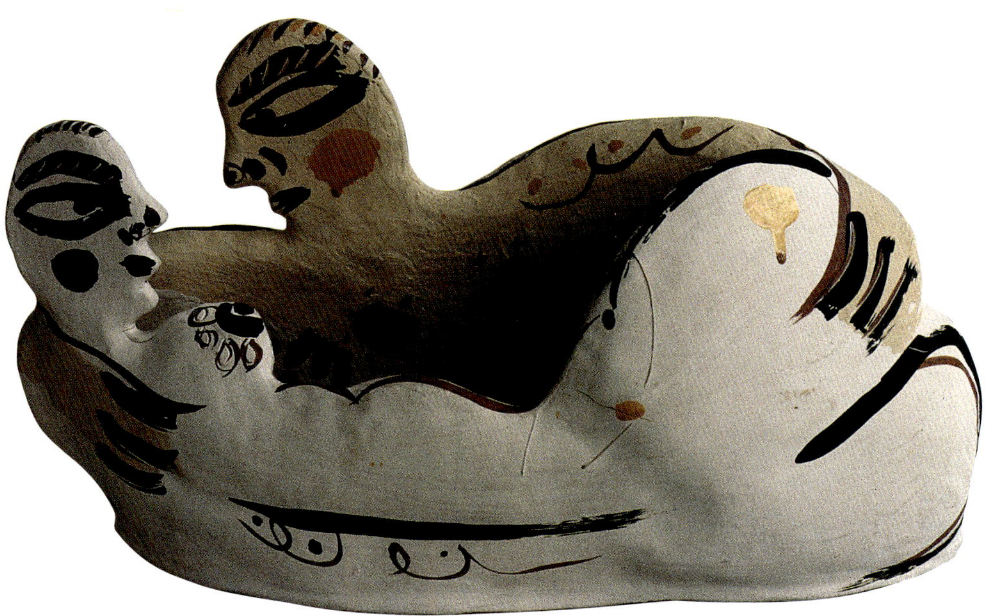

Fig. 1
*Untitled*, 1981, hand-built stoneware, 9 × 14 × 5 in., Collection of Bruce Cochrane. Photo: Bruce Cochrane

of the earliest of Akio's signature envelope vessels. I did not know the artist's name, but I knew immediately that I wanted to represent him. This vessel used the front and the back of a pot in such a way as to transform the space in the vessel into emotional ether. I had never felt a pot do that to me before, and on the basis of that one piece, I offered Akio a one-person show.

A few years later, he shyly reminded me that we already knew each other before this pot sighting. In 1976, I had come to Alfred as part of a nationwide lecture tour for the American Craft Council. He was the charming young Asian man who met me at the airport in Rochester and drove me to Alfred. It was a delightful encounter, and I remember in particular his response to my question, "How do you like living in Alfred?" In limited English, but with his distinctive eloquence already in place, he said, "Ah, it is a good place to become an alcoholic." Given that Alfred was a dry town (no alcohol could be sold within city limits), the comment was all the more droll.

Happily, Akio agreed to have his first solo show at our gallery in Los Angeles. The works were made at that great incubator of postgraduate talent, the Archie Bray Foundation for the Ceramic Arts in Helena, Montana, run at the time by his close friend Kurt Weiser. Akio sent me slides of his works while they were still in the green state and unpainted. They were already so impressive that, armed with these images of unfired works, I went to a number of collectors around the country. In New York, Dan Jacobs, then one of the most perspicacious collectors, immediately bought several based on this limited evidence of what was to come, and others soon followed. By the time the show opened, most of the pots had homes.

This reaction was not surprising. Akio was taking the pot into new territory, a psychosexual landscape that employed the "inside-outside, front-back" mantra of the pottery aesthetic in a completely new manner. True innovation in a medium

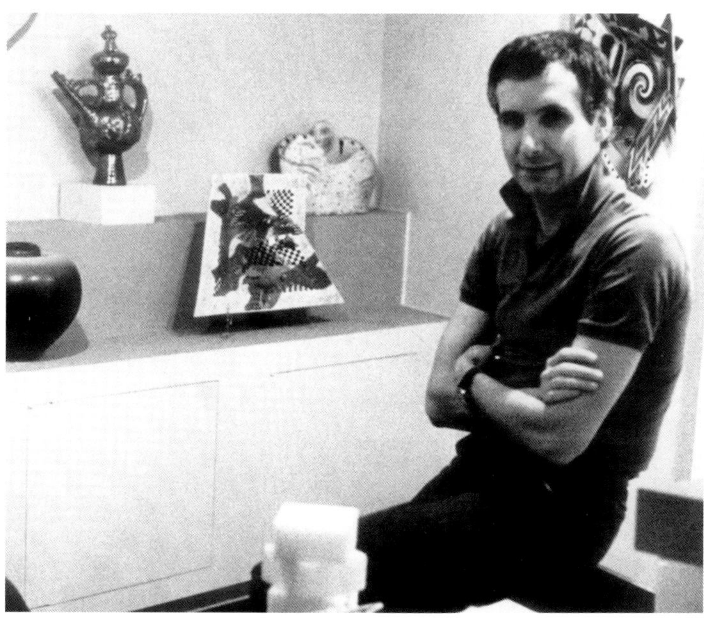

Fig. 2
Garth Clark in his Los Angeles gallery, ca. 1983. Photo courtesy of Garth Clark Gallery, New York

that is eons old is not a minor achievement, and so Akio's arrival on the American ceramics stage was at once startling and a delight.

His inventiveness was sparked not by ceramic influences but by erotic Japanese prints. Many see him as an heir to Rudy Autio, but this is not accurate and misses the point of the vastly different dynamics of space at work in each artist's ceramics. With his envelope form, Akio was able to set up a tableau by raising the back rim of his pot, on which his subject was outlined, and juxtaposing that with what he had painted on the front of the vessel. The implied relationship between the two sides—one inside, the other outside—set up the sexual and emotional tension, and the shallow volume between the two was charged with meaning.

There was no single theme; each pot carried its own karma. Sometimes the situation was chaste, at other times almost lewd. Certain pots were loving and gentle, while others were aggressive and threatening. In many cases, lovers had witnesses, perhaps intruding on their privacy, or participants waiting in the wings. Some viewers found the work too racy, but Akio's view of sexuality has a welcome lack of moralizing, a nonjudgmental objectivity that is distinctively Japanese but that also has deep roots in his childhood, when his father ran the village's medical clinic, where he treated patients with venereal disease and survivors of the atomic bomb. I remember Akio once discoursing on fellatio at a large dinner party at our house for a rather conservative and elderly audience. Despite the initial shock of the topic, Akio's delivery was so removed from vulgarity that it was received with as much comfort as a description of the weather.

Akio's envelope vessels, as they came to be known, were one of the most important developments in the vessel tradition during the 1980s, a time when American ceramics let loose a torrent of creative energy, with many of the major artists coming out of Akio's alma mater, the Kansas City Art Institute, under the challenging tutelage of Ken Ferguson. This group included Andrea and John Gill,

Chris Gustin, Richard Notkin, Chris Staley, Irv Tepper, Kurt Weiser, Arnold Zimmerman, and others.

Let me now fast-forward to 1996 and the European Ceramic Work Centre in 's Hertogenbosch in the Netherlands. The years that preceded this visit were difficult ones for the artist. He was wrestling with his work. I remember us having many conversations at the time about his creative unease. I have to admit that for a long while I just did not understand what he was telling me. When he spoke about his work being "too easy," it sounded as though he was unhappy with the fact that his ability to make and paint his work came with too little struggle or pain. I teased him, remarking that he wanted "to become Basquiat." In return, he wondered whether it was merely part of a typical male midlife crisis and joked that all he needed was "a young girlfriend and a red sports car."

The envelope vessels had grown in scale and drama. The human architecture (now often one figure rather than many) was powerful and grandly sensual, focusing the architecture of the pots on voluptuous, provocative rumps. But he was becoming dissatisfied. One body of work he did for an exhibition in Los Angeles presaged his unhappiness. The works were, to be honest, haphazardly painted, unresolved, almost self-destructive. At the time, it seemed like a lapse in judgment, but it was a message. This way of working was no longer feeding his muse. He was in crisis.

For about three years, we witnessed a struggle. Collectors noted a shift in mood and became uneasy. Works from one body to the next had little consistency or continuity. It was an odd period, but it also produced some wonderfully eccentric works. *Summer of '92 Vase* and *Vase of Voyeur,* both 1992 (pages 96, 97), are a perfect example of the struggle to bring something new into his art that would excite him. They made use of a wonderful new language, but the artist did not follow up on it. Eventually, it became clear that Akio was not at war with his impressive facility but with the lack of challenge in his current format. The vessel was not taking him to the next stage.

It reminds me of the time I asked Ken Ferguson why he had stopped making functional pots. His answer was simple and true: "Because I had reached a point where I could not make them better, I could only make more." Facing that

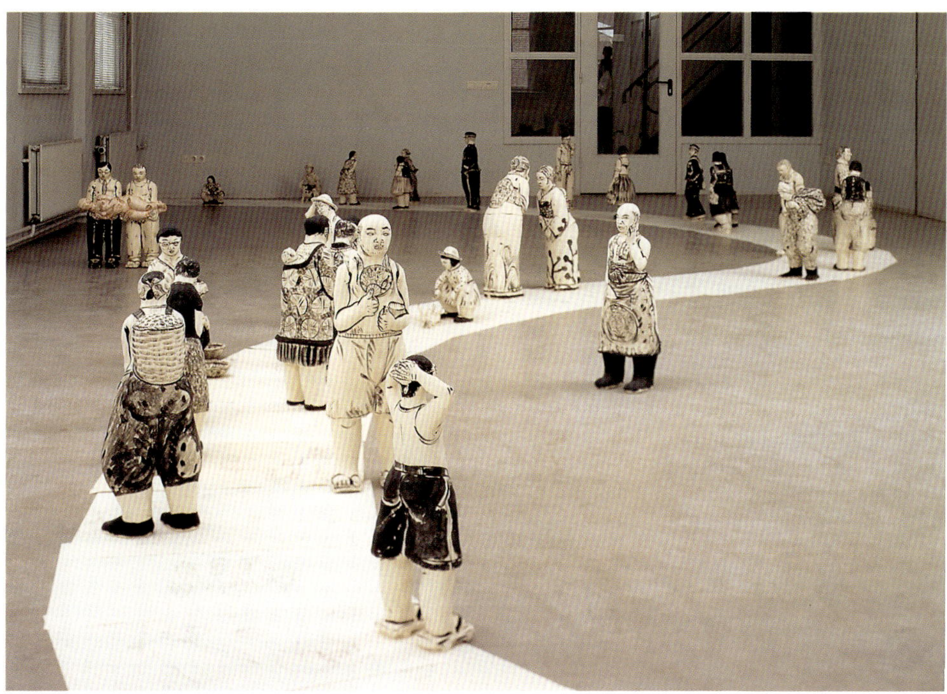

Fig. 3
Installation view of the exhibition *Path* at the European Ceramic Work Centre, 's Hertogenbosch, the Netherlands, 1996. Photo: Peer van der Kruis, courtesy of the European Ceramic Work Centre

dilemma at the European Ceramic Work Centre and given free rein to experiment, Akio produced a body of figures (fig. 3). This was not a brand-new departure; he had made figurative work both in Kansas City and at Alfred. But those figures were small and somewhat abstract. The figures that he made in the Netherlands were closer to realism and blended sculpture and painting. The forms were unpainted, chunky, and roughly modeled but with an authentic figural spirit. Detail was provided by the painting. It was a perfect marriage of 3-D and 2-D.

Akio knew that something important had happened, but he returned to the United States with some trepidation about how that something would be received. Our working relationship was a little strained after a few awkward exhibitions. And Akio had some very specific concerns. Our gallery had been founded initially on championing the vessel to the exclusion of other forms in ceramics, but that had gradually changed. Nonetheless, he was sure that we would not welcome the idea that he had left for the Netherlands a potter and returned a sculptor. I asked several times to see the work, but the slides never arrived.

When they did arrive, the work captured in these 35mm frames was a revelation. The seduction was immediate. It was a parade of childhood memories, capturing the characters of the artist's youth—fellow students, fishmongers, peasants and elegant women, children at play. I remember his surprise and relief when I called to convey my enthusiasm about the work.

The Work Centre figures were shown in New York, to acclaim, on a large tripart structure we termed a "bridge to the past," pouring out the denizens of his memory into the front room of the space. Looking back, it was one of our most important exhibitions, taking the gallery deeper into the other great ceramics tradition, the figure.

Since then, Akio's figures, at first modestly reflective of the artist's formative years, have expanded dramatically. His tableaux of humanity now encompass grand themes, from the Second World War to Old Master paintings (also from memory, as his father had schooled him in images of Western art) to symbolic portraits of powerful women of the aristocracy and the way in which their dress and hair evoke their station as well as an underlying sexual symbolism.

Now there are murmurs that Akio may be preparing to return to the vessel again. There are questions in this format that he still has not asked, and they are again beginning to prod him into response. And so our journey continues. Now we might have to prepare his audience for another sea change in his art.

Friendship with Akio is rewarding. He encourages intimacy, is caring, even loving, and has great empathy—factors that certainly contribute to his success as an educator. Discussions are open, without boundaries, and even the deepest and darkest emotion can be expressed. This is true from both sides, even though Akio comes from a nation known for its reticence. And when he surprises one with an inner feeling or thought that many might think twice about revealing, one feels a kind of honor to be entrusted with this fragment of his psyche. There are few in the field with whom I enjoy discussing art itself more than Akio, whose insights are always as unexpected as they are revealing. Then there is the matter of sex. If only Kinsey were still alive. Their conversations would have been extraordinary. And what mixes it all together so well is a sly sense of humor, often self-effacing, but with a rare understanding of the ironies involved in standing between two strong, different cultures.

So the memories that this retrospective mid-career exhibition evokes in terms of Akio and his artistic trajectory are a complex matrix of commerce, friendship, and art, with the strands of each so tightly and closely interwoven that it is difficult (and unnecessary) to separate one from the others. I can cite example after example of moments shared: the celebration of sales to great collections and acquisitions by prestigious museums; encounters at conferences and exhibitions around the world; times when he has buoyed my spirits—a richness of events and camaraderie, of tensions confronted and of ease enjoyed.

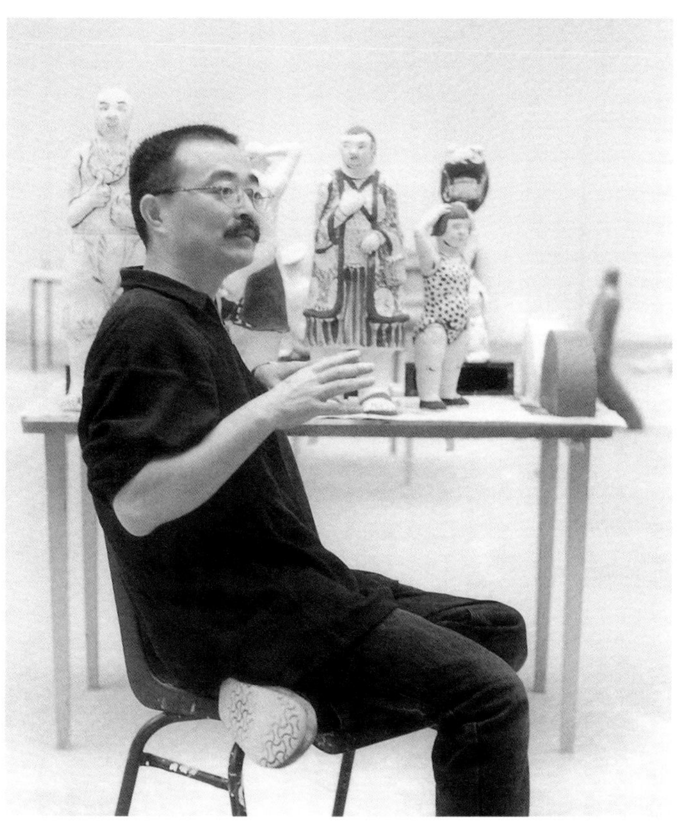

Fig. 4
Takamori working in his studio at the European Ceramic Work Centre, 's Hertogenbosch, the Netherlands, 1996. Photo courtesy of the European Ceramic Work Centre

But selfishly, for me as a dealer, this relationship is one of my defining, anchoring achievements. I am reminded of a wonderfully satiric pot that Mark and I once acquired. It bore the maxim "A man is only as young as the women he feels." Ignoring the obvious political incorrectness of the statement, it can be paraphrased to say, "A dealer is only as good as the artists he represents." Given the dominant stature of commerce in American culture, and the frequent arrogance of art dealers themselves, we sometimes lose track of the fact that dealers in contemporary art are not primary players. No matter how visionary, resourceful, or innovative in our approach to this profession, we who represent talent remain secondary players, and we are both defined and limited by the quality of the art in our time.

So, as complex as the narrative of nearly a quarter century of working with Akio may be, the cumulative feeling that results is, surprisingly, not complex at all. It is, simply, a profound sense of privilege at having been there at the outset of this career, at being awarded (and hopefully earning) the trust to accompany him on his journey, fueled by his remarkable creative spirit and boundless humanity.

# Between Clouds of Memory *by Peter Held*

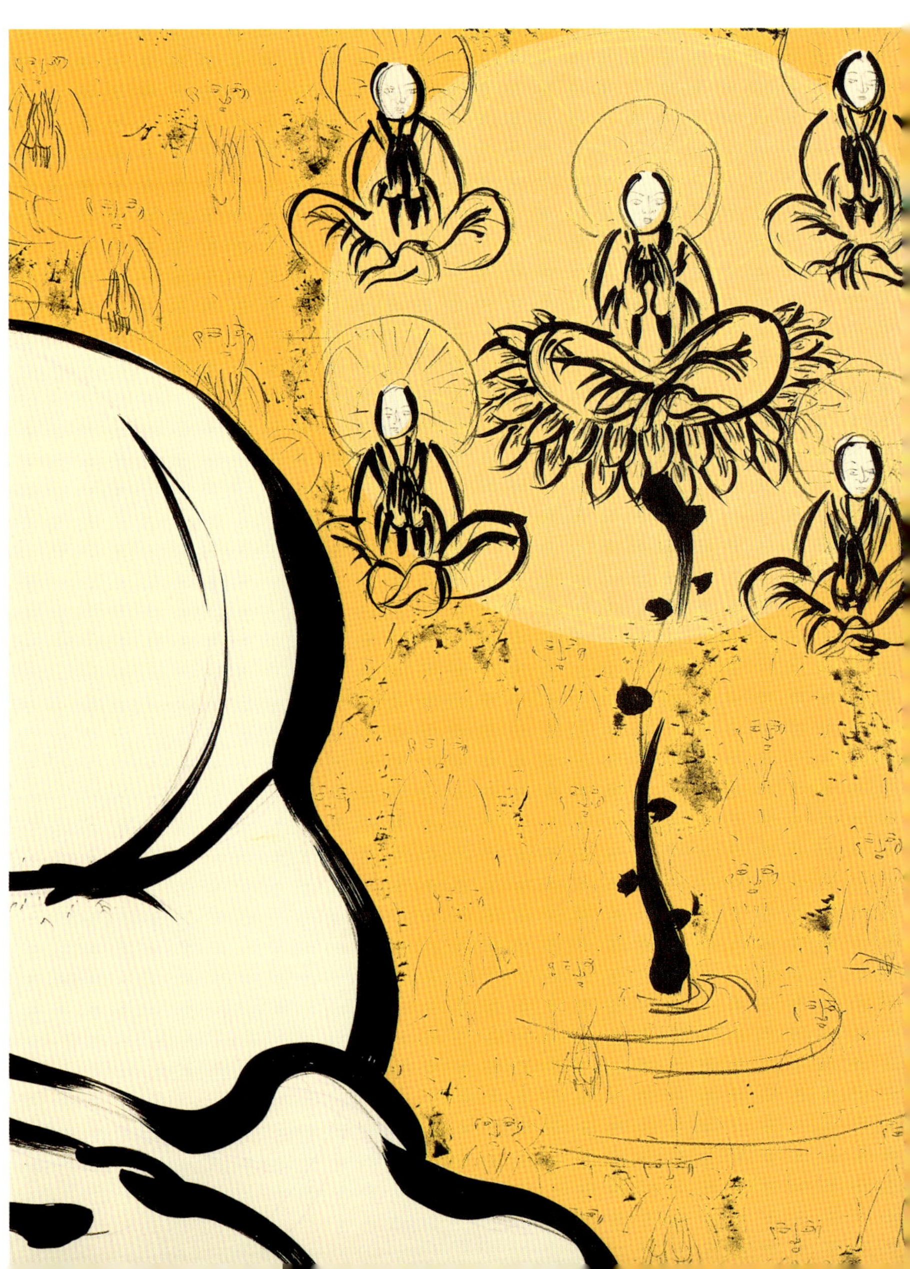

**Memories are like clouds, moving restlessly between** heaven and earth, stimulating imagination and stirring emotion. They live and die, ever shifting, leaving us adrift with fading remembrances of their brief passage through our consciousness. Clouded by time, the accumulated memories we hold are building blocks to our personal and collective identities, redefining history along the way.

In his account of Japan in the wake of the Second World War, John W. Dower, a historian specializing in U.S.-Japanese relations, remarks that patterns of remembering and forgetting are most meaningful when seen in the broader context of public memory and mythmaking, especially during times of traumatic events. Ravaged by war, the Japanese were searching for, at times inventing, something familiar with which to brace themselves against an uneasy era.[1]

Akio Takamori was born in 1950, five years after the ending of hostilities and two years after Allied forces, under the leadership of General Douglas MacArthur, withdrew from Japan. Though the tragic events of the war were not directly experienced by the artist, they nevertheless left an indelible mark on his psyche. His first memories of war relate to the rebuilding of his impoverished hometown of Nobeoka, where he played in the remnants of caves that had been used as bomb shelters along the flanks of the local mountainsides. Although Japan was being reinvented and there were signs of hope for the future, the Takamori family went through times of suffering and living in fear. Two uncles were imprisoned; one was captured by the Soviet army, spending years in a Siberian prison, and the other was interred in a Japanese prison as a suspected communist sympathizer. And Takamori's mother (fig. 1) told him of a harrowing experience she had when an American military jeep came up behind her on the road and slowed down as it approached; nothing happened, aside from a loudly shouted greeting, but the fear she felt was palpable and real.[2]

Takamori spent his childhood in the small industrial town of Nobeoka, in Miyazaki prefecture, located on the southernmost island of Kyushu. His father (fig. 2), a dermatologist and urologist, managed a clinic whose clientele included some of the prostitutes of Nobeoka's red-light district. Takamori, the youngest of three children, witnessed a constant influx of patients, an exposure that provided an unvarnished vantage point in witnessing the fullness of humanity. "I was

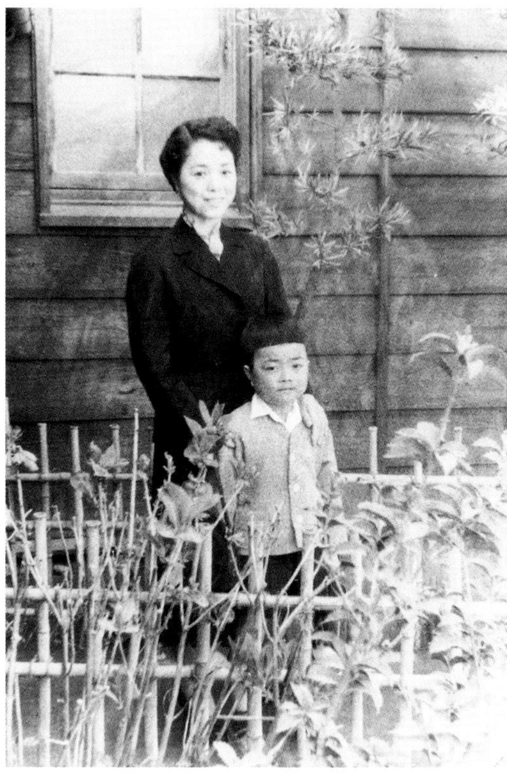

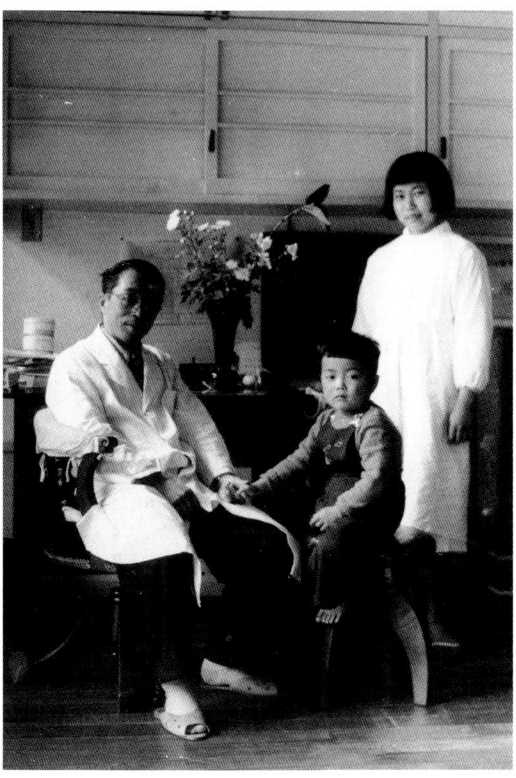

Fig. 1
Takamori with his mother, Nobeoka, Miyazaki, 1957. Photo courtesy of the artist

Fig. 2
Takamori with his father (and unidentified nurse), Nobeoka, Miyazaki, 1954. Photo courtesy of the artist

fascinated by the patients and the different bodies coming and going and by all the people who came through our house," Takamori recalls.[3]

The household teemed with relatives, a handful of housekeepers, and a parade of people coming to see his father. There were also five or six young nurses in training, mostly "daughters of farmers," who came to work at the clinic. His father's office became home to an extended family, with nurses, students, aunts, and uncles all living under one roof. For some, coming from the remote countryside, the clinic provided their only access to schooling.

Steeped in a nurturing home environment and regaled by ancient stories of his homeland, Takamori reveled in the mysteries of everyday life.

> Religious experiences for me as a child in Japan were made tangible through traditional customs and ceremonies to celebrate and grieve. Most of these experiences were transmitted by narrative storytelling. Religion to me was a collection of fantastic otherworldly stories, mythologies, and folktales when I was growing up. There were many gods here and there, hiding behind stones and living in rivers. Perhaps I grew up without knowing the meaning of faith and religion. I enjoyed visiting places where people attended and participated in some kind of spiritual experiences without much of the authoritarian persuasion.
>
> My grandmother's family ran a Shinto shrine. It was built on the spot, as the story goes, that a samurai warrior's eyeball had landed after gouging his own eye and [throwing] it many miles away. I suppose that people still

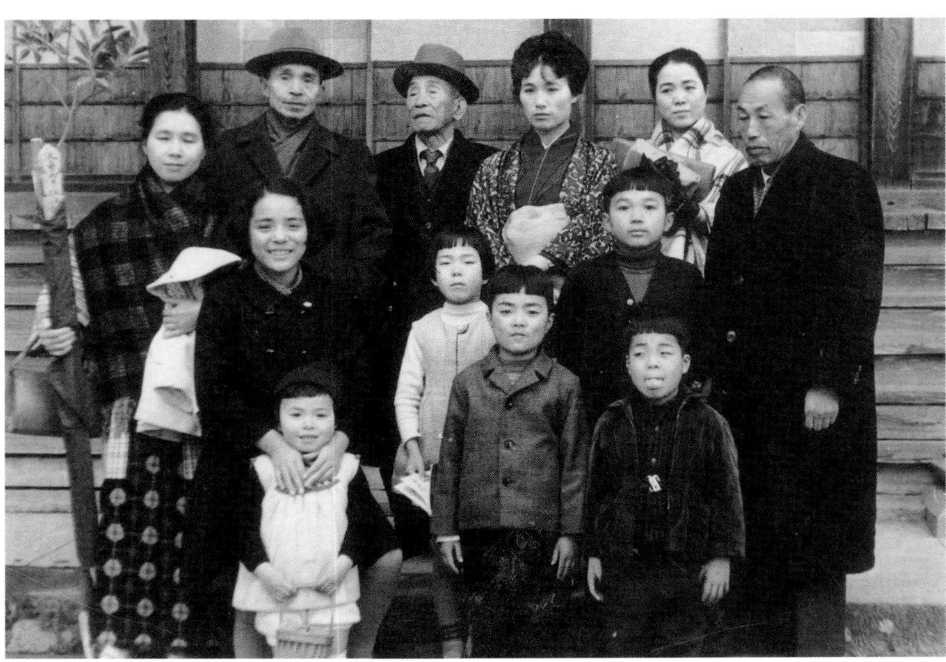

Fig. 3
Temple gathering in father's hometown of Yamage, Miyazaki, 1958; Takamori is standing in the front row, center. Photo courtesy of the artist

go there when they have ailments relating to sight. When I was a child, people still liked to talk about such outrageous stories to me. They remained believable as they were associated with real and tangible places.[4]

Dr. Takamori, a humble man who was an ardent supporter of the arts in Nobeoka, embraced the itinerant puppeteers who would visit the Takamori home. This left a permanent impression on the young Akio, who remembers his father riding a scooter through town, with a young performer holding on for dear life, waving a flag to advertise an upcoming performance. When artistic productions were held at the local schools, Akio would watch the performers from behind the stage, captivated by the dramatics. These performers would often be invited home to share meals with the family, staging impromptu performances that aroused the children's already vivid imaginations.

Takamori's father also welcomed myriad painters, printmakers, and poets into the home. One old man in particular, who was "monklike" and preferred living in honest poverty, would stay with the Takamoris when traveling through Nobeoka. Another family friend, an aged poet, admired one of the artist's papier-mâché sculptures, a copy of a Picasso goat. These visitors encouraged Takamori's already heightened inquisitiveness toward art.

This curiosity extended through high school, where Takamori joined the art club. Students were trained in Western art concepts, seeking inspiration from Impressionism and modernist movements. There was an emphasis on charcoal drawing and oil painting, at times imitating the work of modern masters such as Van Gogh, Picasso, and Modigliani. Early on, Takamori recognized that he was drawn more to expressive figuration and abstract art than to purely representational subject matter. Frustrated by the discipline his teachers imposed, he was never comfortable with overt academic instruction. Seeking a niche in which he could excel, Takamori explored more tactile media such as papier-mâché, which better suited his early artistic inclinations.

After graduating from high school in 1969, and desiring to continue his arts training, Takamori applied to a four-year program at Musashino Art University located in Tokyo. He was rejected from the four-year program, so he enrolled in the two-year program, with a focus on industrial design. His main professor had been trained in Sweden and was a proponent of a modernist design aesthetic, stressing drafting and mold-making in his coursework. According to Takamori, students were unmotivated and he was personally dissatisfied with the program. He found greater satisfaction pouring his energies into the growing student protest movement targeted at American involvement in the Vietnam War. A self-described poor student, Takamori struggled even to graduate: a lamp he made for his final project was rejected. A second object—a mailbox—finally met the basic requirements for graduation.

That year, 1971, Takamori saw a touring exhibition at the National Museum of Modern Art, Kyoto. *Contemporary Ceramic Art: Canada, U.S.A., Mexico, Japan* exposed him to the works of American ceramic artists such as Jim Melchert, Richard Shaw, Henry Takemoto, and Peter Voulkos. Finding the work anti-authoritarian, he was impressed by the freedom of expression—the antithesis of the Japanese ceramics establishment, which he saw as rigid, exclusionary, and tradition-laden.

Shortly after graduation, Takamori's parents sent him on a European tour organized by the Japan Folk Art Museum based in Osaka. He was the youngest in the group. The whirlwind itinerary, which began in Amsterdam, included visits to Madrid, Barcelona, Lisbon, Rome, Florence, and Athens, among other cities. Back in Japan, Chuichi Miyake, who was the head of the Folk Art Museum and had been the tour leader, suggested a pottery apprenticeship to develop Takamori's interest in ceramics. For the twenty-year-old artist, who was entering adulthood and feeling unsettled by the sociopolitical upheavals taking place around him, the idea of an apprenticeship struck an appealing chord. It validated the rigor of work, which coincided with his idealistic belief in manual labor as the great equalizer.

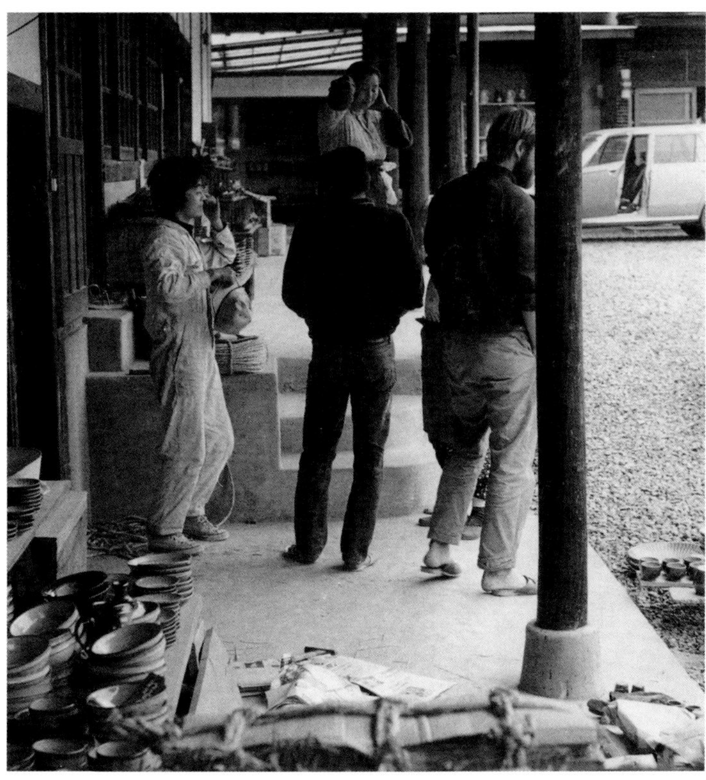

Fig. 4
Takamori (in overalls), with Tetsuzo Oota (center) and Chris Holmquist (right), at the Oota pottery, Koishiwara, Fukuoka, 1972. Photo courtesy of Chris Holmquist

Koishiwara is a small pottery village in the mountains of Fukuoka prefecture in Kyushu, sparsely populated with ten active potteries owned by old pottery families. Like most traditional potteries, their clay source was dug from the hillside adjacent to the village. Each facility consisted of the family house, a pottery building, and a *naborigama,* or hill-climbing wood kiln. Takamori studied with the Oota family. Kumao Oota, the patriarch, was sixty years old and had two sons who also assisted in the family enterprise. They created work in the Koishiwara style and considered themselves to be stewards of the *mingei* folk tradition. In exchange for room and board and a small stipend, apprentices worked long hours with only two days off each month. Although the range of work produced was limited, the experience confirmed a strong work ethic in the aspiring potter.

A visiting American student, Chris Holmquist from Minnesota, was also apprenticing at the time (fig. 4). Takamori, being the "college boy," was assigned by Oota-san to assist the American, in the process improving his English-speaking skills. To the envy of Takamori, Holmquist, being a guest, was allowed to make more than just the standard tea bowls the rest of the apprentices produced by the hundreds on a daily basis. Holmquist recalls:

> When I arrived in Koishiwara I was introduced to everyone by an interpreter because none of the Oota family could speak English. That was when I first met Akio. He had been there for two months already. When I met him he was working in the back part of the pottery where clay was prepared for throwing, smoking a cigarette. He greeted me

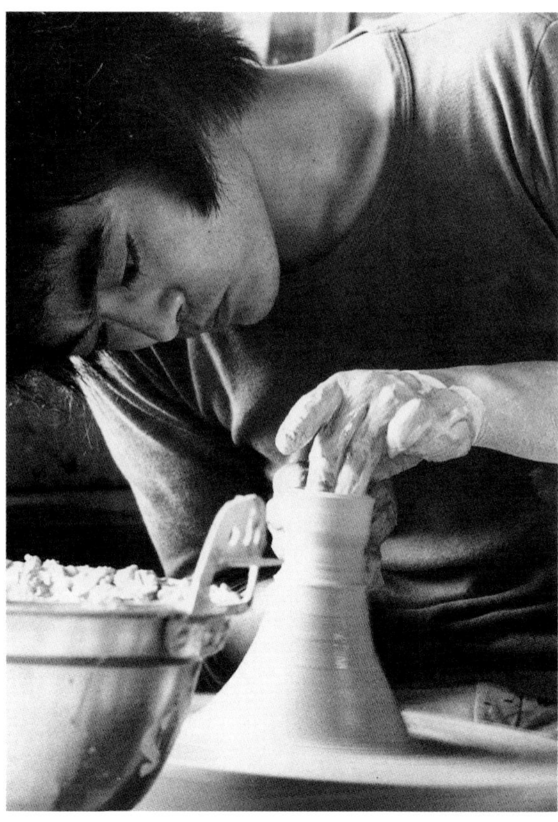

Fig. 5
Takamori throwing off the hump while apprenticing at the Oota pottery, Koishiwara, Fukuoka, 1972. Photo courtesy of the artist

> in what sounded like English, but I wasn't quite sure. We both did a lot of clay preparation and were being taught to throw small teacups off a mound of clay (fig. 5). The eldest son, Takahiro, was our teacher and boss. We worked at wheels on either side of him and learned by watching. The father, Kumao, and the youngest son, Tetsuzo, worked in a different room. Akio and I both learned to make the teacup and then were expected to throw them in quantity. This teacup was a pot that the pottery needed in large numbers. We made this same teacup for many months.
>
> One vacation I went with Akio back to his parents' home. It was on this visit that I could see a glimpse of Akio's earlier art. In Akio's room there was a collection of small papier-mâché painted figures he made while in middle school. There were circus characters made in a wonderful and unique style. I loved them because they were so full of life. I now realize that this was the real feeling of Akio and that he was just sidetracked making traditional *mingei* pots.[5]

This meeting encouraged Akio to think about going to the United States to further his education.

It was during this time that Ken Ferguson, head of the ceramics program at the Kansas City Art Institute and an innovative clay artist in his own right, visited the Oota pottery while touring Japan. Ferguson felt an instant rapport with the young apprentice and urged him to come to Kansas City to further his studies.

Based on his interactions with Ferguson, coupled with the excitement he felt when he had seen American ceramics in the exhibition in Kyoto, Takamori accepted Ferguson's invitation to study at the Kansas City Art Institute.

However, the offer was not fully realized for another year. Prior to enrolling at the Art Institute, Takamori first lived in Chicago, where he studied English at Loyola University and roomed with a doctor from El Salvador. His original plan was to study for a year and gain language proficiency before entering his art studies. After sending Ferguson a postcard to inform him of his plans, he was encouraged to come to the school immediately, even though the semester was in full swing. Takamori hopped on a bus to Kansas City.

He still lacked self-confidence because of his limited English but was bolstered by Ferguson's unbridled support. Beginning with what he knew best, Takamori produced wheel-thrown pots, still under the regimented spell of Koishiwara ware. But soon, taken with the energy and vitality of fellow classmates, including Allan Winkler, who approached his work with conceptual savvy while retaining the influence of folk traditions, Takamori began his search for a truer artistic voice. The department encouraged experimentation and curiosity and organized visits to local collections such as the Nelson-Atkins Museum of Art. Immersed in American culture and emboldened by his fellow students' energy and passion for their work, his own work started to transform.

During this interlude of rediscovering himself in a new land, he began to draw on childhood memories. His first tentative steps in hand-building harked back to his youthful efforts in sculpture. As Takamori recalls, "Ken Ferguson looked over my shoulder at my tiny pieces and told me, 'They are very nice. Make lots of them.' It was like magic. I can't explain how much that remark meant to me at that moment. I felt as if I had finally rediscovered something that was truly mine, and it was okay to make it."[6]

Ferguson, a distinguished alumnus of New York State College of Ceramics at Alfred University, encouraged him to apply to the school's M.F.A. program. In retrospect, Takamori wished he had devoted more time to improving his English as Alfred's program placed a stronger emphasis on art theory, and it was still a challenge for him to grasp concepts and engage in meaningful dialogue

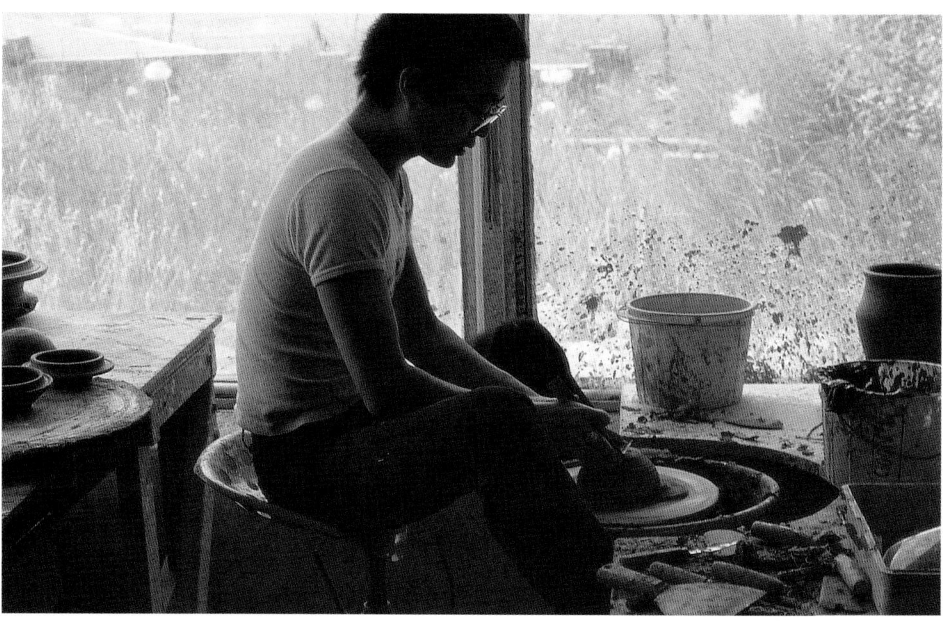

Fig. 6
Takamori at the Archie Bray Foundation for the Ceramic Arts, Helena, Montana, 1978. Photo: Kurt Weiser

with students and professors. "I really didn't take advantage of the professors coming to my studio for biweekly critiques," he has observed. "Instead, I had to learn very quickly to satisfy the faculty to show progress."[7]

The most memorable experience for him was an informal critique with faculty member Ted Randall, who remarked that Takamori's figures looked like weak attempts influenced by Picasso's figurative work done years ago. Feeling compelled to make "real art," Takamori was unsure about how to achieve it: by scaling up his work or by becoming more abstract? By the time he finished his degree, he was still dissatisfied, feeling his work was not yet genuine. When his M.F.A. show came down, it was assigned to the dumpster, a cathartic reaction by the artist to his Alfred experience. In retrospect, Takamori realized that the experience had been necessary for him to understand his own limitations, marking a coming to terms with his true self.

At the invitation of Kurt Weiser, the newly arrived resident director of the Archie Bray Foundation for the Ceramic Arts in Helena, Montana, and himself a protégé of Ken Ferguson at the Kansas City Art Institute, Takamori relocated to Montana for the summer (fig. 6). The generous open spaces of the West and the collegial atmosphere of a nonacademic setting provided a recipe for instilling a renewed sense of vigor and experimentation in Takamori's work. Since 1951, the Bray has acted as an incubator, a halfway house for ceramic artists building their careers. Takamori was in good company; his fellow resident artists included Larry Bush, John and Andrea Gill, Wendy Mueller, and Allan Winkler, all alumni of the Kansas City Art Institute. Once more, Takamori started loosely throwing pots, painting the contoured surfaces, and attaching clambering figures to the flanks.

At the end of the summer, Takamori returned to Japan, with the idea of setting up a pottery in order to craft a livelihood. A fortuitous call came from Jun

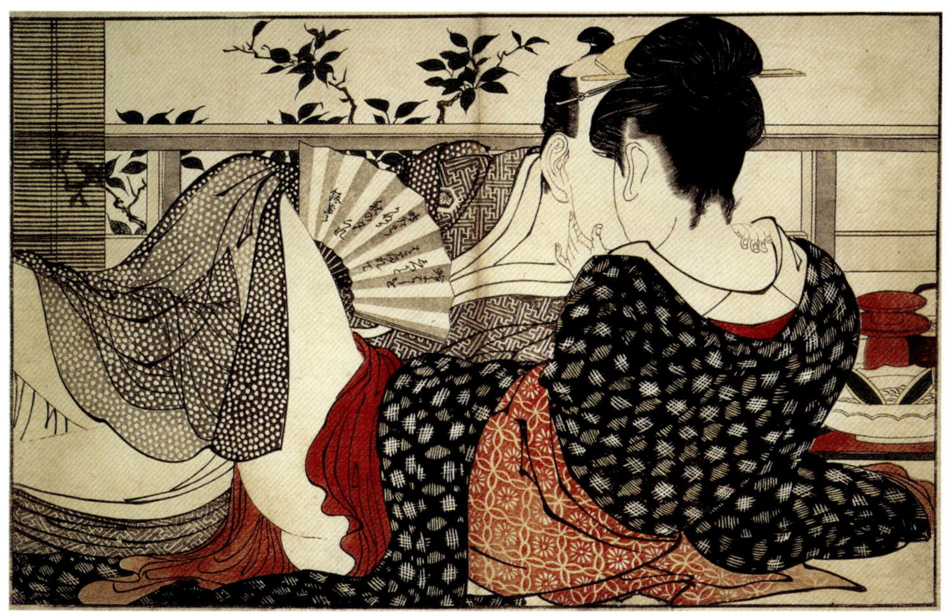

Fig. 7
Kitagawa Utamaro, *The Lovers*, 1788, color woodblock print, frontispiece from *Utamakura* (Poem of the Pillow). Photo © Victoria and Albert Museum, London

Kaneko, whom Takamori had met briefly in the United States. Kaneko was returning to the States to teach at the Cranbrook Academy of Art, and he asked Takamori if he wanted to work at his home and studio in Nagura, Japan. The timing was perfect. Kaneko assisted Takamori in many ways, perhaps remembering his own personal and professional challenges when he went to America in 1963 to study art; he introduced Takamori to ceramic artists such as Goro Suzuki and took him to the potteries in Shigaraki.

During this transitional period, Takamori accepted several short-term teaching positions, thinking it would be beneficial in honing his skills and would provide additional income. At Sheridan College of Applied Arts and Technology in Ontario, Canada, he filled in for Bruce Cochrane, a former classmate at Alfred. At Sheridan, Takamori developed his breakthrough slab-constructed envelope sculptures, inspired by Japanese printmaker Kitagawa Utamaro's *The Lovers* (fig. 7), which the artist first saw when he was a graduate student at Alfred. As Garth Clark eloquently describes in his introduction to this book, it was at Cochrane's house that he first saw one of these envelope vessels. Enthralled with it, he extended an invitation to show Takamori's work in his new Los Angeles gallery. Initiated during the burgeoning studio crafts movement, the relationship between Takamori and Clark was forged by enthusiasm, passion, and mutual respect that continue to this day.

In 1983, Takamori moved to Bozeman to teach at Montana State University as a one-year sabbatical replacement. He reconnected with a former classmate from Kansas City, Vicky Lidman, and they married a year later. While in Montana, he resumed working at the Archie Bray Foundation for several more years, returning numerous times over the next decade (fig. 8).

Following the birth of their first child, Takamori and his wife began their search for a permanent home, finding a suitable living and working environment

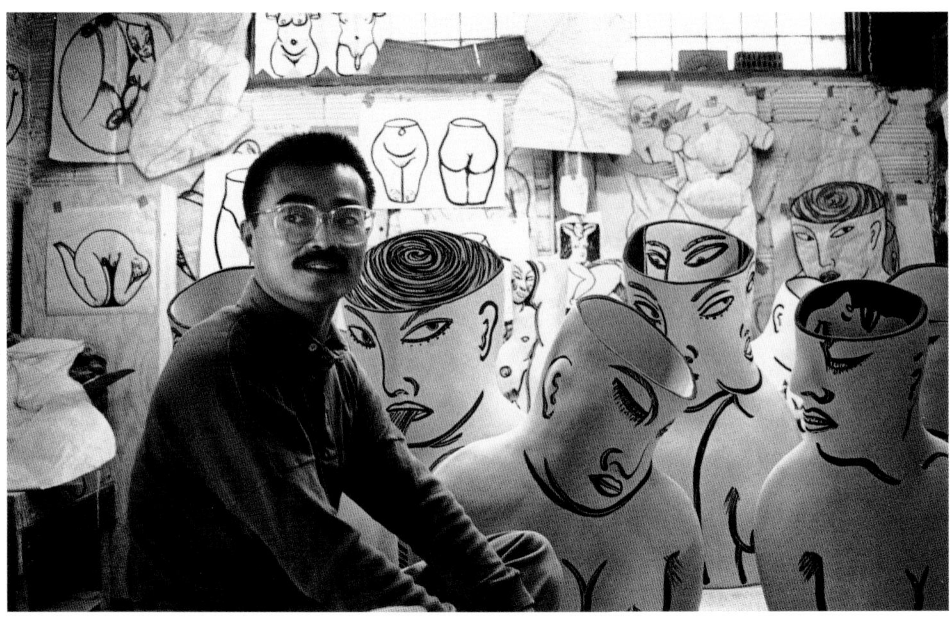

Fig. 8
Takamori at the Archie Bray Foundation for the Ceramic Arts, Helena, Montana, 1986. Photo: Vicky Takamori

in the Pacific Northwest. They bought a home in Vashon, Washington, a verdant island in Puget Sound, abundant with plant and animal life and just a short ferry ride away from Seattle. Takamori quickly fashioned a studio and kiln. His relocation also provided him an opportunity to connect with the local Asian community, something that became important in raising the children. A bucolic lifestyle ensued for five years, with Takamori teaching intermittently at the University of Washington.

In time, mold grew underfoot, and restlessness set in. Though living in close proximity to the city, the family nonetheless felt isolated. Simultaneously, Takamori's work was starting to evolve; a summer residency at the European Ceramic Work Centre (EKWC) at 's Hertogenbosch, in the Netherlands, foretold a new and exciting direction. Upon returning home, he was offered a full-time teaching position at the University of Washington, joining Jamie Walker and Patti Warashina. The family moved to Seattle in 1994, establishing a new rhythm, embracing city life, and adjusting to the stimulation of academia. Takamori recognized how much he had enjoyed meeting new people in different parts of the country during previous short-term teaching positions, and he appreciated that each situation offered unique experiences. His energetic, nontraditional approach to teaching and easy rapport with his students have had a lasting impact on many of those who studied with him.

Jeanne Quinn, currently on the faculty at the University of Colorado, Boulder, recently reminisced about Takamori's inspiring and unorthodox teaching methods:

> For the first meeting of our graduate seminar at UW, he showed a video of an MFA opening at Alfred, where he had been teaching the previous spring. At the time, I wondered why he was showing us someone else's

> MFA opening. It was oddly enjoyable, but seemed a little random. Later, I realized that he was giving us a sense of what was to come, offered something to strive toward. It was the next step for us, and he was showing us both that it was possible, as well as what was possible. It was very smart.
>
> He then showed us slides of the work he had made that summer at the European Ceramic Work Centre. I totally enjoyed hearing about his experience, and as a new graduate student, I was again somewhat mystified. His work at the EKWC seemed to me totally beautiful and resolved. In retrospect, I think he was showing us two things—another step, after graduate school—that we could continue to be supported as artists at places like the EKWC. But more important, by describing his own questions about his work, he was showing us that the process of being an artist never changes radically. One never "arrives," never makes a perfectly resolved piece. We just keep working, and the problems are always there; we get better, as an accidental by-product of continuing to work. I admire him for his desire to continue to evolve as an artist.[8]

In 1996, Takamori returned to the European Ceramic Work Centre, which proved to be another turning point in his artistic development. It was during this residency that he sculpted his first freestanding figures (fig. 9), creating a body of work that, when displayed at the Garth Clark Gallery in New York in 1997, startled devotees familiar with his signature envelope vessels of the past fifteen years. Drawn from the artist's memory bank, the figures "had long been the ghosts in Takamori's mind," recalling the villagers in Nobeoka.[9] Free from the demands of teaching and working toward exhibitions, Takamori, while ensconced in a supportive atmosphere working with other artists and trained technical support, unleashed vestiges of the past that were joined with the present and the future, engendering a distinctly new vision. No longer a producer of stunning single objects, the artist created groups of people in dialogue with one another and with the viewer.

Through each of his ceramic evolutions, Takamori has challenged our readings of his art. A leader in the field of ceramic sculpture, yet never resting on past

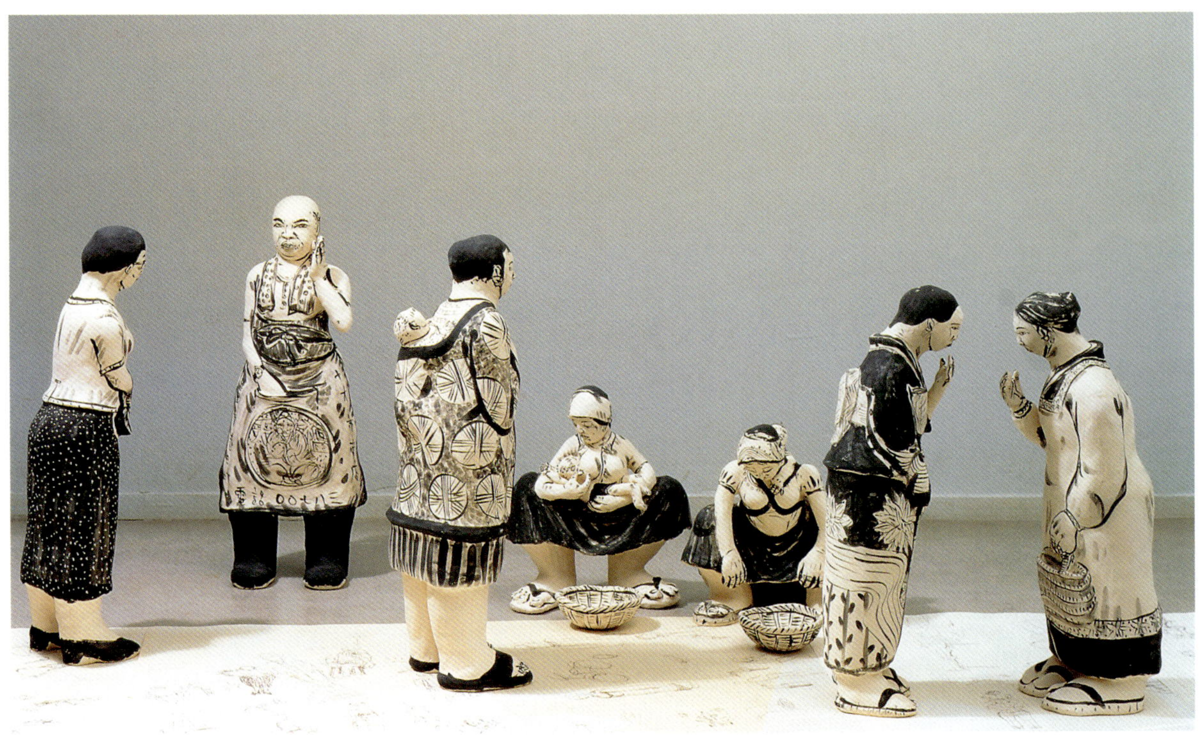

Fig. 9
Installation view of the exhibition *Path* at the European Ceramic Work Centre, 's Hertogenbosch, the Netherlands, 1996. Photo: Peer van der Kruis, courtesy of the European Ceramic Work Centre

accomplishments, he is a true innovator. Each twist in his work announces new realities. His work triggers a host of associations in his viewers; some are close to the surface, others buried deep within us. Assessing the last twenty-five years of his career, we witness an unfurling worldview, flexing time and space in reconstituted identity, caught between clouds of memory.

## Notes

1. John W. Dower, *Embracing Defeat: Japan in the Wake of World War II* (New York and London: The New Press, 1999), 30.

2. One American soldier stationed in northern Japan had a keen interest in folk pottery and purchased children's music to bring back to America. His name was Ken Ferguson, an extraordinary man with a deep sense of humanity and a curiosity about Asian cultures, who would go on to mentor a young Akio Takamori when the artist came to America almost three decades later.

3. Akio Takamori, interview with the author, May 16, 2004.

4. Akio Takamori, correspondence with the author, October 19, 2004.

5. Chris Holmquist, correspondence with the author, October 13, 2004.

6. Akio Takamori, interview with the author, May 16, 2004.

7. Ibid.

8. Jeanne Quinn, correspondence with the author, September 1, 2004.

9. Garth Clark, *Akio Takamori* (New York: Garth Clark Gallery, 2000), 22.

# It Takes a Village: The Ceramics of Akio Takamori

*by Edward Lebow*

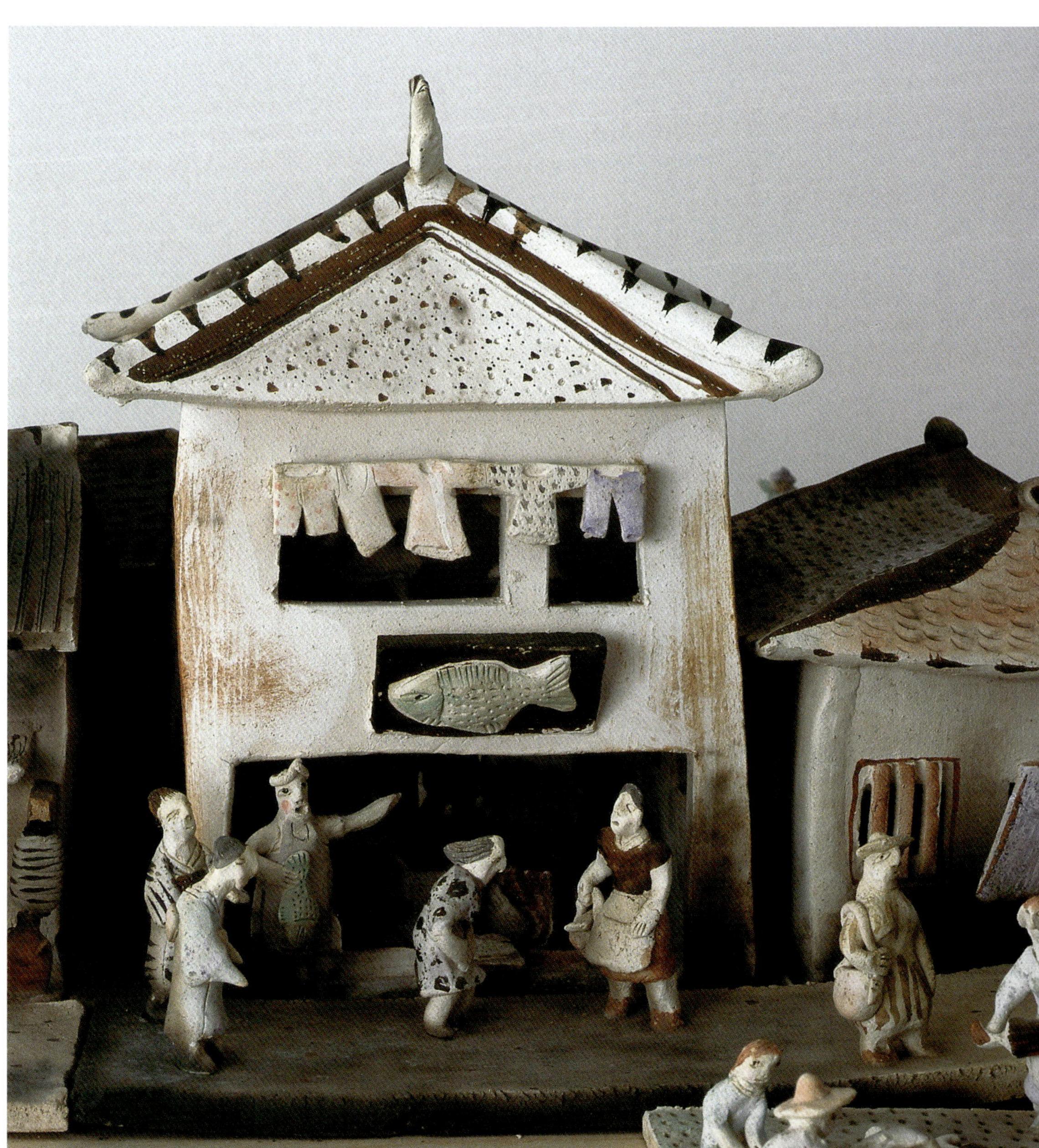

The memory doubtless is, so to say, the belly of the mind, and joy and sadness like sweet and bitter food. —*The Confessions of Saint Augustine*

MEMORY IS CERTAIN, BUT NOT ALWAYS ACCURATE. WE FORGET facts, not feelings. This loss is imagination's gain, and Akio Takamori has made the most of it. For the past twenty-five years, he has reached into the "belly" of his mind to create some of the most distinctive and self-revealing images in contemporary ceramics. Their lyrical candor appears so matter-of-fact that one could easily believe, as Takamori's friend and fellow artist Kurt Weiser once facetiously put it, that "what you see in Akio is what you get." His erotic vessels of the 1980s and 1990s convey frank sensuality without breathing a trace of squeamishness, shock, or self-consciousness. His more recent groups of figurative sculptures deliver equally plainspoken accounts of his ongoing search for personal and cultural identity in an era of increasingly global influences and contradictions.

That identity is tangled, at best. Takamori has rummaged the attics of Eastern and Western art to make works that follow the conventions of neither. His trail of visual breadcrumbs extends far beyond the arts of his native Japan and adopted America. He is "a true cosmopolitan, a citizen of the world," writer Rick Newby observed, and not just a citizen of *his* world, of *his* age.[1] Takamori—like most moderns—travels through time, borrowing and snatching images from other artists, cultures, and epochs. His swath extends from his own childhood doorstep in Japan to Picasso, pre-Columbian pottery, Velázquez, Goya, and Persian miniatures. He has shopped the aisles of Greek mythology and European and Asian cave paintings and filled his studio cart with delicacies produced by Han, Ming, and Tang Dynasty Chinese ceramists as well as folk artists of all stripes.

From this melting pot, Takamori has managed to concoct personal fictions that tell his own truths about basic human themes. Ranging initially from love and sex to childbirth and family, those themes have matured along with the artist, touching the wider world of culture, history, and myth. What's clear is that he has always inched ahead by looking back. His rearview mirror doesn't hold a single iconic image but, as his latest works suggest, the cumulative scene of a sprawling village. Part past, part present, his village is both a remembered and an invented place. Above all, it's a place Takamori can point to and say, as Saint Augustine did, "There also I meet myself and recall myself."[2]

Takamori's *Village,* 1976 (pages 70–73), is the first of his major works to reimagine the past and attempt to bridge the discrepancy in memories between facts and feelings. Made while he was a student at the Kansas City Art Institute, *Village* was modeled on the urban layout of buildings and shops in Nobeoka, the Japanese town where the artist was born and raised. Takamori didn't precisely miniaturize the town; rather, he built the nostalgic memorial to home from recalled and imagined scenes. "I was a little person then," he says of the time when he first glimpsed the town, "so my perspective was like fiction."[3] He transferred that fiction into the way he peopled the shops and streets with doll-like caricatures outfitted with just enough detail to convey their identities.

At the fish store, a fishmonger in black boots carries the day's catch; old folks tote their fish in baskets. In a plaza outside, a hatted man squatting on a tatami mat fixes umbrellas. "He squatted there all day," Takamori recalls. "All the neighbors would bring their broken umbrellas. And I would squat beside him and watch."

*Village* embodies the material and spiritual dualities that would appear with far greater sophistication and subtlety in Takamori's later works. The buildings, shop signs, tables, and merchandise are the material remnants of memory—things to touch, things that remain. The fleeting throngs of people and scenes he once knew and glimpsed are not. *Village* is filled with ghosts. Yet its back-to-the-future gesture let Takamori tap the rich psychology of his past and begin his escape from the abstract austerity of Japan's ceramics tradition.

Peter Held points out in his essay in this volume that Takamori's upbringing provided him with a unique window on the facts of life and gender. The full-frontal view he had of the beauty and baseness of human sexuality could easily have been warping, but as historian Garth Clark, who is also Takamori's dealer, has observed, "for Takamori, it produced a kind of leveling, a nonjudgmental acceptance of sexuality" that left its mysteries and conflicts intact.[4]

Those mysteries were heightened by his father's extensive collection of textbooks and art books. "Spending a day in my father's library was heaven to me,"

Takamori has recalled, adding, "I developed this almost clinical, biological approach to the human body from looking at his reference books."[5]

Volumes on Picasso, Pieter Brueghel, and photography, including Edward Steichen's *The Family of Man,* fueled an early interest in the world outside Japan. "I was always a little more interested in Western culture," he says. So much so that in elementary school he once made his own version of Picasso's sculpture of a large-teated she-goat. This isn't to say Takamori avoided his own roots. He worked both sides of the cultural aisle, sneaking into his father's library every so often to thumb through Junichiro Tanizaki's erotic book *Kagi* (The Key), which was illustrated with starkly beautiful black-and-white woodcuts from the master printer Shiko Munakata. "The picture I really liked," says Takamori, "was of a woman naked on the bed, and the man's glasses had fallen on her belly." It was so matter-of-fact and real, he recalls, "nothing like a Hollywood scene of love." Years later, Takamori summoned Munakata's spare lyricism to create his own drawings and paintings on clay forms.

Other riveting images arrived in full and memorable color. One day, peering into the darkened pit of his family's outhouse—the only option in an era when indoor plumbing was rare—he glimpsed pools of menstrual blood left by the women living with his family. Another time, Takamori noticed maggots in the pit. He fetched some boiling water to kill them, but one of the young nurses stopped him. Dousing the pit with hot water was forbidden because, as Takamori recalls her telling him, "a beautiful goddess lives there. She is very beautiful with long black hair, but she is blind."[6]

The ceramics world that Takamori entered in the late 1960s and early 1970s offered neither the forms nor the freedom to present such tales and images. An austere utilitarian simplicity then dominated Japanese pottery. Takamori had glimpsed the freedom that was characteristic of works made by innovative American ceramists, such as Richard Shaw, Henry Takemoto, and Peter Voulkos. But he didn't know how to put that freedom to use in his own pursuits. So, in 1972, he signed on as an apprentice with the *mingei* pottery master Kumao Oota in the village of Koishiwara (fig. 1). The production routine epitomized the top-down authority and stoicism of Japanese pottery. Takamori did what was expected of

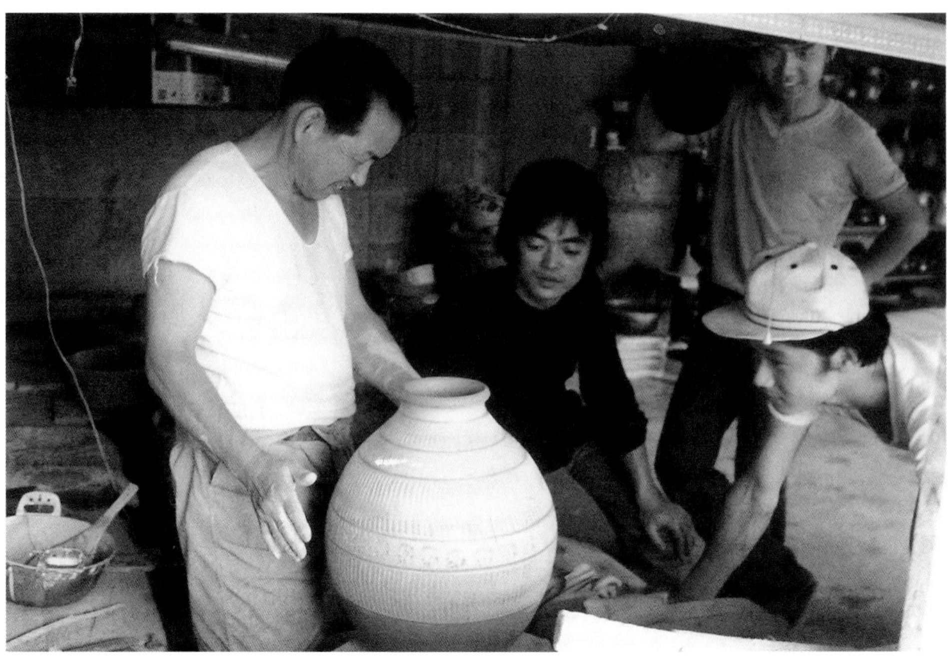

Fig. 1
Kumao Oota demonstrating on the wheel for Takamori (second from left) and apprentices from Takatori pottery, 1972. Photo: Chris Holmquist

him, cranking out 250 tea bowls a day. He learned little about the medium, he says, but the repetition drilled him in the discipline of work. What's more, the stint introduced him, in 1973, to the renowned American potter Ken Ferguson, who headed the ceramics program at the Kansas City Art Institute and was touring potteries in Japan.

Ferguson opened the American door, inviting Takamori to attend the Art Institute. Takamori remembers thinking the venture would lead him to produce a more creative line of utilitarian ware. But his involvement with the school and with Ferguson, which began in 1974, fundamentally altered his outlook on clay. Ferguson, like Takamori, was just beginning to think about diverging from functional ware. Ferguson made his escape by following Voulkos's departure from symmetry and the scale of hand-held pots. Takamori did it by abandoning the wheel for hand-building. He initially made small figurative pots that mimicked the Coke-bottle-shaped dolls he had made using papier-mâché as a child. Like Ferguson, he also dabbled in erotic images. Yet eroticism didn't emerge as Takamori's focus until the end of the 1970s, after he was done with the Art Institute and had secured a master's degree in art (1978) from the New York State College of Ceramics at Alfred University.

Teachers at Alfred had pushed him to move beyond the figurative. But, as works such as *Couple,* 1980, *Leda and Swan,* and *Lovers with Onlookers,* both 1982 (pages 74–76), suggest, his persistent subject was the secret, sometimes mythic, life of human sensuality. Takamori used these works to lay out his youthful takes on love, courtship, and sexual union. The people and creatures of his early pots are notably wary about their prospects. They are romancers and voyeurs—insiders and outsiders—playing out the divided acts of making love and watching it.

Their wary, one-eyed gaze mimics the one Takamori had seen in Persian miniatures and Japanese erotic prints. As he had with the inhabitants of *Village,* Takamori scratched and brushed on just enough detail to tell the story of the creatures and characters in his scenes. His simple, expressive lines follow Munakata's calligraphic lead. Compared with later vessels, the pale surfaces of these early ones seem almost raw. Takamori moistened Leda's nipples with dabs of glaze, but otherwise the surfaces have the look of parched clay, rather than the damp sheen of skin that gives such later works as *Spring,* 1988 (page 86), and *Lovers,* 1995, their unabashed sensuality.

The envelope-like form of these vessels was a breakthrough. Its broad surfaces and shallow volume solved a problem Takamori had been wrestling with for several years. Since leaving Japan for Kansas City and Alfred, he had gravitated toward making figurative vessels decorated with drawings. Yet traditional cylindrical pots presented a problem. Their narrow, upright forms revealed only one glimpse at a time of the entire surface drawing. To see decorations whole, one had to walk around the pot. "Basically, I wanted to be able to grasp the image of a horizontal nude woman at once," says Takamori. "I wanted the form to be more of a canvas."

The wide structure of *Couple* gave Takamori room enough to recline the woman across the front of the pot and stretch the man and his enveloping arms across the back. The shallow inner space of the container became the intimate gap between them. The idea for the form came from an erotic woodcut print by the eighteenth-century Japanese printmaker Kitagawa Utamaro. Takamori had snipped an illustration of it from a book at Alfred and tucked it away for several years before drafting it into his cause. It depicted a couple lying together. The woman, her back to the viewer, fills the foreground, the man the background. In his vessel, Takamori separated them spatially and let the drawing define the form. He did that, according to Garth Clark, by releasing "the rim of the pot to become a free form, a fluid line with which he can draw the outlines of animals, figures, or heads."[7]

The rim outlines the bodies of the reclining lovers in *Couple;* it contours the onlookers in *Lovers with Onlookers;* and it rings the hips, breasts, and head of Leda with the neck and wings of the swan. This fluid shift from line to form represents something more than the expected inside/outside, surface/form dichotomies of pottery. It becomes the starting point for all of the transitions and transformations that take place in Takamori's vessels and helps to imbue his themes with the poignancy of a private mythology.[8]

In the sweep of a rim, a woman morphs into a swan, a man into a woman, and a boy into a dog. Takamori ushers these changes along by modeling the anatomy of his figures—rounding the breasts, hips, and thighs of Leda, for example, and bulging the rump of the woman in *Couple*. These three-dimensional shifts establish the contours of his works' overt sensuality. Takamori wasn't the first artist to push and pull clay in this way. Centuries of artists—Rudy Autio, Mary Frank, Reuben Nakian, and Picasso, to name just a few more recent ones—modeled their forms to bolster the interplay of surfaces and volumes. This trick goes far beyond ceramics to the floating world of animals the ancients carved and drew on the uneven outcroppings of cave walls.

In Autio's works, the undulating rim and spatial heave of forms amplify the linear power and sensuality of the decorative surfaces. In Takamori's, as Clark points out, the "image on the vessel and the shape of the pot merge to become one."[9] Takamori's aim wasn't simply to turn drawings into pots or to pump them up with a steroid bulk. He used the physical to reveal the spiritual and more. "Physicality could be an entrance to instinct and intuition where we might find something beyond spirituality and intelligence," Takamori once wrote.[10] Here, the artistic invites the psychological. According to the Swiss psychoanalyst Carl Jung, writing in 1916, the physicality of art gives "visible form" to the vague content of dreams and other unconscious expressions. "Often the hands know how to solve a riddle with which the intellect has wrestled in vain," he went on. "By shaping it, one goes on dreaming the dream in greater detail in the waking state."[11]

Takamori's reveries in clay of the 1980s and 1990s may have begun with the wet dreams of sexual intimacy and pleasure. However, their autobiographical themes evolved in step with the artist's own maturity and changes. What's clear is that his preoccupation with telling stories with clay made a permanent return to

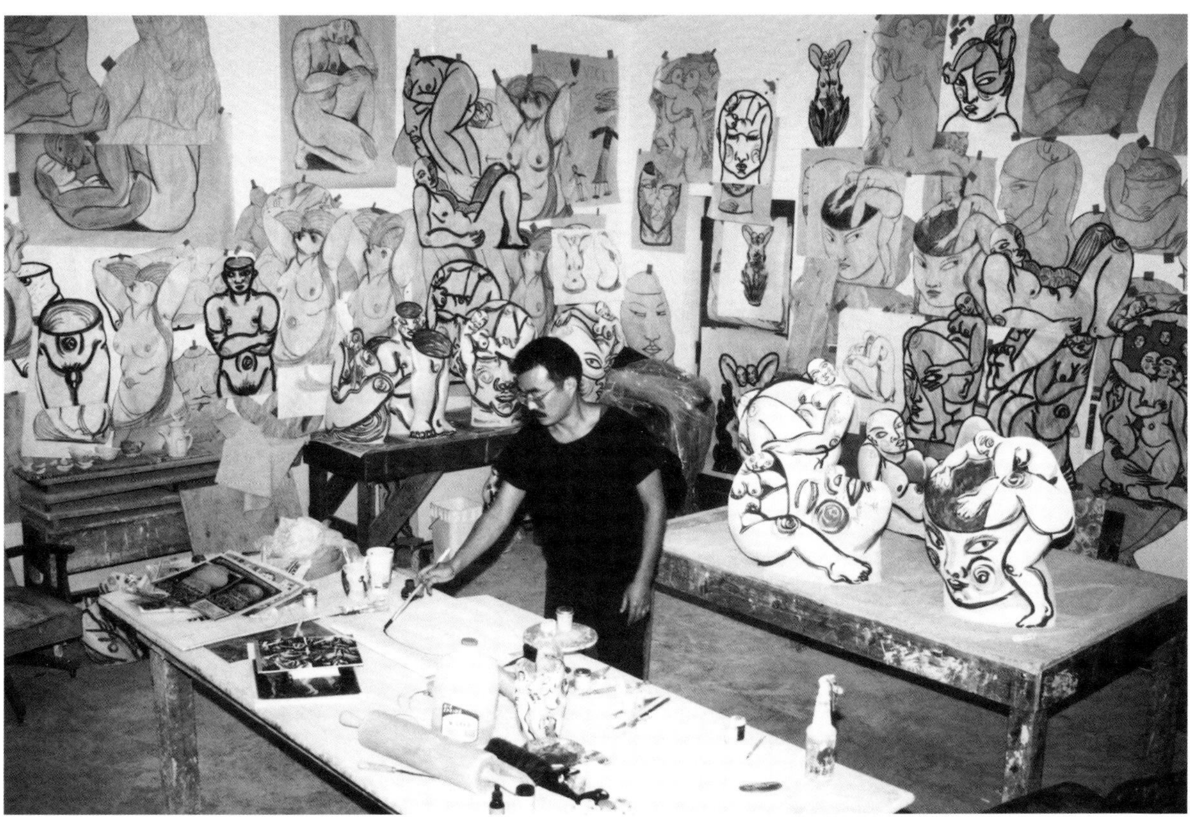

Fig. 2
Takamori working in his studio at the Archie Bray Foundation for the Ceramic Arts, Helena, Montana, 1987. Photo courtesy of the artist

Japan all but impossible for him. Through the late 1970s and early 1980s, Takamori had shuttled between the United States and his homeland, holding temporary jobs teaching ceramics while looking for a place to live and work. He tried to find a Japanese niche for himself, but it proved to be a difficult fit. He recalls: "In ceramics, narrative doesn't really exist there. They prefer abstraction." He lacked the personality, he says, "to fight and break the wall down." So, in the early 1980s, he set his sights on settling in the United States. He married Vicky Lidman in 1984 and a year later began an extended period as a resident artist at the Archie Bray Foundation for the Ceramic Arts, in Helena, Montana (fig. 2).

At the Bray, Takamori settled into refining and pushing his clay envelope, using the form to tell increasingly complex tales of a changing inner world. Shedding his naive ideals about sexual and emotional intimacy, he managed to tap the more ambiguous and turbulent streams of married and familial love.

His *Boy Holding Dog,* 1983 (page 78), made in Japan, and *Self-Portrait,* 1984 (page 79), which he made in Bozeman, Montana, before landing at the Bray, hint at this shift toward denser psychological expressions. The forlorn fellow in *Self-Portrait* isn't merely navel-gazing. Posed as a pot, he is wrapped around his own void. He isn't as acrobatic about it as the guy Takamori later depicted peering up his own tail in *Looking at the World,* 1988. But he might as well be staring up his own dark hole. He is the stoic fretter over a question with no particular answer.

There's also no clear answer as to what's going on between the dog and the boy. Their vigilant stares suggest they're not just posing as Timmy and Lassie sharing a happy hug. The narrowed, darting eyes and slightly bared canines seem to pop the question, "Is this love, or is this entrapment?"

These works begin to show the sharper, more colorful palette that distinguished Takamori's best pots of the 1980s and 1990s. He would often fire his works several times, building up detail and depth to his colors during each pass through the kiln by adding layers of china paint and lusters. Though he relied on a pinkish earthenware for his *Self-Portrait,* he used a white-bodied clay for *Boy Holding Dog.* This shift to white clay, both stoneware and porcelain, brightened his surfaces and helped Takamori achieve a lyrical precision with his coloring and a flurry of brushwork and markings. His companion works *Portrait of Ms. M* and *Portrait of Mr. W,* both 1986 (pages 80, 81), are sensational examples of that.

*Mr. W,* with his upturned head set off by black strokes and incised lines, is a wide-eyed, bird-brained daydreamer, who is thinking about a woman and birds whose reddish outlines seem to drift or fly across his skin. *Ms. M* is the mister's complement, her entire being permeated by the image of a striding man reaching for one of numerous birds and other beasts in flight across her face and torso. Both figures are naked. The open tops of their flattened heads flip the lid on what they're thinking: more birds on the brain.

Takamori distinguished the thinkers from their thoughts by defining the faces and torsos of Ms. and Mr. with fat black strokes and letting the thinner red lines carry the dreams, obsessions, and imaginings. This duality of the dreamer and the dream, act and image, paves the way toward the greater complexity and virtuosity of forms and images found in *Her Love* and *Mother and Son: Homage to Bronzino,* both 1987 (pages 82, 84), and such later works as *Spring,* 1988 (page 86), and *Birth of Lena,* 1990 (page 88).

These and other works from the 1980s and 1990s indicate that Takamori was making his pots more fully dimensional. He extended his decoration across the back of the forms and beefed up the volumetric modeling of his figures. Though works such as *Mother and Son* and *Birth of Lena* began as drawings, their knees, bellies, breasts, and bottoms protrude and swell from their walls as full-bodied players in a drama that comes close to encircling the form. In *Mother and Son,* that drama relates the cycle of emotions and expectations between mother and child. As in many other works, Takamori uses the vessel's hollow as the physical and metaphorical gap of intimacy.

Despite these moves toward in-the-round dimensionality, Takamori never fully abandons his stage-set approach to his works. They always hold a preferred view. That's due in part to his interest in presenting the entire story in a single scene, laying it out across the whole surface. The basic structure of the works also reinforces their frontality. The taller back wall of his envelopes invariably serves as backdrop to the vessel's lower front side. This configuration reflects his forms' beginnings as drawings. Takamori would start each vessel by drawing the figures he wanted to incorporate on large sheets of paper. He would then use the images as patterns to cut the three slabs—back, front, and bottom—that constitute the forms.

In the 1980s, Takamori began playing up the sensuality of his forms by misting their surfaces with salt glaze. In *Spring*, the sheen helps to make the clay appear more skinlike and to sell the sense of a woman transported. Head tossed back, eyes closed and relaxed, one hand hooked around her lover's neck, she is adrift on an ocean of pleasure, a world away from the open-eyed man. There's little ambiguity about the contrasting worlds and perceptions of the lover and the loved. One is black, the other white. One sits on the outside, looking in. The other has gone inward, as far as she can go.

If *Spring* represents the sensual climax of love and lovemaking, then *Mother and Son* and *Birth of Lena* embody some of its inevitable consequences. What's striking about these and other later vessels are their growing dimensionality and realism. Takamori's depiction of his daughter's arrival into the world bears none of the cartoonlike simplicities that accompanied some of his earlier works. The image teems instead with the softness, resolve, endurance, effort, and pain of birth. The helping hands and faces escorting Lena from womb to world signify the new village that surrounds and bolsters every newborn. This may not be a virgin birth, but it comes with its own true-life and life-altering myths of miracles. Takamori's version of it is a scene witnessed and deeply felt, not merely one heard about and retold.

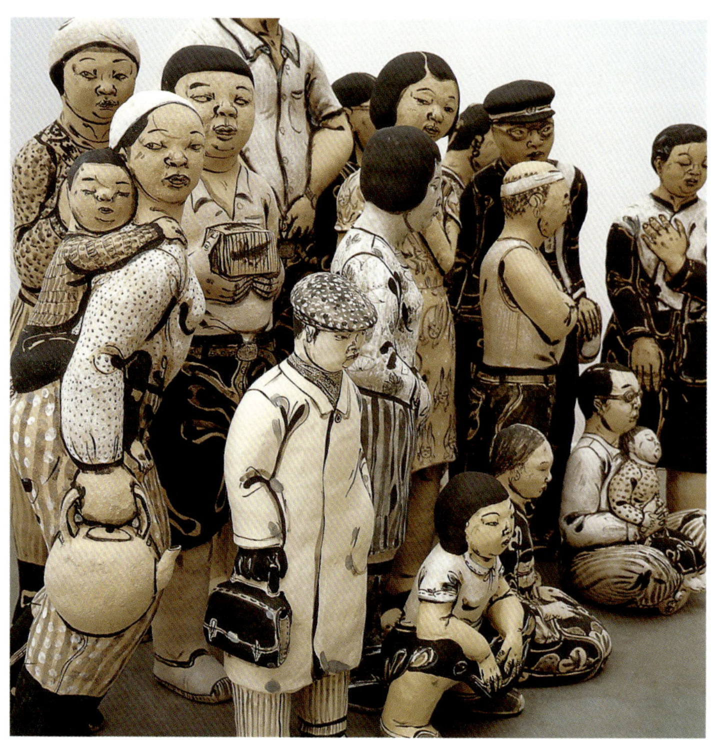

Fig. 3
Studio view of work in progress, 1999.
Photo: Ayumi Horie

These autobiographical images resonate far beyond Takamori's experience. The events and themes they depict—love, birth, sacrifice, deception, and redemption—are common to the tales and images he borrows from Eastern and Western mythology. Yet the figures remain intensely personal, moving easily from those shared mythologies to the one Takamori appeared to be evolving for himself. It's one that always seems to pair outsider with insider. The relaxed woman in *Laocoön,* 1994 (page 98), her arms folded, is not a character from the ancient tale. She is a modern-day reader, perusing Lord Byron's account of Laocoön in *Childe Harold.* She is on the outside, looking in at an event long past.

In his earlier sexually oriented works, Takamori's onlooker could easily pass as a voyeuristic peeper. Yet, over the course of his career, his preoccupation with the emotional and cultural dualities of outsider/insider has come to signify more than that. It underscores Takamori's own efforts to bridge the divide between the world he came from and the one he inhabits. He is not Laocoön warning the Trojans about the danger of the false gift of the wooden horse. Instead, he is a man engulfed by efforts to discern estrangement from belonging and to uncover the roots of identity buried in the cultures that have defined his sense of home.

This is borne out by the tableaux of figures he has produced in the past eight years (figs. 3, 4). Begun at the European Ceramic Work Centre in the Netherlands in 1996, they are as much a departure from the vessels as his *Village* was from the pottery that had preceded it. As he had at the beginning of his career, Takamori returned at this time to the subject of his village to refuel his ideas and depart from the forms he'd been making. This time, it was a village without buildings. The people were the place. The place was a global and intellectual one,

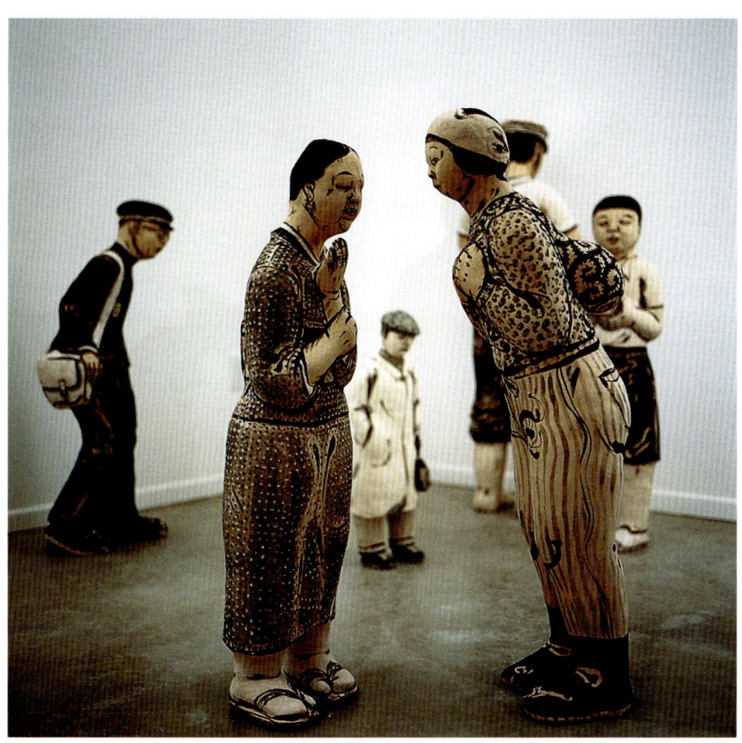

Fig. 4
Studio view of work in progress, 1999.
Photo: Ayumi Horie

made up of figures drawn not merely from Takamori's own past but from the broader streams of political, social, and cultural thought and history he had since come to know. The figures marked the first time that Takamori enclosed the forms and left behind all reference to pottery.

The first of Takamori's clay troops appeared as nostalgic guides to his vanished youth. Garbed in traditional Japanese attire, his *Female Student* and *Male Student,* both 1996 (pages 102, 103), could have easily wandered in from the streets and markets of Takamori's childhood Nobeoka. Like many of his other early figures, these students aren't specific individuals; they are types of people. They get their identities from their poses, clothing, bags, and satchels. Even without knowing the title, we would recognize in the ladies in *Conversation,* 1997, the solicitous postures of people sharing a few words in passing.

These and Takamori's other figures aren't meant to perform as solo sculptural acts. They're meant to act as an ensemble. Their interplay hinges on their identities and proximity to one another. His pairing of figures and the distance he puts between them are similar to how he paired figures in his vessels and used the vessel's hollow space to play up the emotional distance between them. However, unlike the vessels, the overall narrative of the sculptural works seems always to be a story in motion. "Usually when I'm making vessels the story ends when they come out of the kiln," Takamori says. "What's different with the groups is that I begin playing with the pieces and seeing how they fit together after they come out of the kiln."

This open-endedness gave Takamori the flexibility to do more than merely play mix and match with his big clay dolls. By moving and repositioning the

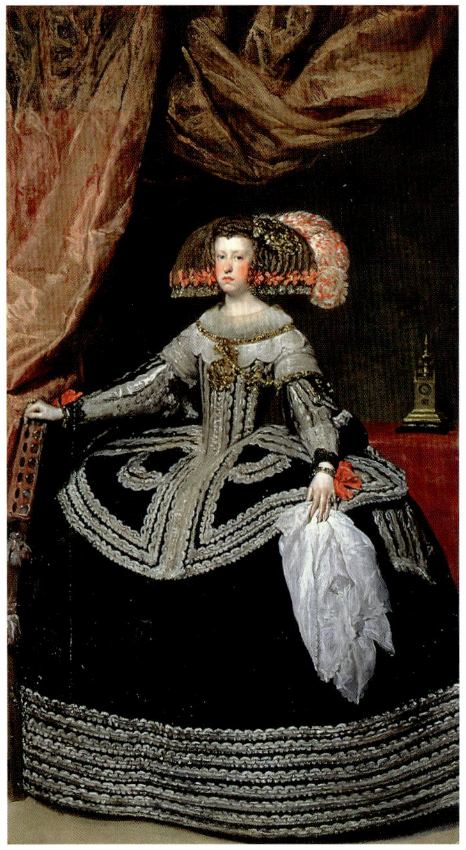

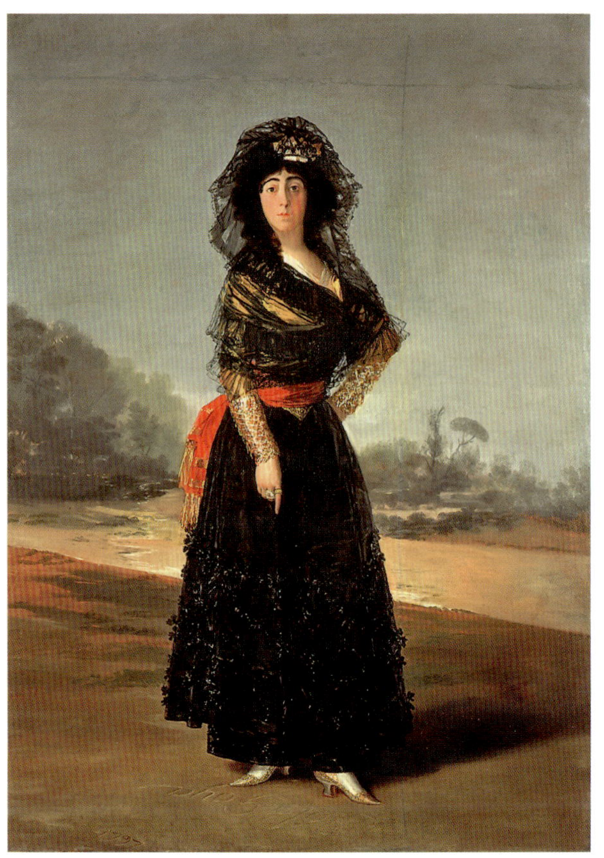

Fig. 5
Diego Rodríguez de Silva Velázquez, *Queen Doña Mariana of Austria*, 1652–53, oil on canvas, 90$^{15}/_{16}$ x 51½ in. Photo © Prado National Museum, Madrid

Fig. 6
Francisco Goya y Lucientes, *The Duchess of Alba*, 1797, oil on canvas, 82¾ x 58¾ in. Photo © Hispanic Society of America, New York

figures, he compounded their inferences and amplified their contrasts of class, culture, and politics. This social and historical engineering could easily be lost in the context of a retrospective display, where a sculpture from one series might get paired with one from another. Yet the impact is clear in the original tableaux, where the figures functioned as both mirror and lens on their made-up worlds. Their warps of time and history put the Jane and Joe punch-clocks of one era and culture elbow to elbow with those of another. The tableaux allow peasantry and royalty to mingle, and political and military winners and losers to share the stage.

The resulting collisions of culture and images often reflect equivalences of class. *Empress* and *Queen*, both 2003 (pages 112, 113), offer a dress-up duel of royalty in a world where size and opulence are indicators of power. That's evident enough in the billowing skirt and blooming hairdo of the Queen, inspired by Velázquez's *Queen Doña Mariana of Austria* (fig. 5), and the phallic dimensions of the Empress, whose swollen shaftlike torso rises from a base of twin bulbs, her sexualized form crowned by a bulbous wig. The shape of the hair, like the rest of her form, comes from Tang figures. Their suggestion of "ripe fruit, genitals, or breasts," as Takamori once put it, could hardly have been accidental. The point is clear enough. Royal is royal, in any setting. The cumulative erotic, social, and political power of the throne is packaged in the costume and the coiffure. Yet Takamori presents his *Queen* and *Empress* as rulers victimized—their power compromised—by the very trappings of style. Swaddled and bound by the

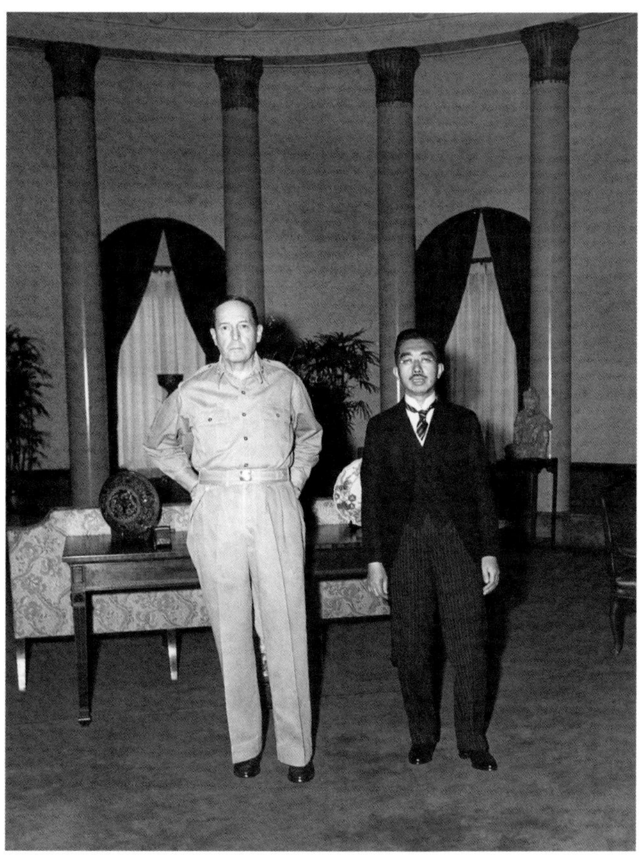

Fig. 7
Photograph taken at the first meeting of General MacArthur and Emperor Hirohito, September 27, 1945. Photo © U.S. National Archives and Records Administration, Maryland

unyielding lavishness of their costumed forms, they have no visible feet, no mobility. They appear to be frozen in their power roles and robes.

These aren't the only images in which size and costume matter. In *General and Emperor,* 2001 (page 107), the khaki-clad figure of General Douglas MacArthur, the Pacific victor of the Second World War, rises above that of the defeated Emperor Hirohito, who is dressed in Western-style formal wear (fig. 7). In *Dance,* 2001 (page 106), a uniformed American soldier towers over a kimonoed partner who appears to eye him uneasily. And *Duchess,* 2000 (page 108), meant to represent Goya's *Duchess of Alba* (fig. 6), originally appeared beside the diminutive figure of an old Japanese woman.

However, West doesn't always trump East. Takamori sometimes reverses scale and size. In one tableau (not included in this exhibition), as critic Matthew Kangas has pointed out, "a Japanese child may tower over an Old Master painting figure, or a boy reading a magazine may overwhelm a European farmer."[12]

This "tension of scale and cultural encounter," as Kangas described it, underscores the uneasy relationship between East and West. Yet Takamori's tableaux are more than an impersonal rehash of cultural and political struggles and domination. His images are history made personal. His pairings of queens and empresses, generals and emperors, East and West reflect his own sense of dual cultural citizenship. Takamori straddles the world of his birth and his chosen world as both an insider and an outsider. As *Sleeping Woman and Child* and *Sleeping Woman*

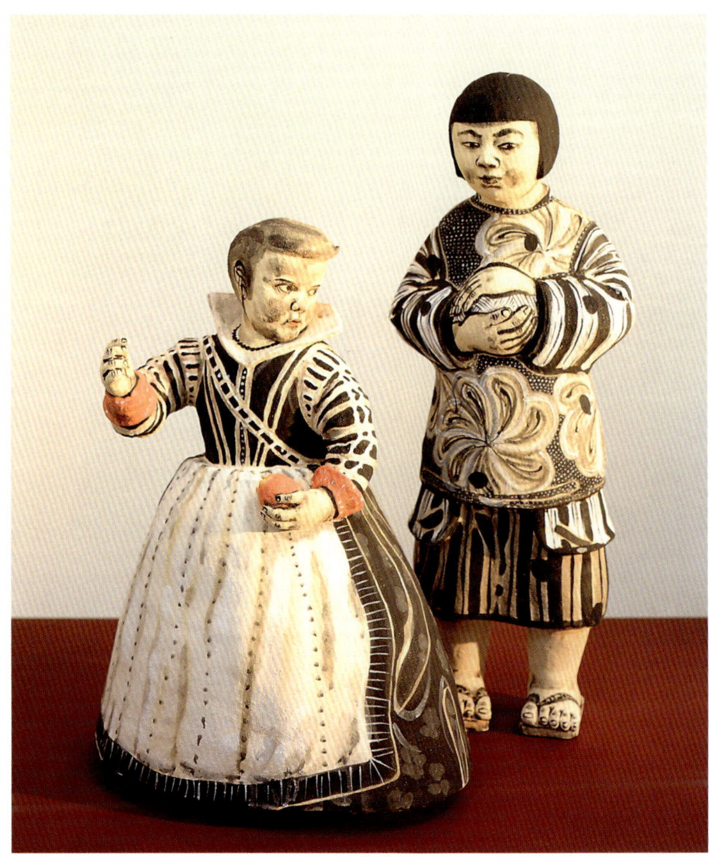

Fig. 8
*Dwarf* and *Girl with Ball*, both 2000, on view in the exhibition *Ensemble* at Grover/Thurston Gallery, Seattle, 2000. Photo: Kate Preftakes, courtesy of Grover/Thurston Gallery, Seattle

*in Checkered Skirt,* both 2003 (pages 110, 111), suggest, his position is suffused with the vulnerability and power of sleepers and watchers.

Eyes closed, bodies inert, and minds appearing to be unaware of all but the limits of their skin, the sleepers would seem to be the exposed ones in the room. The rosy-cheeked *Sleeping Woman in Checkered Skirt* lies in an unguarded pose of comfort, her body curved slightly inward, her hands pillowing her head. The youngster in *Sleeping Woman and Child* nestles in the protective contours of the woman, whose arm is draped across him for good measure. It's difficult to come upon these figures without feeling a twinge at having intruded on a rare intimacy. Yet Takamori twists that response by flip-flopping ideas of strength and weakness, dominance and submissiveness. At home and at ease in their unconscious worlds, the sleepers play the insiders in their scenes. Awake, upright, and free to walk around them, we are nudged to the outside, conscious of all that we can never know about what lies beneath the surface of these works. As he has done throughout his career, Takamori compels us to peer at these figures from across a fundamental divide. In this case, it's one that gives us the dreamers, not the dreams; the visible facts, but not the feelings.

## Notes

1. Rick Newby, "To Stave Off Death: Akio Takamori's Life Studies," *Ceramics: Art and Perception,* no. 8 (1992): 33.

2. *The Confessions of St. Augustine,* trans. Albert Cook Outler (Mineola, N.Y.: Dover Publications, 2002), 179.

3. Unless otherwise noted, all statements by the artist are from an interview by the author, July 2004.

4. Garth Clark, in artist biography materials for the Garth Clark Gallery.

5. Akio Takamori and Peter Ferris, "Vessel Concepts," *Ceramics Monthly* 36, no. 2 (February 1988): 27.

6. Ibid.

7. Garth Clark, *American Ceramics: 1876 to the Present* (New York: Abbeville Press, 1987), 222.

8. Andy Nasisse made a similar point in "The Battleground of Eros: Akio Takamori," *American Ceramics* 5, no. 1 (1986): 32.

9. Clark, *American Ceramics,* 22.

10. Akio Takamori, in *Master's Touch,* exh. brochure (Tempe, Ariz.: Tempe Arts Center, 1996).

11. Carl Jung, *Portable Jung,* ed. Joseph Campbell, trans. R. F. C. Hull (New York: Penguin Books, 1971), 294.

12. Matthew Kangas, "Exhibits Feature Work of Ceramic Sculptors," *Seattle Times,* October 20, 2000, sec. E, p. 8.

# The Image of Ordinary Japanese People in Akio Takamori's Art

*by Toyojiro Hida*

高森暁夫 (Takamori Akio) の日本人像 (Individual Figures)

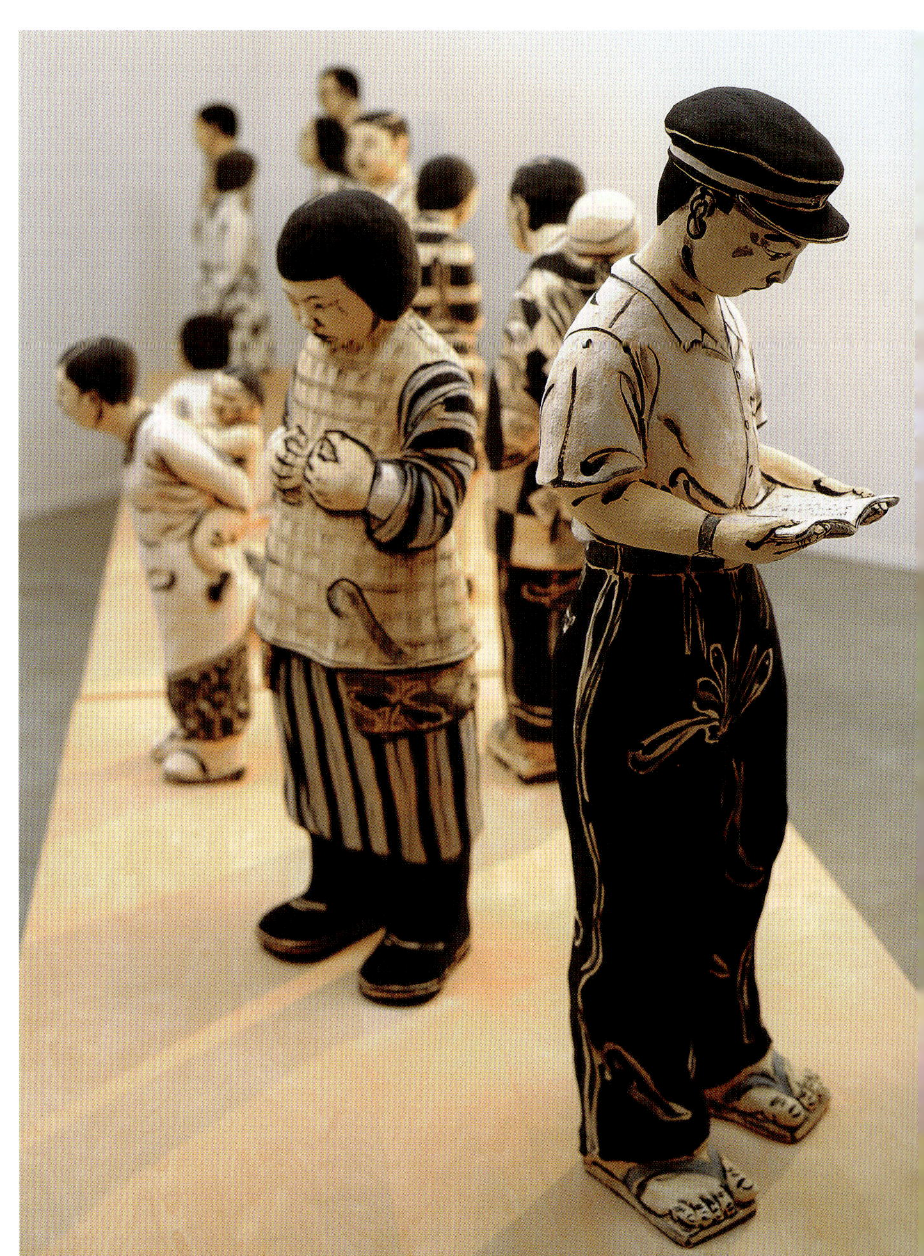

WHEN I FIRST SAW AKIO TAKAMORI'S *Villagers (Figural Group),* 2000 (fig. 1), I was immediately reminded of the *manga* works of Yū Takita depicting scenes of working-class life in Tokyo during and immediately after the Second World War (fig. 2). Takita's people are lovingly portrayed amid settings complete with the smallest details of everyday life. However, Takita started to draw *manga* of this style only in the late 1960s, when the details captured in his works had already vanished and thus were remembered with nostalgia and some idealization. His portrayals can be seen then as a lamentation for the loss of the old ways. The men, women, and children in Takita's world—with their very human weaknesses and surrounded by the details of daily life—seem to have much in common with the people in Takamori's figural group.

Wanting to better understand Takamori's art, with its focus on ordinary people's lifestyles, I looked at the whole of postwar Japanese art and found that photography was the medium that took up this theme most often. The earliest examples (though not by Japanese artists) are the photographs taken shortly after the war, and printed in *Life* magazine, that reported the destitution of the people in this defeated country (fig. 3). They are more photojournalism than fine art, perhaps, but one can recognize in them how much the news photographers sincerely cared for the people they were recording, which adds a layer of subjective expression to these images. This is especially evident in the images of children playing in worn, patched clothing. When the photographers looked at these children, they saw simply children, not citizens of a nation that had been defeated by their own. Examples of this kind of endearing photography are included in John W. Dower's landmark history of postwar Japan, *Embracing Defeat: Japan in the Wake of World War II.*

One of the most notable postwar works by a Japanese artist is Ken Domon's *Children of Chikuho,* 1960 (fig. 4), which captured the unbroken spirit of people living in dire poverty. As the coal industry declined, the people working in the coal mines suffered from drastically reduced incomes. Domon was an outsider to the poverty-stricken area, someone just visiting from a more affluent city. Yet he was acutely aware that Japan's overall economic growth, which was gaining momentum at the time, was contributing to the poverty and hardship of the coal miners. Unlike the earlier American news photographers, Domon felt a personal

Fig. 1
Akio Takamori, installation view of *Villagers (Figural Group),* Garth Clark Gallery, New York, 2000. Photo: Kate Preftakes

挿図1
高森暁夫
『ヴィレッジの人々』、
2000年、個人蔵

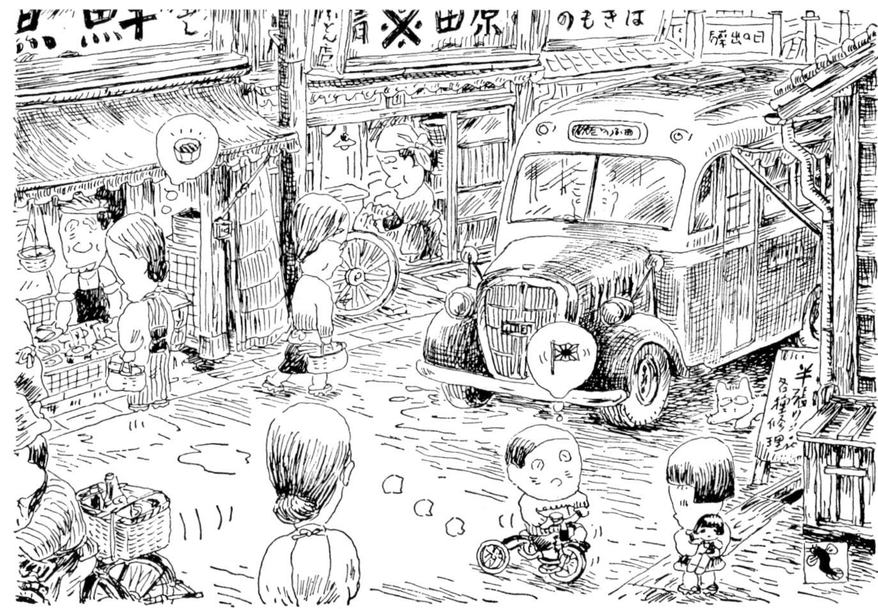


Fig. 2
Yū Takita, "Bus Route Street," from *Dreamy Episodes from Shōwa* (Shōwa Yume Zoshi), Shincho-sha, 1980.
Photo © Asako Takita

挿図2
滝田ゆう
「裏町バス通り」、
『昭和夢草紙』、
1980年、新潮社

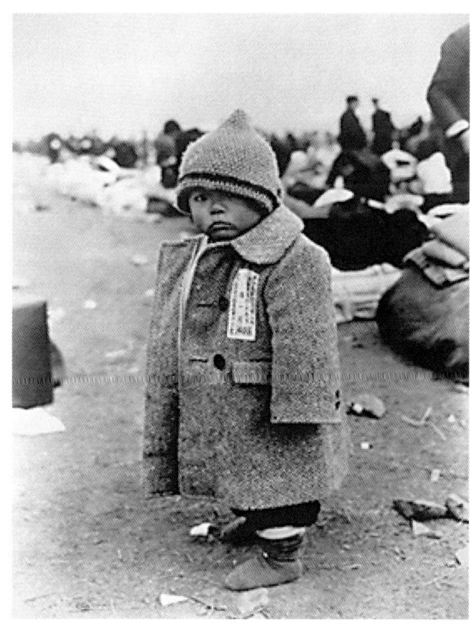

Fig. 3
Repatriated child, 1946.
Photo: Keystone/Staff
Hulton Archive

挿図3
キーストン／スタッフ
『引揚者の子供』1946年、
ハルトンアーカイブ

高森暁夫の『ヴィレッジの人々 (FIGURAL　GROUP)』(2000年) という作品を見たとき、わたしは滝田ゆうの漫画を思い出した (挿図1, 2)。滝田が漫画の舞台としたのは、戦中から戦後、つまり1940年代から50年代の日本の下町である。そこで生きる人たちの姿を、滝田は細密なタッチで丹念に描いた。もっとも滝田がそうした漫画を発表しはじめたのは1960年代末になってからのことである。そこで描かれた下町情緒はもはや現実のものではなく、すでにポエジーであった。消えゆくものへの哀惜がそこには込められていた。その滝田の漫画に登場する飾り気のない、そして生活感あふれる子供や大人たちが、高森のつくる人物像と通じ合っているように思えたのだ。

滝田の描く人物の顔立ちはだれもが童顔である。漫画だから当然だともいえるが、登場人物はみな嘘のつけない人柄を表している。この点でも、高森が表現する庶民のあどけない表情と共通しているように思えた。

高森の作品に触発されて、戦後日本で庶民の素朴な生活に関心を寄せた造形表現を探してみると、「写真」がそこに視点を当て続けてきたことに気づかされる。早い例としては、敗戦直後の貧しい生活を捉えたグラフ雑誌『LIFE』の写真がある。これは造形表現というよりも、報道というべきものだが、とくにつぎはぎの服で遊ぶ子供たちにカメラを向けた特派員の目には、なぜかしら愛情が感じられる。相手が子供であるだけに、そこには勝者と敗者の関係を一瞬忘れた人間を見る目の優しさがあり、それが報道写真にも広い意味での主観的表現を与えていったのではないだろうか。そうした写真は、1999年に出版されたジョン・ダワーの『敗北を抱きしめて』 (John W. Dower,『Embracing Defeat』) でも、微笑ましい戦後のスナップとして紹介されている。

外部のアメリカ人によってではなく、日本人自身の目で戦後の庶民生活、とくに貧困とそれを跳ね返していく生命力を捉えた写真としては、土門拳の『筑豊のこどもたち』(1960年2月) がある。石炭産業の崩壊に

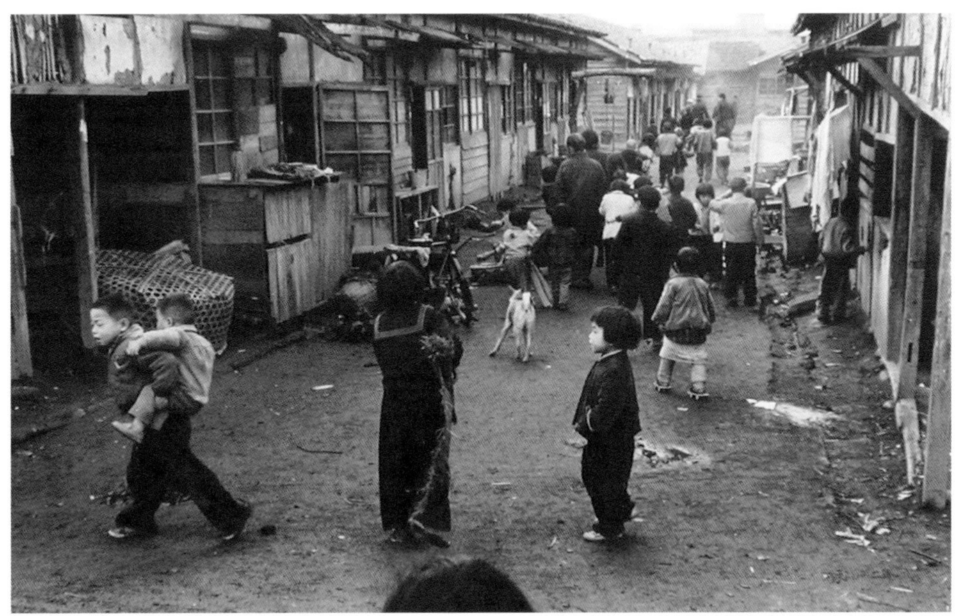

Fig. 4
Ken Domon, *Children of Chikuho,* 1960. Photo © Ken Domon Photography Museum, Sakata City, Japan

挿図4
土門拳,
『筑豊の子供達』
1960年，土門拳写真美術館

responsibility, to some extent, for the scenes he was recording: he captured the images of children playing around the miners' housing as a case history of how some segments of the population inevitably lose a previous lifestyle as other segments of the economy gain new affluence.

Nobuyoshi Araki's first collection of photographs, *Satchin,* 1964, has a similar viewpoint, though Japan's social structure was not his central theme (fig. 5). In this series, Araki records, in the style of a straight documentary report, the daily life of a fourth-grade boy and his pals in Mikawajima, a district in the working-class area of Tokyo. The photographer would later become very popular—dubbed "Araki the Genius"—for his works capturing scenes from contemporary sex culture, but it should be noted that he began his career by portraying the working-class lifestyle in a neighborhood that seemed to be left out of the urbanization that was transforming other, better-off parts of Tokyo. In other words, he was like many Japanese at the time who appreciated modernization but were also somewhat dismayed by the rapidity of change, looking back on the older lifestyle with a certain nostalgia.

Takamori's figures share the same theme—the nostalgia for an older, now vanished lifestyle. Since the end of the war, many photographers have aimed their cameras at social realities in Japan; but fine art, in both painting and sculpture, has almost exclusively pursued new aesthetics, detached from and independent of the realities of life. The latter has been true as well in the crafts, and only a handful of artists has taken an interest in exploring the changing society and lifestyle. Takamori's ceramic figures embody a rare exception. They are probably based on people in his hometown of Nobeoka and are not in any way unusual in themselves. But the fact that they were chosen as the subject for a work of craft art is very unusual, because ordinary people, treated in a realistic manner, have never been taken up in Japanese crafts, except in the form of dolls.

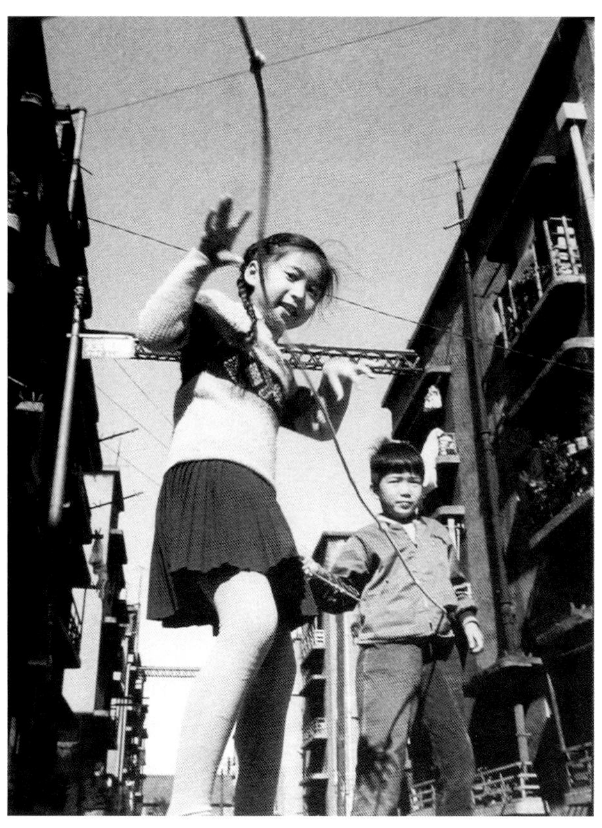

Fig. 5
Nobuyoshi Araki,
*Satchin*, 1964

挿図5
荒木経惟、『さっちん』
1964年

よって貧困のさなかにある炭坑住宅で生きる子供たちを見つめる土門の目は、やはり都会人という外部からのそれではあった。が、しかし、高度経済成長の始まりが炭鉱労働者を失業させていると認識していた土門の目は、自分も含めた日本自体の選択がこうした困窮生活を引き起こしていると自覚していた点で、『LIFE』誌の特派員のそれとは大きく違っていた。土門は、いわば、自分も加担している日本経済の成長が不可避的に生じさせる古い庶民生活の喪失例として、筑豊の炭坑住宅で遊ぶ子供たちを撮影したのである。

土門の場合ほど日本の社会構造にたいする関心はつよくなかったが、荒木経惟 (ARAKI Nobuyoshi) の処女写真集『さっちん』(1964年) にも同じ視点があった。これは東京の下町である三河島の小学4年生の少年とその仲間の生活を、ルポルタージュのように記録したものである。後に「天才アラーキー」と自称して東京の新しい性風俗を激写して売れっ子写真家になる荒木だが、その原点が身近にあってしかし徐々に社会の発展から置き去りにされていく下町生活にあったことは見落としてはならないだろう。つまり、多くの日本人は変貌する東京に共感をもちつつも、その速さにとまどいや不安を感じて古い東京への郷愁を抱いたのだが、そのなかのひとりに荒木もいたということである。

高森暁夫のつくる人物像も、庶民生活を懐古するこうした戦後日本の視点に連なるものである。戦後の「写真」が日本の現実に目を向けてきたのにたいし、絵画や彫刻などの純粋美術は、むしろ生活から遊離した新しい芸術運動それ自体を追求してきた。工芸にしても状況は同じで、社会と連動した生活の変化には、一部の作家を除いて関心を払ってこなかった。そうしたなかで、高森の陶彫による人物像は希有な例である。彼の作品は生まれ育った延岡の街で子供の頃に目にした人たちの姿を再現したものと思われるが、そもそも市井の人々を「工芸」が表現の主題とすること自体、「人形」を除けば日本ではなかったのである。

Even though they share a certain theme with Domon's photographs and Takita's *manga,* Takamori's ceramic figures differ in one important aspect: the sense of loss and sadness that tinges the images of the former was an emotion felt by all Japanese, who were witnessing massive social changes in the 1960s and 1970s, but Takamori's figures exist outside this social context. They are removed from the shared sense of loss for the older ways for two reasons. One is that Takamori was living in the United States and therefore was not driven by a need to create works that took up as their theme contradictions in Japanese society resulting from the recent economic growth. The other is that Takamori lacked the sense of involvement, the guilt of having taken part in this destruction, that was felt by artists in Japan, who witnessed these changes firsthand. It is telling that he started to make these figures of the people of Nobeoka in 1993, when the old lifestyle was already long gone, and during his stay at the European Ceramic Work Centre in the Netherlands.

One may ask then what motivated Takamori to create these works featuring innocent facial expressions and humble clothing long after these characteristics had disappeared forever from Japanese society. One can understand this, I believe, by seeing how Takamori discovered his own, new approach to art-making. But before I go on to discuss his approach, I would like to make this point: the sense of loss that was felt by the Japanese did not mean that they wanted the old lifestyle back; rather, it was a kind of reminder not to forget the values of the past, when people were poorer but cared more for one another, before society changed all around them through the rapid modernization that was, for the most part, a process of Westernization.

No one can clearly define what these traditional values were that gave the Japanese a spiritual strength in their daily life. It is certain, however, that the Japanese, when facing the flood of Western ideas and values that entered Japan after the opening of the ports at the end of the Edo period (1603–1867), made a constant effort to maintain their cultural identity by reminding themselves that their traditional value system, which was still very much alive in certain aspects of their lives, was as effective as the new Western one. That is why, when the last remnants of the older lifestyle started to disappear in the wake of rapid economic

しかしながら、こうした根本的一致があるのにもかかわらず、高森の陶彫像と、土門の写真や滝田の漫画との間には決定的差異もあった。それは土門や滝田の場合、消えゆく庶民生活への眼差しは個人的興味であるだけではなく、日本社会全体の関心事でもあったのにたいし、高森の眼差しには、いうまでもなく、そうした社会的関心が重なり合ってはいなかったということである。

高森の場合、二重の意味で1960年代から70年代に日本で高まった庶民生活の喪失にたいする関心とは無縁だった。ひとつには、アメリカ社会で生きる高森にとって、日本の経済成長がもたらす社会的ひずみを持ちだしたところで、それはお門違いのメッセージでしかなかったからである。

そしてもうひとつには、高森の目には最初から、日本の古い庶民生活の喪失を他人事として見過ごせない共犯者的感覚が含まれていなかったからである。そのことは、高森が人物像を本格的につくりだした時期が端的に物語っているだろう。彼の作品に延岡の人たちの立体像が登場するのは、日本の町並みからすでに古い情緒が消えてしまった後である。それは、1993年にオランダのヨーロッパ陶芸センター (European Ceramic Work Centre) で研修制作して以降のことだった。

それでは高森はなぜ、日本人の顔からあどけなさが失われ、その身なりから質素さが消えてしまった後になって、それらを作品化しはじめたのだろうか。そこにこそ高森独自の着眼点があったに違いない。だが、その話しにはいる前に、日本人にとってかつての庶民生活への哀惜は、かならずしも郷愁の念にかられてのことではなく、むしろ、戦後の生活が際限なく近代化、実態としては西洋化していくなかで、貧しいけれども人情の深かった生活を律していた価値観まで忘れてしまいたくないという気持ちの表れだったことを思いだしておくべきだろう。

もっとも、生活の精神的側面を支えてきた日本固有の価値観といっても、それがどのようなものであるのか、誰も定かには示せない。しかし、日本人は幕末の開国からというもの、西洋の価値観が押し寄せてくるのを体験して、日本にもそれに対抗しうるだけの価値観があったはずだし、いまでも残存しているはずだと想定し続けてきた。だから高度経済成長によって、生活のすみずみまでが根こそぎ西洋化されだしたとき、炭坑住宅の生活や下町情緒に多くの人の目が向いたのもことの必然だった。ほんとうにそれらの場に、生活の精神的アルカディアがあるかどうかはわからない。それらは西洋流の生活にたいするカウンターカルチャーとして、いささか強調していえば「仮構」されたのだ。

こうして西洋が流入してくることへの防波堤として、そうしたものがあると想定されだした日本固有の価値観は「伝統」と呼ばれてきた。明治維新後にその名前が登場する日本舞踊、日本画、工芸などは、見かけは旧来の舞踊、絵画、手仕事を踏襲していたが、その内容は土着的伎芸と近代芸術の複合物であって、文明開化期の発明品だった。

growth, people were drawn to scenes of coal-mining towns or working-class districts. It would be wrong to say that such areas were actual Arcadias. But the concept of the older lifestyle was "created" out of necessity, as a way to balance out the Western elements that have come to dominate Japan.

The values that were believed to be indigenous to Japan, and that were supposed to function as a bulwark against the influx of Western elements, fell under the rubric of "tradition." After the Meiji Restoration in 1868, what qualified as "traditional" Japanese dance, Japanese-style painting (*nihonga*), and craft were in fact mixtures of indigenous heritage and modern art, inventions that were characteristic of the era when Japan was undergoing the first stage of industrialization.

The cultural heritages of Japan, which had long-established schools such as the tea ceremony, ikebana (flower arrangement), and the incense ceremony, also saw a general revival in the Meiji period (1868–1912). Noh, Kabuki, and crafts techniques were given renewed recognition after the Second World War when legislation ordained that such heritages were to be protected to ensure their preservation.

These things make up what is called "traditional culture" in Japan today. In discussing Japan's modernization, Western critics sometimes argue that, through such legislation, Japan has been able to successfully preserve older cultural elements while promoting general modernization. But one cannot tell if these laws have been beneficial simply by looking at what has been preserved. I sometimes even suspect that such arguments, which applaud Japan's acceptance of Western values without too much fuss, are in fact a ruse to keep the status quo.

Japanese-style painting, craft art, the tea ceremony, ikebana, Kabuki, and other forms of Japanese heritage have survived not because we had this thing called "tradition" a priori but because new explorations by artists in each of these fields enabled them to adapt these forms to the new era and to create the concept of tradition as a new value system. Tradition cannot be given a concrete definition. It is a spiritual homeland, something invented in order for the culture to survive the clash of foreign and indigenous elements that has been going on constantly since Japan started its modernization.

江戸時代からすでに流派が形成されてきた茶道、華道、香道にしても、明治時代になって再活性化されている。また、能、歌舞伎、職人技などは、戦後になって伝統芸能、そして、伝統工芸という枠組みのもとで、その保護と継承が法律で規定されてきた。

これらが今日の日本で「伝統」文化と総称されているものの中身だが、こうした近代の文化史および施策に着目して、日本は近代化政策のなかで古いものをうまく残してきたという論調が、ときおり西洋の側から聞こえてくる。しかし、これは結果を元にして原因を探ろうとする予定調和的な見方に過ぎる。深読みすれば、日本は西洋の流儀を押しつけられても反撥しないでうまく対処してくれる、という政治的発言とも聞こえる。

日本には先験的に「伝統」が存在しているから、日本画、工芸、茶道、華道、歌舞伎などの分野が、それを忠実に表現してきたのではない。それらの分野ごとの独自な模索が、新たな価値観としての「伝統」を創出してきたのである。「伝統」には具体的な実体がない。それは近代日本における外来と固有という対立「構造」が生みだした、日本人にとっての精神的家郷なのである。

さて、ここで話しを高森睦夫に戻せば、高森は人物像をつくるのに際し、日本の生活を律してきた固有の価値や、それを芸術の立場から解釈した「伝統」を、作品の主題として掲げなかった。外来と固有の対立という「構造」が生じさせるアポリアは、それこそ日本固有の問題であった。高森はむしろそうした「構造」にとらわれることなく、日本の生活から庶民の風貌を「切り取って」見せてくれた。だからそれでなくても、庶民の顔立ちは芸術作品のなかではあどけなく表現されがちなのに、高森のそれは無垢 (innocent) と呼べるほど屈託のない表情を与えられている。高森の表現する人物のあどけなさには、加速度的に日本が西洋化していくことへのとまどい、そして、淋しさを、誰に向かって訴えることもできないが、ともかく表明しておかなければ気が収まらないという、大方の日本人がかつて抱いた心情が託されていなかったからである。

ところで、高森の人物像が日本の生活から「切り取られ」ているといったのは、なにもそれらのモデルが太平洋の向こう側から持ち込まれたことを指しての比喩であるばかりではない。造形的にもそうなのだ。

それは高森が大学時代に図書館の本から引き剥がし、いまでも大切にとってある日本の春画 (頁29, 挿図7) を見るとよくわかる。これから得たインスピレーションが、彼の初期の作品である『カップル (COUPLE)』(挿図6) に結びついたそうだ。その春画は、具体的には喜多川歌麿の『歌まくら』(1788年頃) のなかの一場面だったが、日本の春画にしては珍しく男女の重なり合う姿だけが画面いっぱいに描かれている。男の脚にいたっては、画面左にはみだしている。

私は春画の専門家ではないが、江戸時代の春画はたいてい室内全体を視野に納め、そのなかに男女が配置されている。つまり、愛し合う男女は絵の主題であると同時に、重要な点景にもなってい

Which leads us back to Takamori and his approach to the theme of ordinary people. In creating his human figures, he doesn't address the values that once governed the Japanese people—the "tradition," from an artistic viewpoint. The aporia arising from the conflict between foreign and indigenous elements was a strictly Japanese phenomenon, which did not concern Takamori. He was thus able to portray ordinary Japanese people severed from the realities of Japanese society. Working-class people tend to be given ingenuous-looking faces in artworks. In Takamori's case, liberation from the social context makes these figures even more ingenuous, bordering on pure innocence, because their expression is not informed by the once prevalent need among the Japanese to voice bewilderment and sadness about the country's rapid Westernization.

When I say that Takamori "severed" ordinary people from the larger Japanese society, I mean not only to use it as a metaphor to acknowledge that he modeled these figures while across the ocean from Japan but also to emphasize that they are severed in an artistic sense. This becomes clear when we look at the erotic ukiyo-e print he removed from a library book when he was a university student and has kept with him over the decades (see page 29). He says that this print inspired his *Couple,* 1980 (fig. 6). The print is a scene from Kitagawa Utamaro's *Utamakura* (Poem of the Pillow), ca. 1788, and is unusual in presenting the couple making love close-up, with their bodies filling the whole picture plane and the man's legs extending out of view to the left.

I'm no expert on erotic prints, but examples from the Edo period generally present the couple within the environment of their rendezvous. In other words, the couple usually functions both as the main subject of the picture and as the focal point in the overall composition, which tends to make it ambiguous as to whether the main interest of the picture is the couple having intercourse or the sentiments evoked by the setting of their secret meeting. These pictures are typically dotted with props that provide atmosphere, such as beds screens, sake bottles and cups on a tray stand, a tobacco tray, a bin in which to throw removed clothes and, of course, the futon.

The ukiyo-e print Takamori has long cherished has an almost complete absence of atmosphere. The patterns on the couple's clothing are carefully rendered,

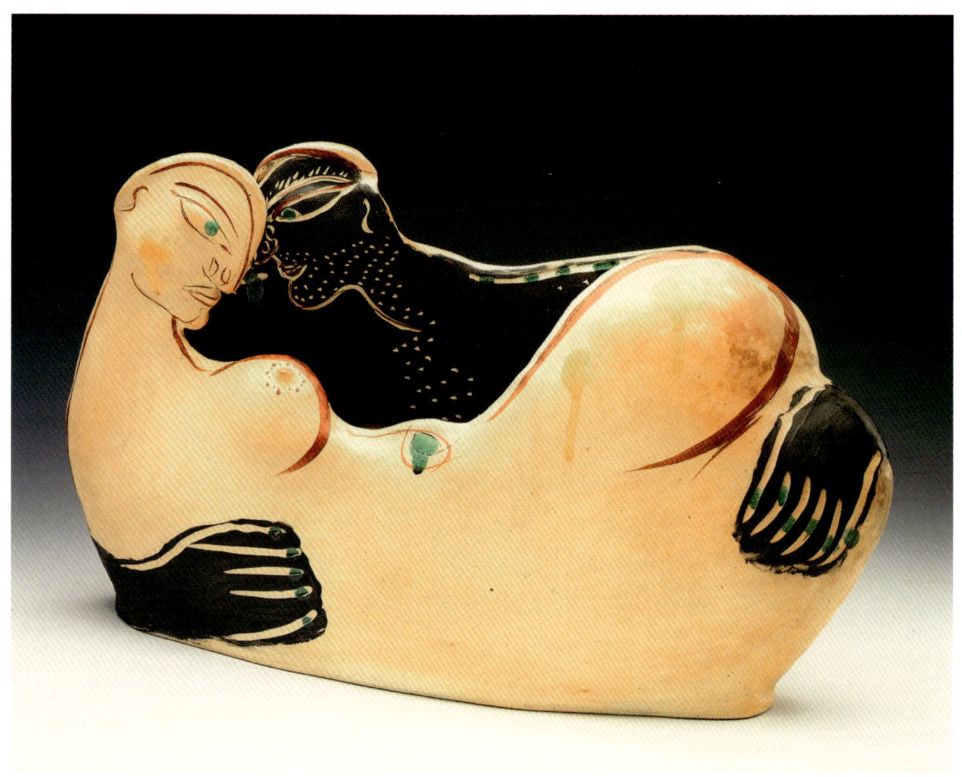

Fig. 6
Akio Takamori, *Couple,*
1980, cat. no. 2

挿図6
高森暁夫
『カップル』、
1980年、個人蔵

て、春画がほんとうに表現したいのが、男女の物理的交わりなのか、それともその交わりが醸し出す「淫靡」、「秘め事」といった情緒なのか、そのどちらであるのかが判然としないものが多い。それが証拠に、春画には枕屏風、膳に載った徳利と猪口、煙草盆、脱いだ衣服を入れておく乱り箱、そしてもちろん布団といった、雰囲気を掻き立てる小道具が描き込まれている。

ところが、高森の愛蔵する春画にはそうした周囲の描写がほとんどない。その分、服の文様が細かく表されているが、女の方は絣でとても地味だ。こういう即物的な春画に着目したところに、高森の非凡さがあった。そして、後に男女間のさまざまな性を題材にして頭角を現していく作家としての原点があった。江戸の春画は郭情緒が表現の重要な味付けになっていたが、高森はそこから男女の関係だけを鮮やかに「切り取って」みせたのである。これなら江戸の遊郭を知らない人にも理解される、そしてこちらの方がより重要なことだが、自分と同時代の物語として親近感をもってもらえる。

もうひとつ例を挙げてみよう。最初に掲げた『ヴィレッジの人々 (FIGURAL GROUP)』なのだが、ここに出てくる人たちも延岡、あるいは日本の街から「切り取られ」ている。日本人の目には身なりから、登場人物の生きていた時代と土地柄がある程度推測がつくのだが、それが分からない人の目には、高森のつくる人物像はたんに見慣れぬ服を着た鄙びた容姿の人たちとして映るのではないだろうか。

実際、高森も最初はこの人物たちを延岡の町並みに入れ込んで制作している。1976年に制作されたカンザス美術大学 (Kansas City Art Institute) の卒業制作『ヴィレッジ (VILLAGE)』(挿図7) がそれである。この作品ならば、なんの予備知識がない人にも、そこに出てくる人物たちが東洋の一隅で生活を営んでいたのだということが一目瞭然であろう。しかしながら、この『ヴィレッジ (VILLAGE)』になると人物は主役ではなくなり、街の雰囲気を演出する点景になってしまう。説明的になると、またしても情緒が作品の主題として浮上してしまうのだ。

but the woman's kimono is a subdued *ikat*. The fact that he chose this print out of so many indicates that Takamori was drawn more specifically to the forms in the print; in fact, his own talent in working directly with form later earned him success with works depicting couples in various sexual contexts. Whereas the erotic prints of the Edo period rely heavily on atmosphere, Takamori's couples are in a severed state, in which the background is completely lacking and all attention is directed at them alone. What is even more important is that, by removing the context from the erotic scene, Takamori gives it universality, making it possible for anyone from any culture to relate to his work.

Let me cite another example. In *Villagers (Figural Group),* the people are severed from their home, whether we consider it to be Nobeoka specifically or Japan more generally. A Japanese person can tell from the figures' clothing alone roughly what period and area they belong to; but for anyone without that background knowledge, the figures appear to be a group of simple-looking people dressed in a somewhat unfamiliar style.

Takamori initially conceived this work as a group portrait set in the streets of Nobeoka, and its first incarnation was as *Village,* 1976 (fig. 7), his thesis work at the Kansas City Art Institute. In this earlier work, you can instantly recognize that these are people who live in some part of Asia. But the environmental elements overshadow the significance of the people themselves; they are there primarily to add a narrative element to the overall atmosphere. This allows sentiments, not the form, to dominate the work.

Sentiments are useful when you are trying to describe the main characters to the viewer, but they interfere with the characters' ability to enter the viewer's imagination and start telling their own stories. Sentiments are predefined, no matter how subtle they are. They can be a source for an artwork, but they don't allow the viewer to arrive at his or her own personal understanding of the work or to be inspired by it to gain a new viewpoint. Takamori must have realized this, and he began to present his Japanese figures in a severed state, devoid of the sentiments that typically accompany erotic ukiyo-e prints or images of the working-class lifestyle. Though they appear as members of a group, the people in Takamori's later work *Villagers (Figural Group)* are in fact separate, independent figures.

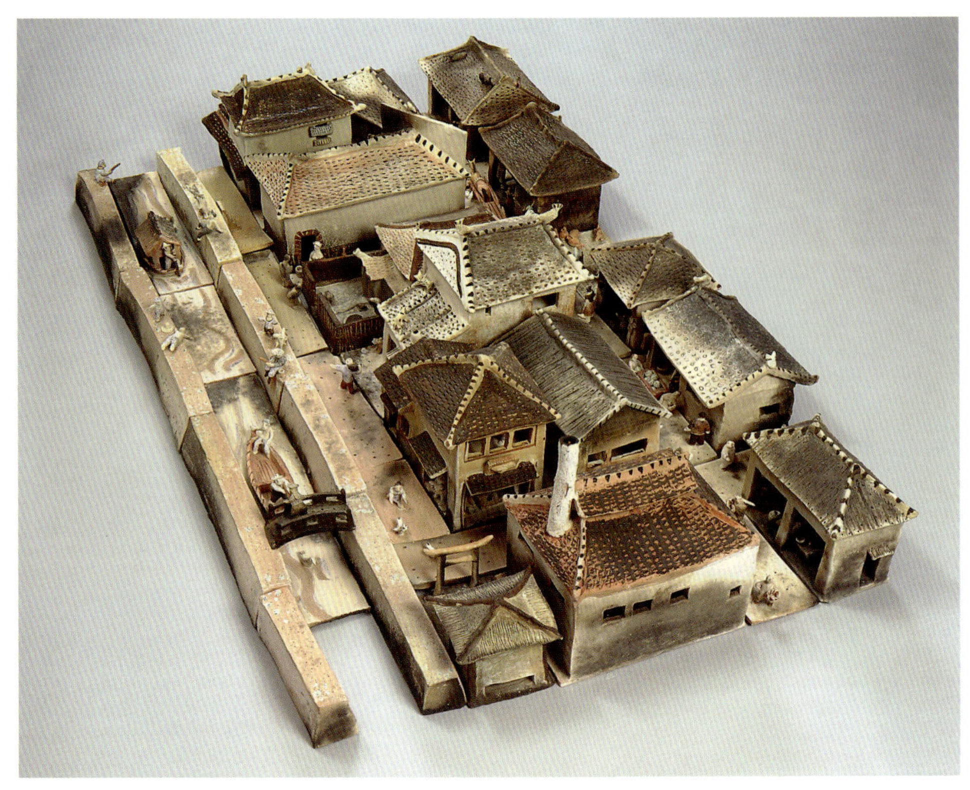

Fig. 7
Akio Takamori,
*Village*, 1976, cat. no. 1

挿図7
高森暁夫
『ヴィレッジ』、
1976年、作者蔵

作品の主人公を説明するには「情緒」は有効だが、主人公が観客の内部でさらに活躍しだすには「情緒」は足手まといになる。情緒はどれほど洗練されていても、既成概念なのである。だから、情緒は作品の生みの親ではあっても、観客が作品を勝手に理解したり、それに刺激を受けて自分なりになにかを把握しはじめるときには邪魔になる。そう気づいたからこそ、高森は日本の人物像を、郭情緒や下町情緒から切り取ってきたのではないだろうか。『ヴィレッジの人々(FIGURAL GROUP)』に出てくる人たちは、集合的に見えて、実は孤立しているのである。

こんな風に日本の風俗文化から、その造形的特色を大胆に抽出してきた高森だから、この作家が陶磁器を素材とするからといって、その作品を戦後日本の陶芸作品と関連づけてもほとんど意味がない。実際、日本の前衛的陶芸についていえば、1950年代から60年代は、ブランクーシやイサム・ノグチの彫刻、そして、アンフォルメルのオブジェを移植し、その後は、抽象表現主義に触発されたアメリカの陶彫作品を受容してきた。

欧米から伝わってくる同時代の立体造形作品は刺激的だったから、日本の陶芸家がそれらに勇気づけられて、陶磁器製作にまつわる従来の規範を片っ端から破っていったのも当然のことだった。しかし、手本があっての前衛というのは、どうしても変わった形の追求や、造形的実験に入り込みやすい。それはそれで記念碑的作品も生まれ、美術館にも収蔵されたが、それをもういちど見に行きたいと思う観客はどれほどいるだろうか。

そうしたなかで、強いて言えばと断ったうえでだが、高森暁夫の人物像に先行する仕事として、中村錦平の『日本趣味解題』と称するシリーズと、柳原睦夫の『オリベ』の名称が冠せられた作品群があった。どちらも、ポストモダンの文脈のなかで、1990年前後から発表されだしている。中村の方は桃山の「変わり兜」にも通じる、日本人の異形を好む趣味を再評価し、柳原の方もやはり桃山に登場した「織部焼」の意表をついた意匠力を再解釈した。

これらの試みは、結局、歴史の見直しである。過去の日本美術が誇ってきた装飾や細工といった造形を発掘しているのであって、必ずしも高森の視点と共通するものではない。が、しかし、同時

What Takamori has done is to boldly extract elements from Japanese historical background and turn them into works that emphasize formative characteristics. This boldness makes it practically meaningless to try to place him within the history of postwar Japanese ceramics, in which avant-garde trends have invariably been variations on outside influences: in the 1950s and 1960s, they transplanted the sculptural forms of Constantin Brancusi and Isamu Noguchi as well as Informel art objects, followed by works influenced by American ceramic sculpture, which had in turn been inspired by Abstract Expressionism. Such contemporary Western three-dimensional work had a very strong impact on Japanese ceramic artists, who grew bolder and started to break conventions in ceramic-making (though often, when avant-garde movements arise in response to outside models, they tend to fall into the pursuit of bizarre and experimental forms).

Perhaps the most significant precedents to Takamori's innovations are Kinpei Nakamura's *Nihon Shumi Kaidai* (Analyzing Japonism) series and Mutsuo Yanagihara's *Oribe* series. Both of these series were produced in the context of postmodernism around 1990. Nakamura's works focus on the long-standing taste in Japan for the "strange form," most notably embodied by the *Kawari Kabuto* (exotic-shaped helmets) of the Momoyama period (1573–1615). Yanagihara, by contrast, turned to the imaginative creativity of Momoyama-period Oribe ware, which he adapted in contemporary versions.

Both of these artists, in short, borrowed from older styles to create new artworks. Their works constitute rediscovered versions of the decorative styles and technical details that make Japanese art of the older periods notable, and in this, their approach is very different in nature from Takamori's. However, Nakamura and Yanagihara share with Takamori a striving to slip out from the grasp of contemporary artistic theories and to destroy the paradigms of formal expression that had been established by these same theories. Nakamura and Yanagihara were attempting to liberate themselves from the obsession with originality that plagued avant-garde ceramic art, and Takamori was trying to eliminate the association with "spiritual homeland" in portrayals of ordinary people.

Unfortunately, Nakamura's and Yanagihara's achievements in terms of historical context in art have not been fully understood in Japan, and no younger artists

代を支配する言説から逸脱し、その言説が構築してきた造形表現のパラダイムを壊そうと試みた点で、両者は共通していたといえるだろう。中村と柳原は、前衛的陶芸における独創性の信奉という強迫観念から抜け出そうとした点で、高森は庶民生活から精神的家郷というイメージを拭い去ろうとした点で、である。

だが、中村と柳原の歴史意識が依然として日本では充分に理解されず、彼らの思想的後継者も現れないように、高森の仕事も日本の陶芸史には組み込まれにくいだろう。また、その必要もないに違いない。高森の人物像はその原産地が日本だというだけであって、それは日本自身が創出しようとしている固有の雰囲気を漂わせていないのだから。そうした固有の雰囲気とはなにかと問われると、これもまた「伝統」のようにその実像はどこにもないのだが……。

要するに、高森の人物像は日本の庶民生活を題材にしているが、その本質はこの作家の創作物なのである。そう思って作品を見渡すと、それらのなかにはベラスケスが描くマルガリーテ王女の像や、最近では唐の婦人俑、さらに、唐子も登場する。

アメリカという多元的文化の国で生きていくためには、すべてが自分の表現になっていることが求められるのだろう。たとえ作品の造形的特色が、自分の出身国に由来するものであっても、それが作品として成立するためには、母国の文化から切り離され、作者の表現として完結しているのでなければならない。そうでなければ、この国では制作物が作品として社会に流通していかないのだろう。作品を自己完結させることは、作品の表現を明確にし、強くすることである。しかし同時に、作品の表現を保証するものを作者自身以外に求めないということでもある。その孤愁に耐えることが、アメリカ社会の掟なのだと思われた。

ところで、高森の人物像は日本から切り離された後、これから先どこに向かって歩きだそうとしているのだろうか。こうしたことに興味をもったのも、最近会ったときに、高森が日本の近代史について熱心に語っていたからである。話題は戦時中の南京大虐殺から、硫黄島玉砕、そして、本人も経験した1970年代の学生運動、大学卒業後に行った小石原 (Koishiwara) での民芸陶器運動まで多岐にわたった。これらの話題を通して、高森は自分の知らなかった、そして、見逃してきた日本を再確認しているようだった。それは日本人のような人物像を、日本のなかにもういちど「埋め戻す」ための準備をしているように思えた。

ただし、高森が作品を「埋め戻そう」としている先の日本は、現実の日本ではないのかもしれない。外来と固有のせめぎ合いのなかで、ちょっと外圧を受ければナショナリズムが高揚しかねない日本ではなく、これもまた作者によって創作された日本であるのかもしれない。

それを感じたのは、『マッカーサーと天皇 (GENERAL AND EMPEROR)』(2001年) が並ぶ像を目にしたときだった。あの有名な写真を立体像に置き換えたものである。これを見れば、多く

have chosen to follow their path. Likewise, it is not likely that Takamori's work will be given its due in the history of Japanese ceramic art. But his work doesn't need to be appreciated as part of Japanese ceramics per se. Although his ceramic figures are based on images of Japanese people, they don't have the distinctive atmosphere that ties them specifically to Japan. And this atmosphere is, like tradition, nothing more than a concept that changes its meaning each time it is defined. Takamori's human figures reference the lifestyle of ordinary people in Japan, but on every level, they are this artist's original creations. When you look at his figures from this standpoint, you begin to recognize among them a whole array of referents, including Velázquez's *Infanta Margarita* and, more recently, Tang Dynasty ceramic figures of women and children.

I assume that in order to survive as an artist in a multicultural nation such as the United States, you need to establish a style in which every element is distinctively your own. Even when the formative elements that characterize your work originate in the country of your birth, they need to be viable as independent forms of expression when seen outside the context of your native country's cultural background. In order to make an artwork independent, you need to make its expression straightforward and strong. On the flip side, this means that no outside endorsements of the work will be provided; the artist is totally alone in creating his or her art and needs to have the inner strength to live with this solitude.

Takamori's human figures are images that have been severed from their origins, and I have been interested in the direction they have been taking ever since I visited the artist recently and listened to his impassioned talk on modern history. He took up diverse subjects, including the Nanjing Massacre of 1937, the battle of Iwo Jima, student activism in the 1970s, which he experienced firsthand, and the *mingei* ceramics production in Koishiwara, where he apprenticed after graduation from Musashino Art University. He sounded as if he were discovering aspects of Japan he had been unaware of or had failed to notice. I felt that, in the process, he was doing preparatory work for replanting his ceramic people in Japan.

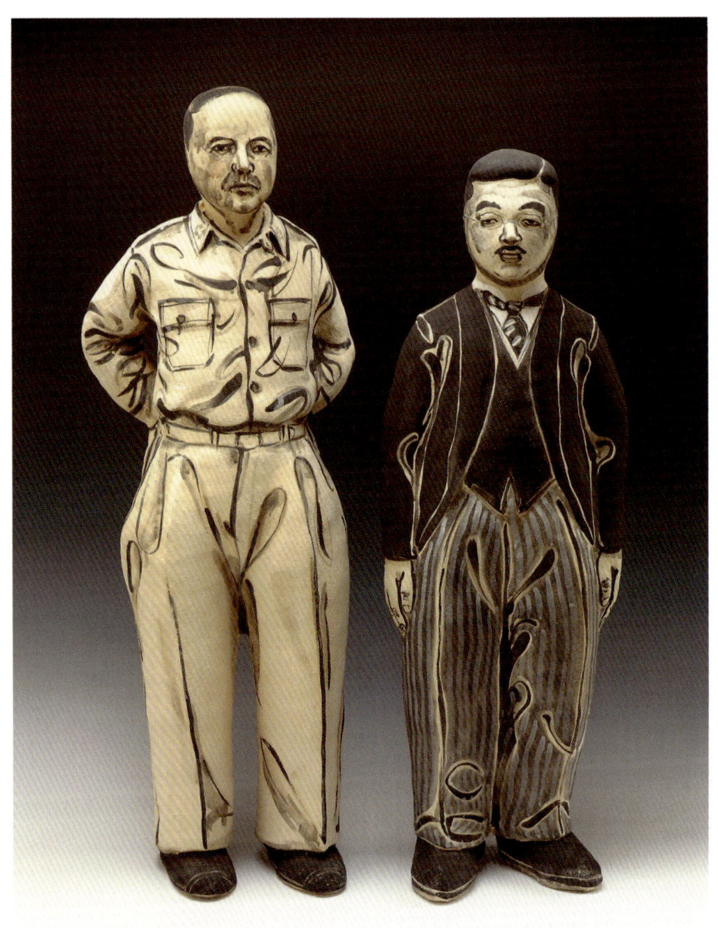

Fig. 8
Akio Takamori,
*General and Emperor,*
2001, cat. no. 36

挿図8
高森暁夫
『マッカーサーと天皇』、
2001年、個人蔵

の日本人は忘れていた敗戦を思い出すに違いない。そして、こうした作品をつくる高森のことを、ネガティヴな意味でセンセーショナルな作家だと感じることだろう。

ところが、この作品をよく見ると、マッカーサーは写真の印象よりも小振りで、そのプロポーションも日本人風に胴長にされている。ひとことで言えば、ウエストラインが低いのだ。あの有名な写真は、武器など使って戦わなくても、日本人ははじめからその肉体においてアメリカ人に負けていたことを否が応でも教えてくれた。しかし、高森の連合国最高司令官にはそんな威圧感はない。この作品では勝者と敗者の関係が、たんなる出会いであるかのように緩和されている。

高森の再発見しようとしている日本は、どこまでいっても、作者の創作する仮想空間のなかの日本なのかもしれない。それはやはりアメリカという国が、高森にこうした作業を促すからなのだろうか。そうだとすれば、さまざまな異文化をフラグメントとして集合していくアメリカ文化の多元性には怖れを感じる。しかし、いまはその怖れを語るときではなく、その前に、どこまでも固有という幻想にしがみつこうとする日本に目を向けるときだろう。日本も少しは「伝統」を解体したらどうなんだ？　高森の人物像は、そう語りかけているように思えた。

京都工芸繊維大学 (Kyoto Institute of Technology) 助教授
樋田豊次郎

But the Japan in which he intends to replant his people might not be the actual Japan. Instead, it will probably be a Japan that is another creation of his, that has greater solidity than its actual counterpart, where the constant clash of the foreign and the indigenous has made the people volatile enough to turn nationalistic overnight.

I felt I had a glimpse of Takamori's Japan when I saw his *General and Emperor,* 2001 (fig. 8), in which General Douglas MacArthur and Emperor Hirohito stand side by side. It is a three-dimensional version of the well-known historical photograph (see page 47). The work is a reminder to many Japanese that their country was once defeated, a fact they would prefer to forget. These same people would accuse Takamori of being an artist who tries to attract attention by taking up politically sensitive themes. But if you look at these figures closely, you will notice these details: MacArthur is presented as being shorter than he was in reality and with a longer torso and lower waistline, more like a Japanese physique. The famous photograph showed us that Americans could have beaten the Japanese with their bare hands because they were so much stronger physically. In Takamori's work, the General doesn't give us this impression. Here, the victorious and the defeated meet as if this were just a casual encounter.

The Japan that Akio Takamori intends to rediscover will probably never overlap precisely with the real Japan but will remain an imagined realm of the artist's own making. I wonder if he feels the need to undergo this phase of rediscovery because he lives in the United States. If this is indeed the case, then I am awed and a little frightened by the multidimensional complexity of American culture, which swallows up fragments of diverse cultures and then reassembles them to make them its own. But this is no time to talk about this feeling of awe. Before doing that, we need to urge Japan to let go of its obsession with indigenousness. I feel that Takamori's human figures are saying, "It is long past time that Japan has deconstructed its 'tradition.'"

Translated from the Japanese by Keiko Katsuya

# Plates

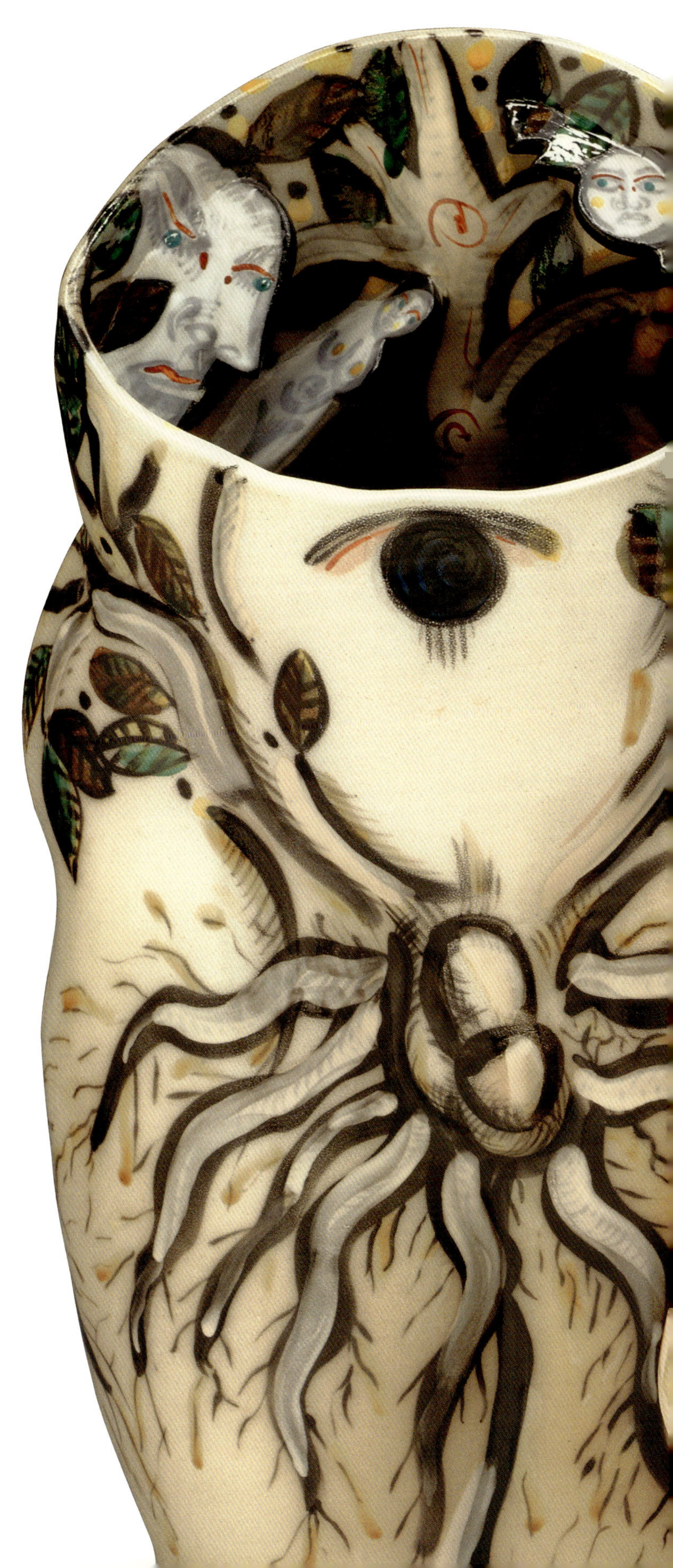

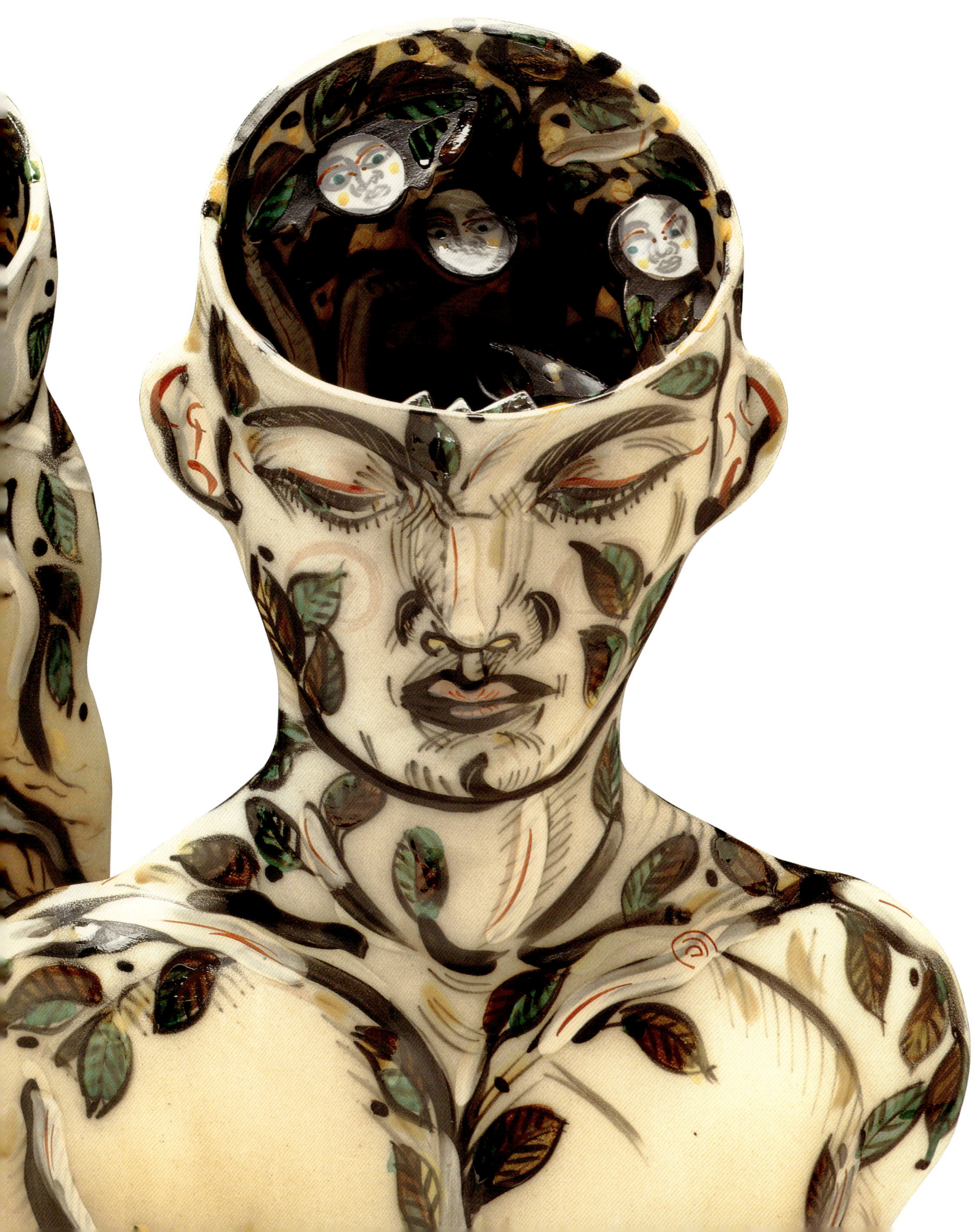

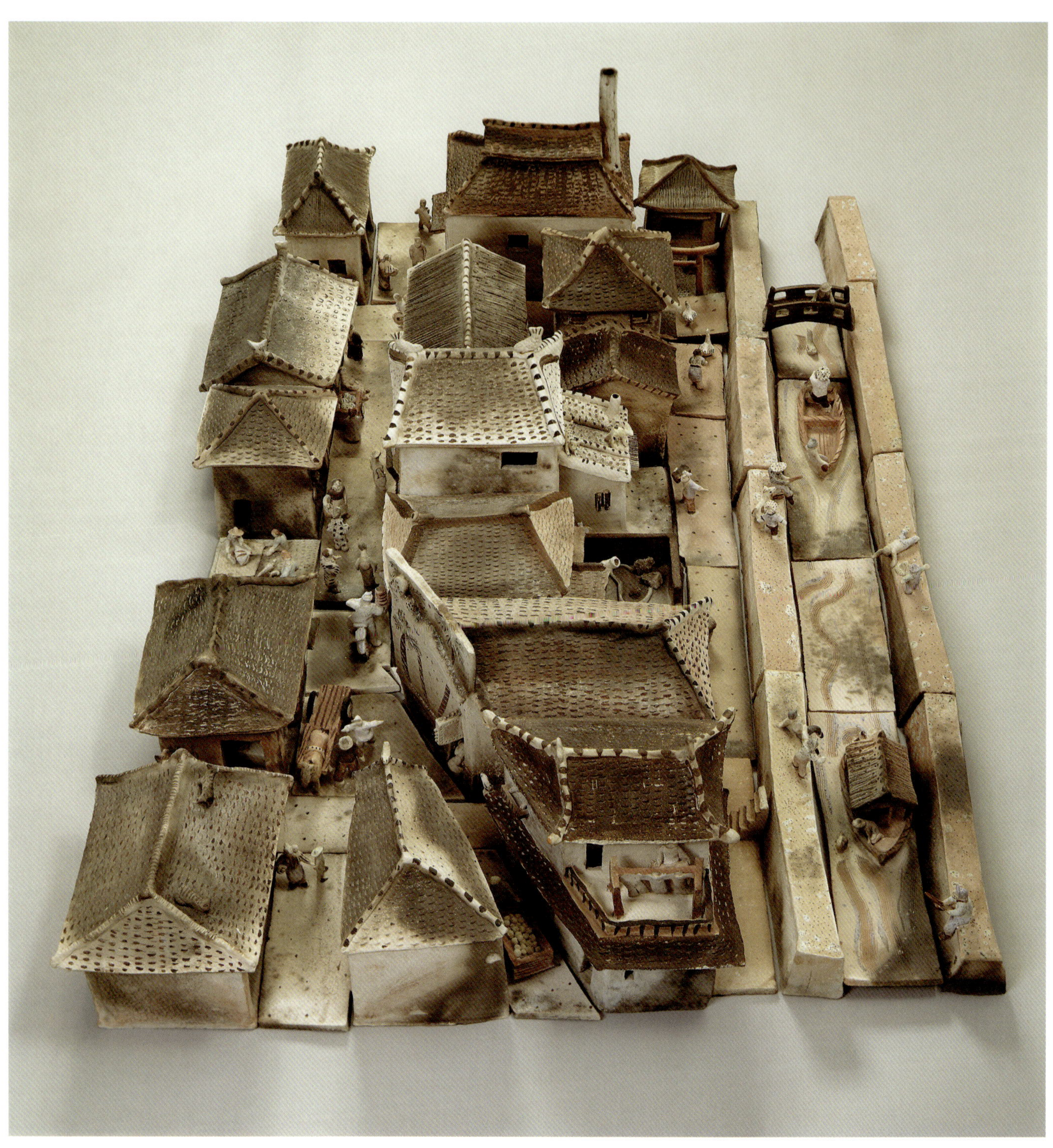

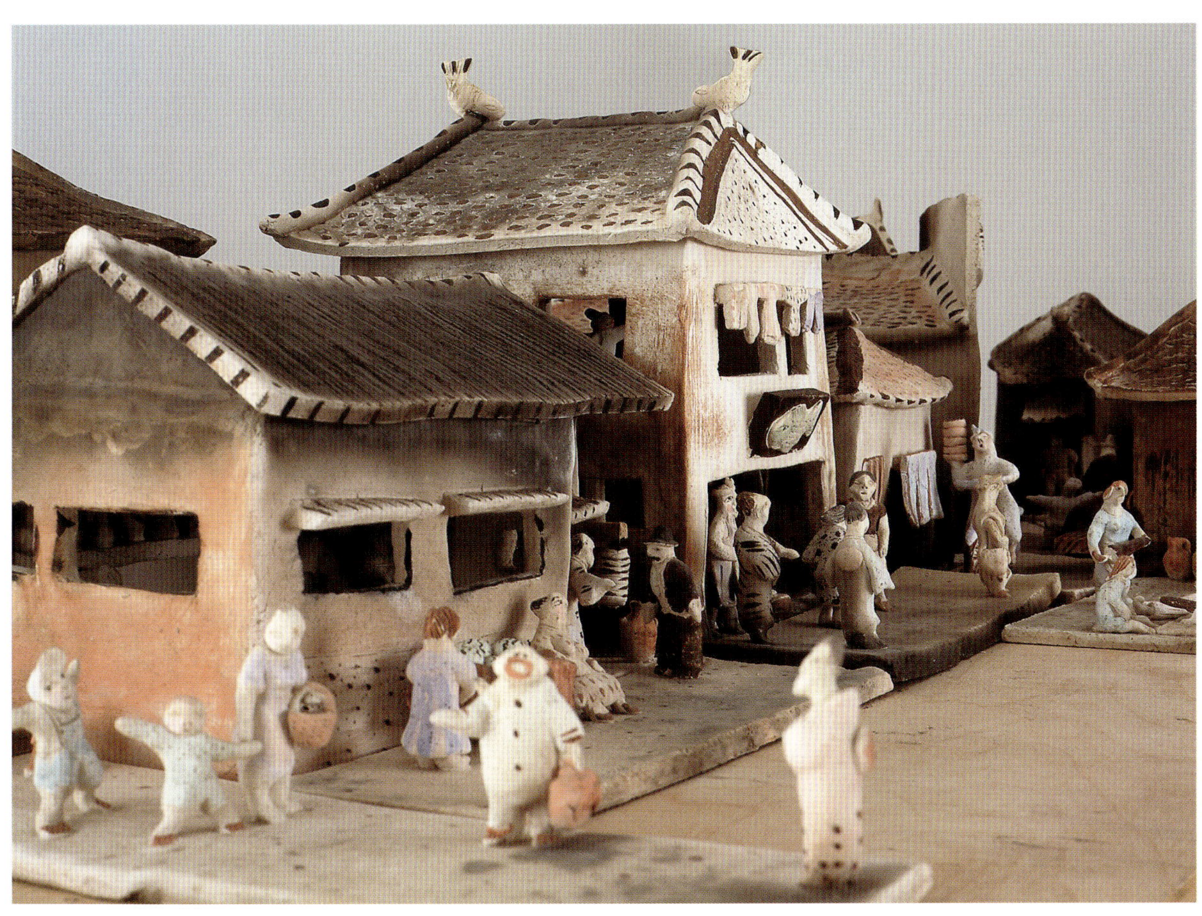

*Village*, 1976
12 × 57 × 35 in.
Hand-built, stoneware, raku-fired
(cat. no. 1)

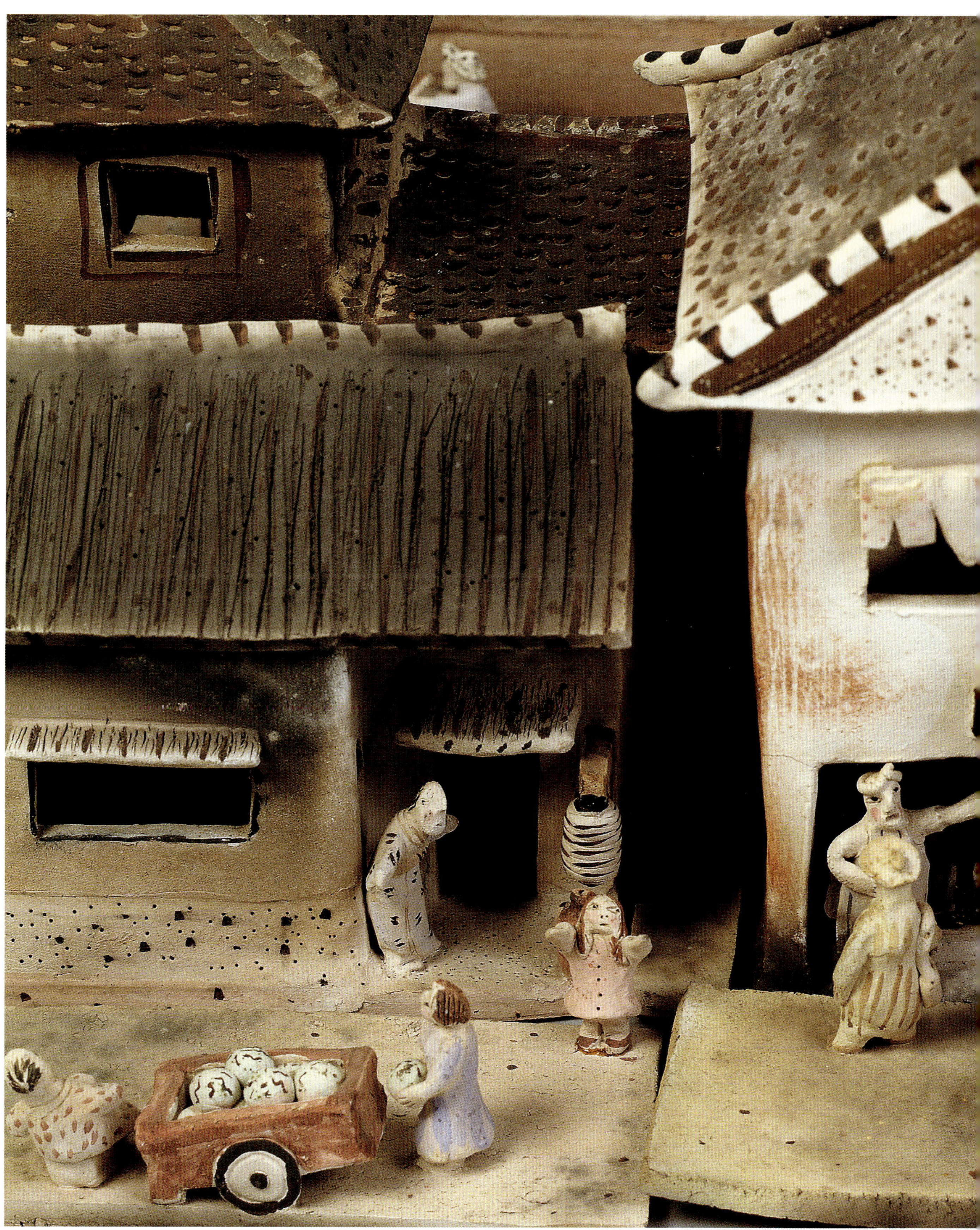

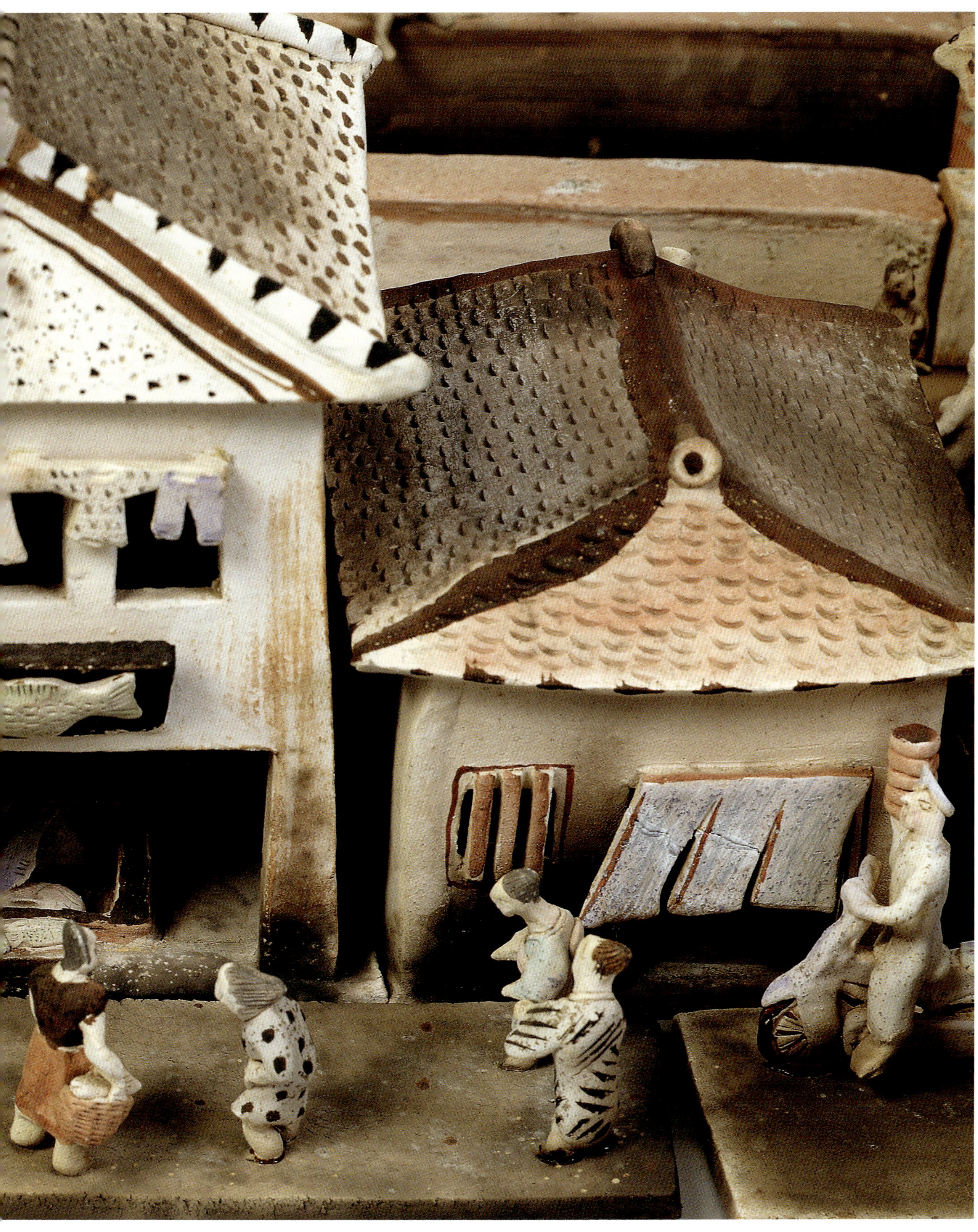

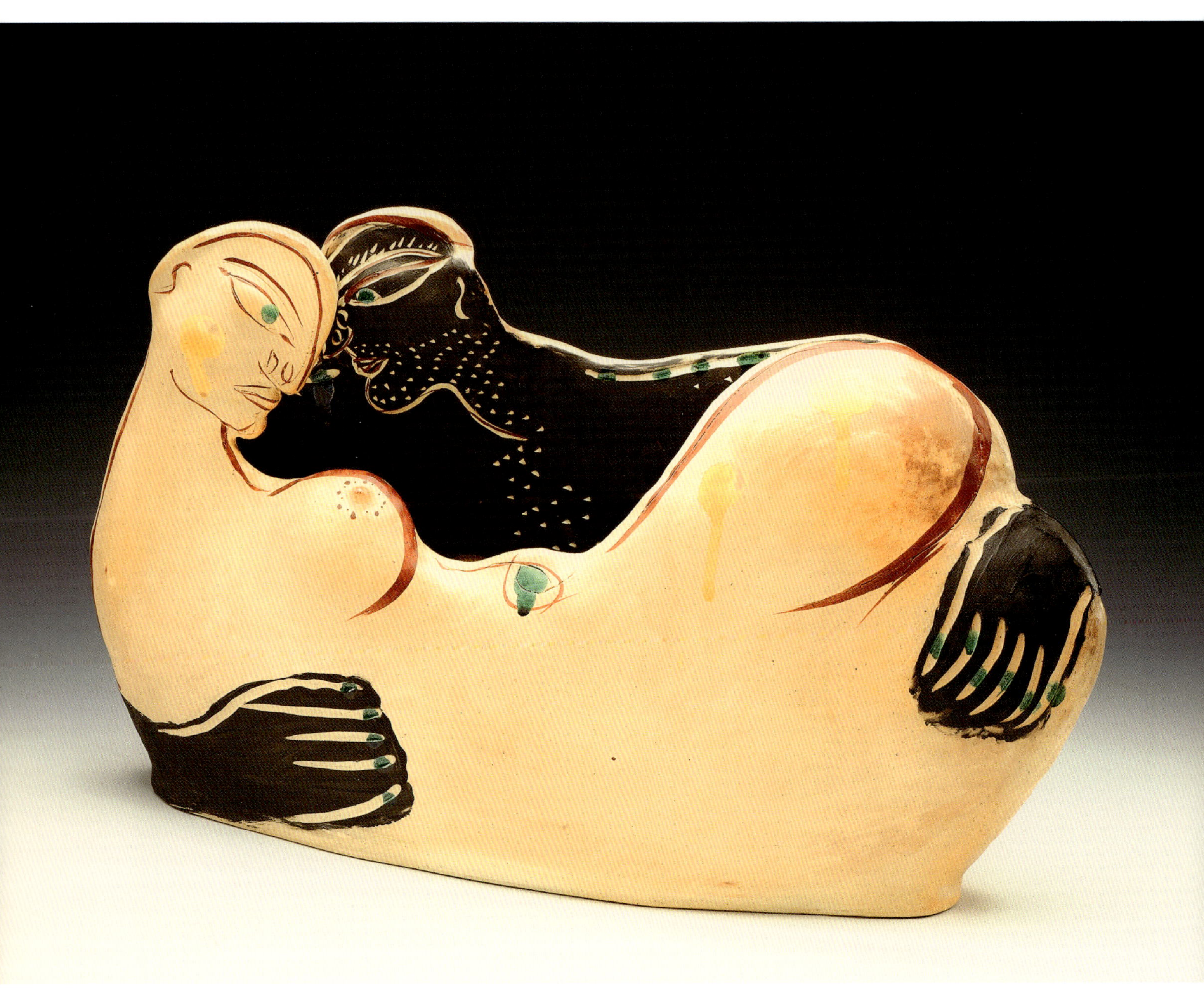

*Couple*, 1980
$12\frac{1}{2} \times 19\frac{1}{2} \times 6$ in.
Hand-built, stoneware, salt-fired
(cat. no. 2)

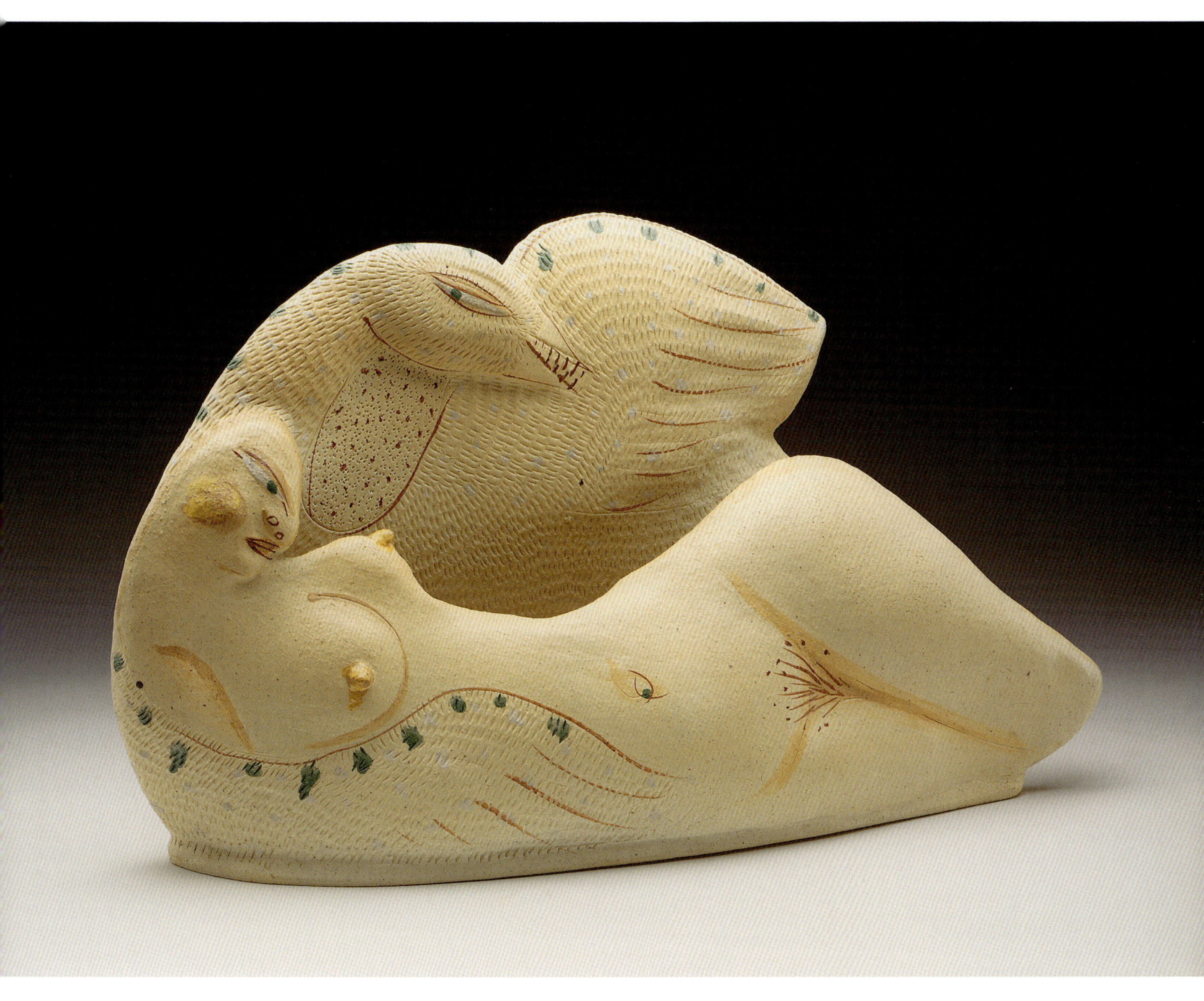

*Leda and Swan*, 1982
13 × 17 × 6 in.
Hand-built, stoneware, salt-fired
(cat. no. 3)

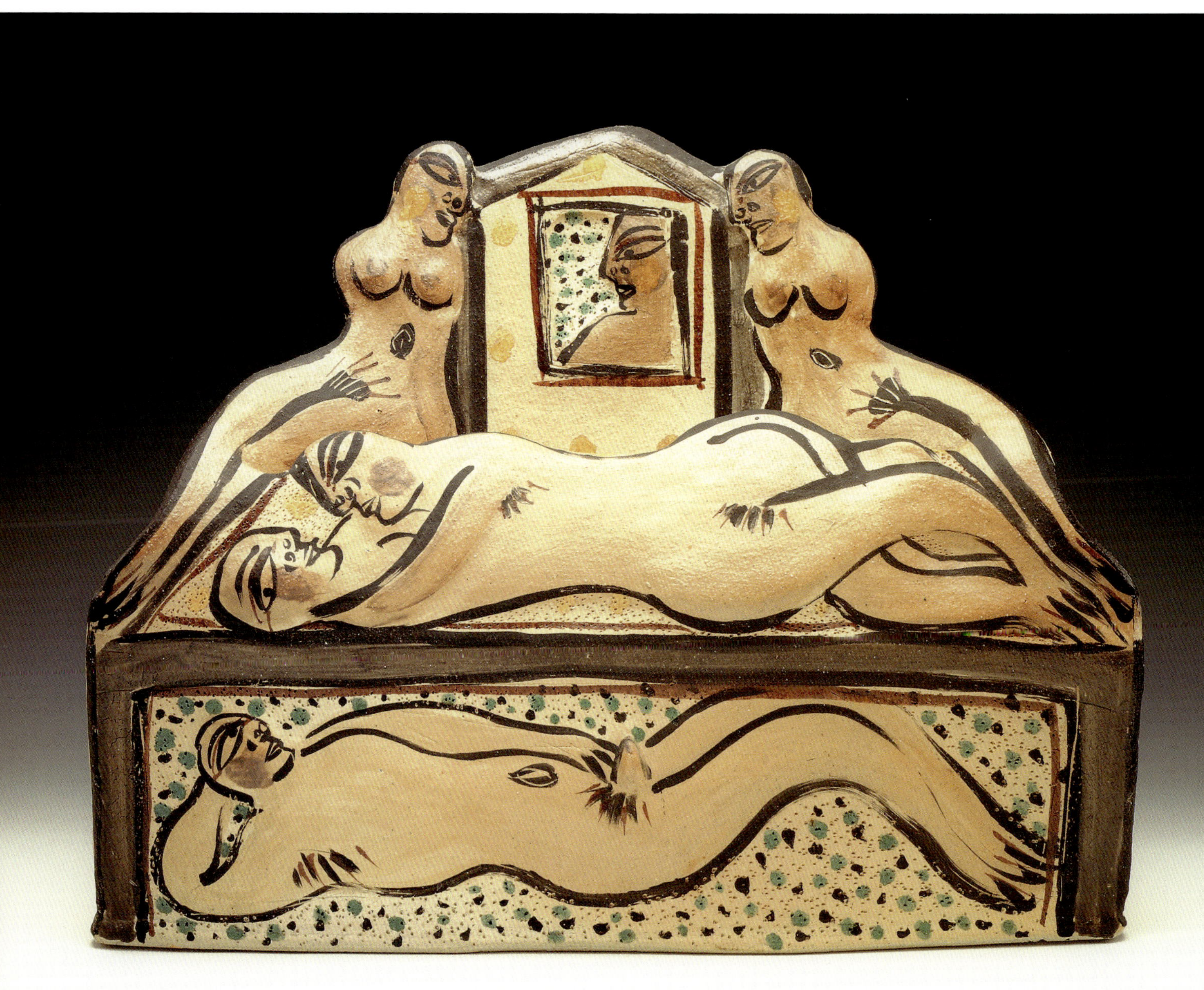

*Lovers with Onlookers*, 1982
14 × 19 × 7 in.
Hand-built, stoneware, salt-fired
(cat. no. 4)

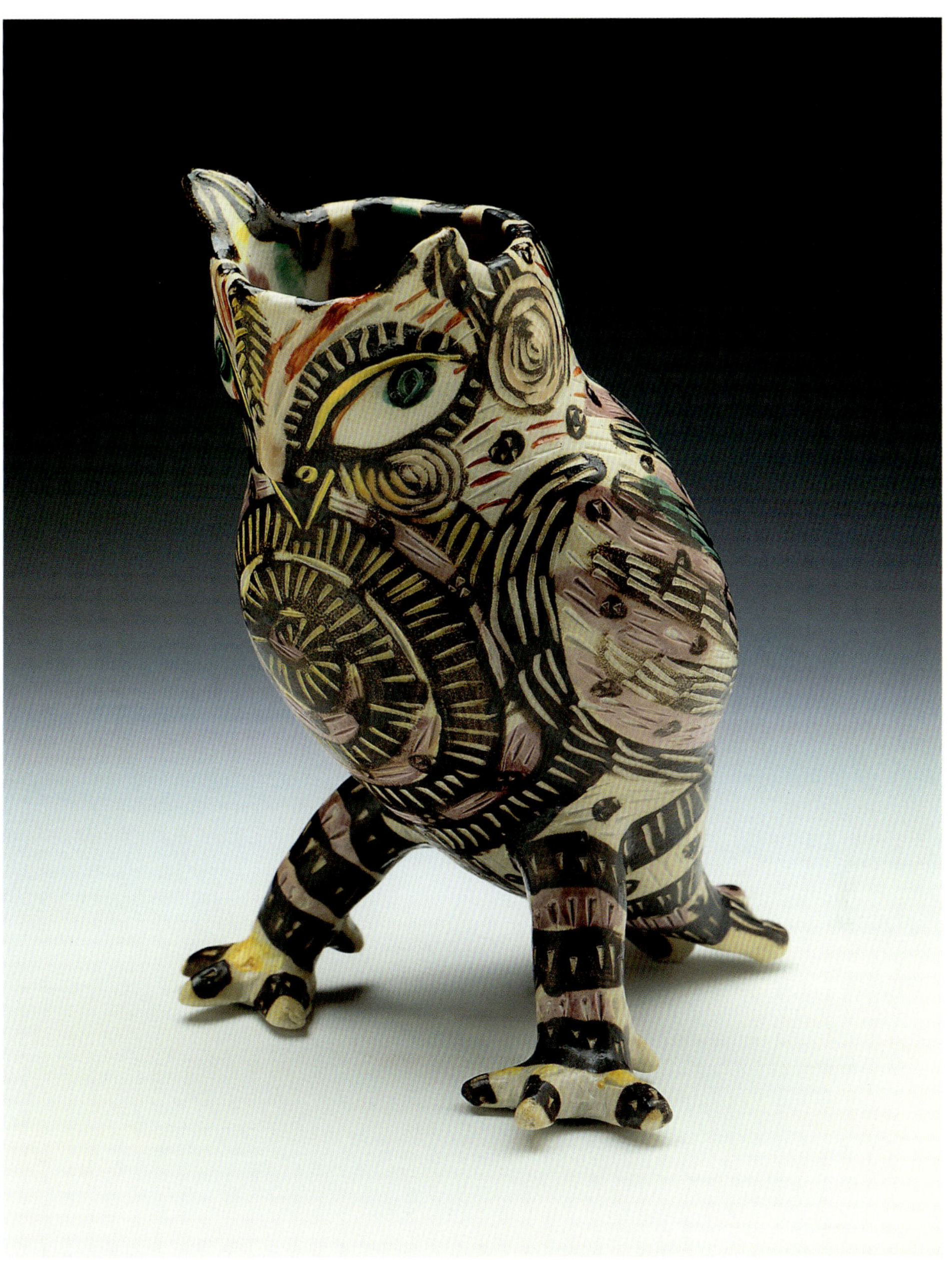

*Owl*, ca. 1982
9½ × 5½ × 6½ in.
Wheel-thrown and altered, porcelain, salt-fired
(cat. no. 5)

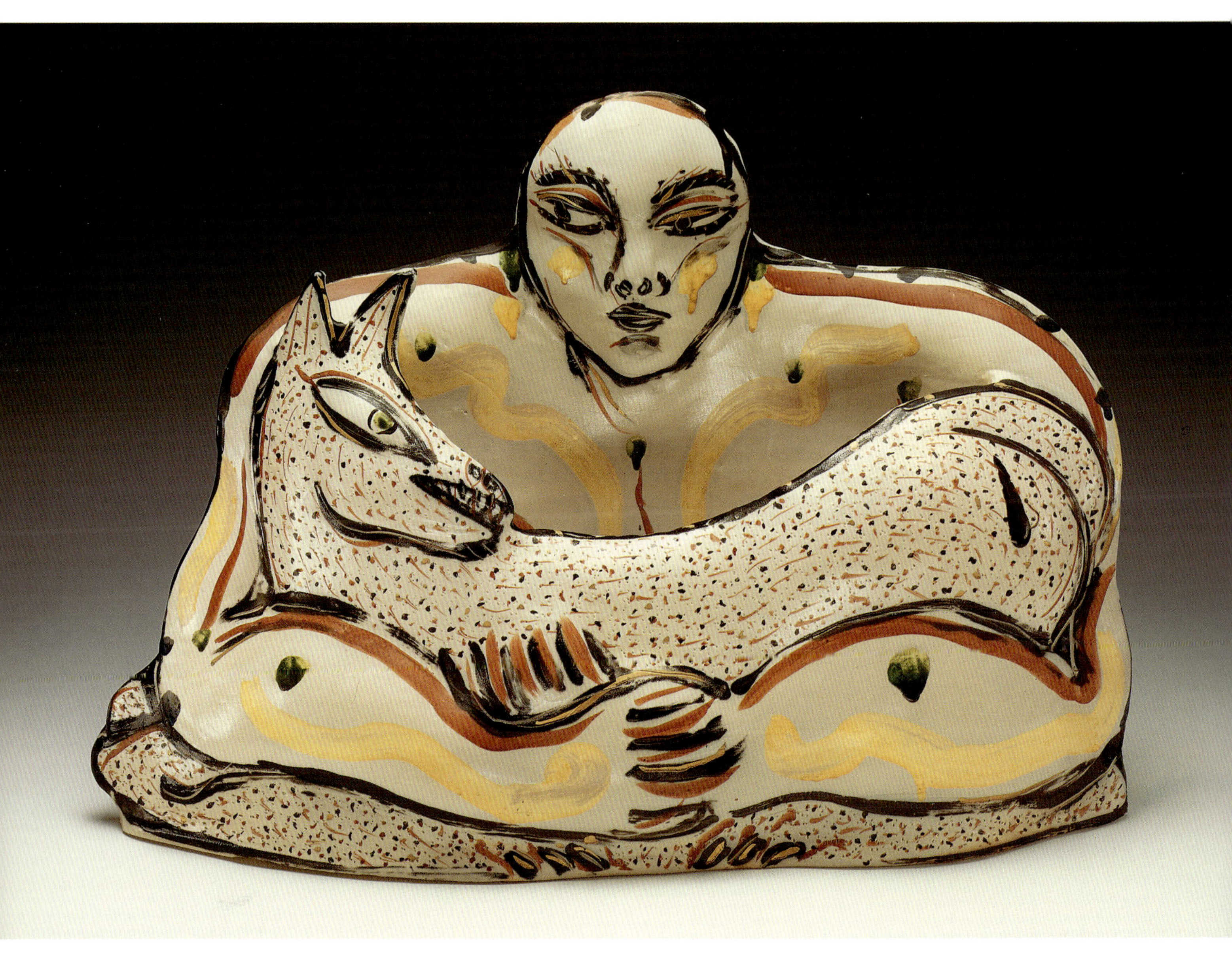

*Boy Holding Dog*, 1983
17½ × 25 × 7½ in.
Hand-built, stoneware, salt-fired
(cat. no. 6)

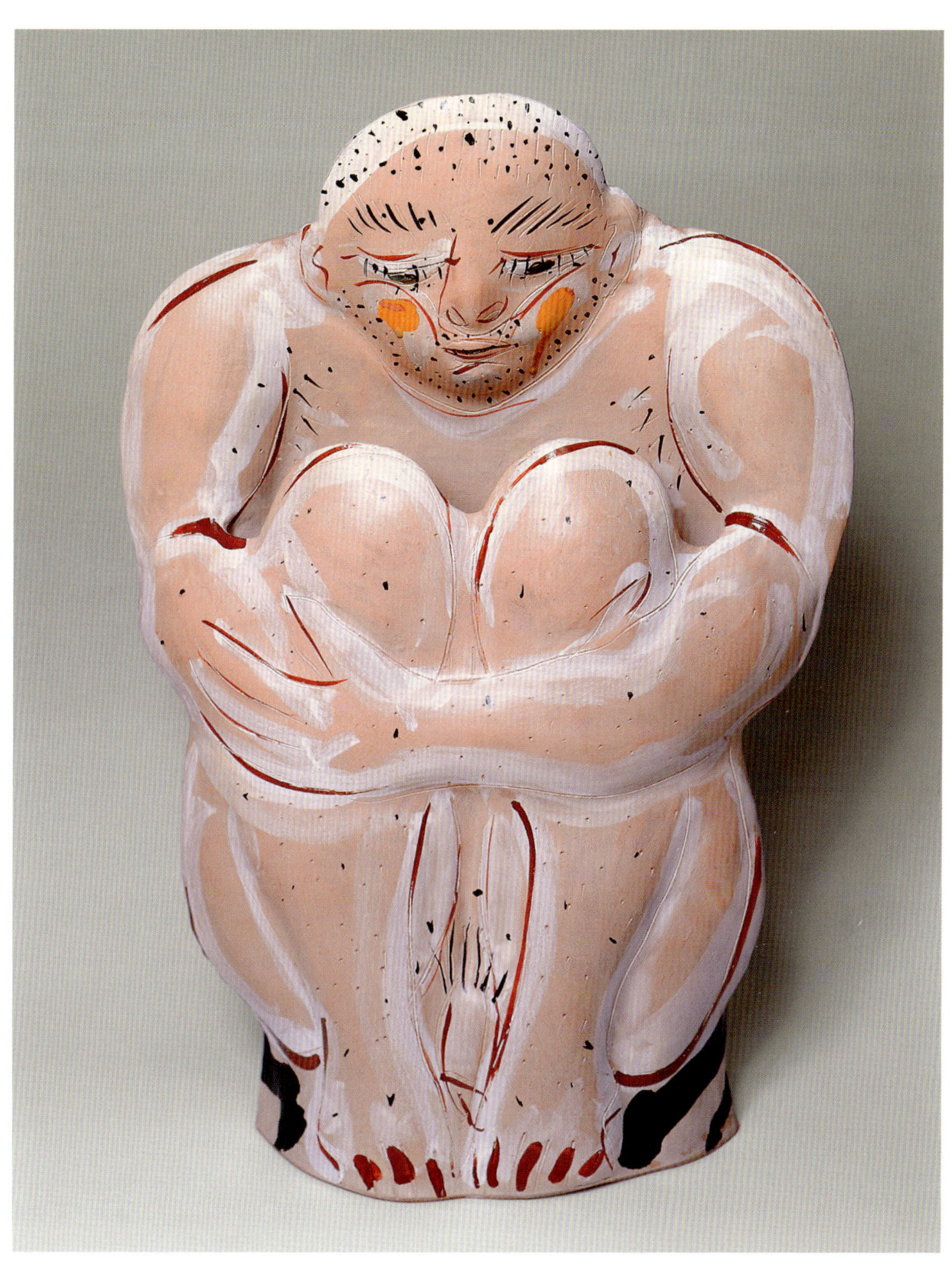

*Self-Portrait*, 1984
14 × 8 × 9 in.
Hand-built, earthenware
(cat. no. 7)

*Portrait of Ms. M*, 1986
22 × 19 × 10 in.
Hand-built, porcelain
(cat. no. 8)

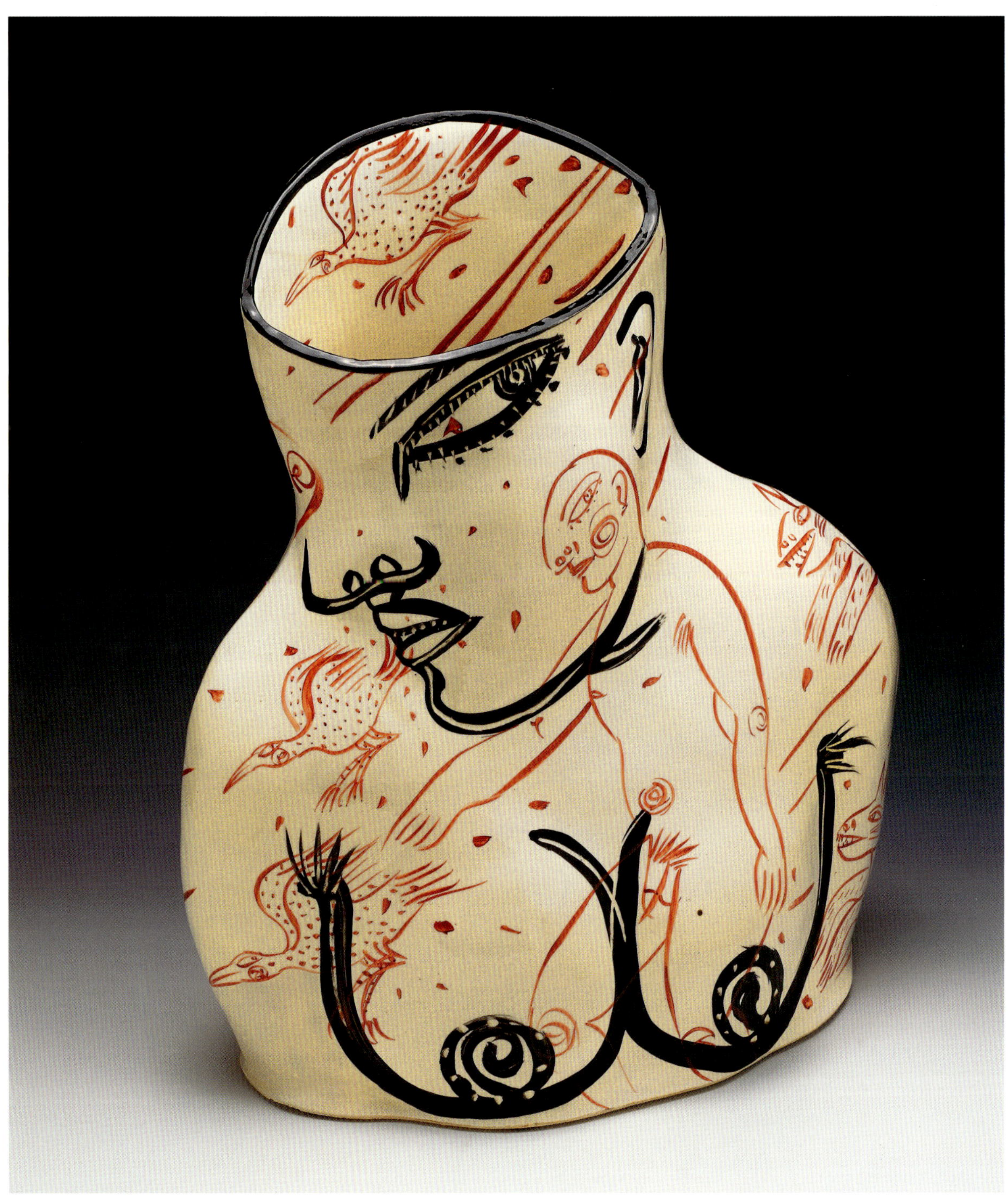

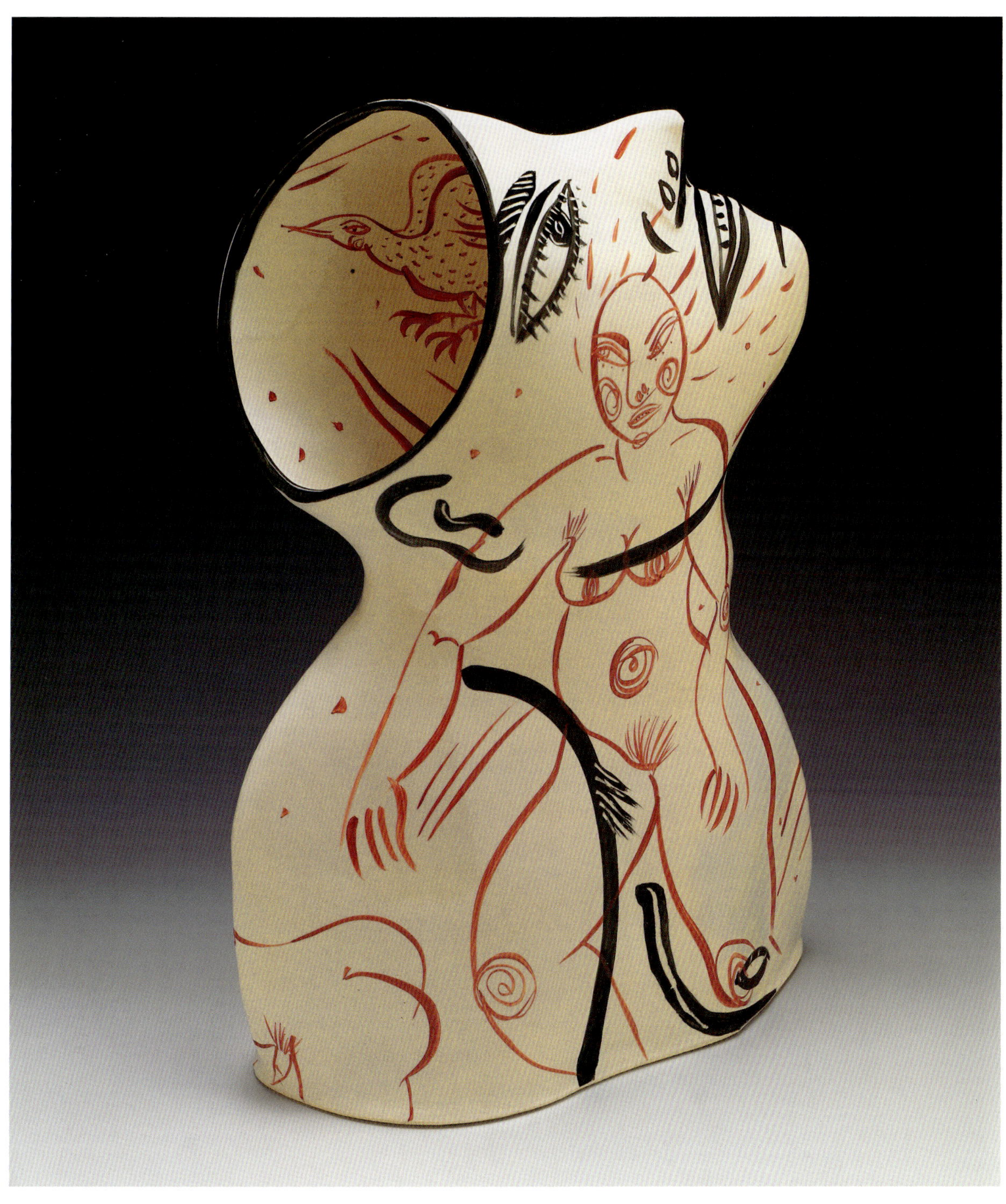

*Portrait of Mr. W*, 1986
24 × 16 × 7 in.
Hand-built, porcelain
(cat. no. 9)

*Her Love*, 1987
21½ × 14½ × 7 in.
Hand-built, porcelain, salt-fired
(cat. no. 10)

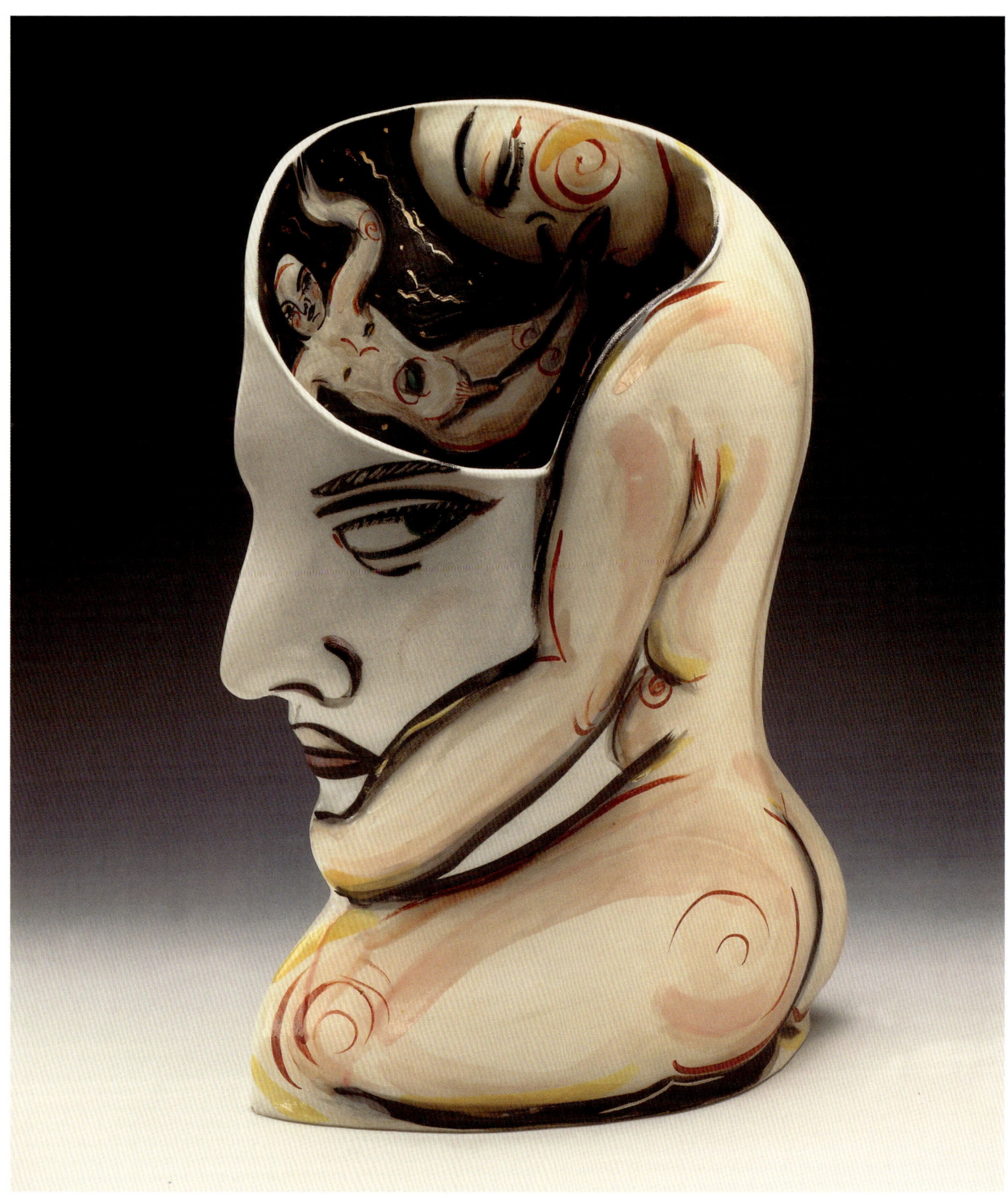

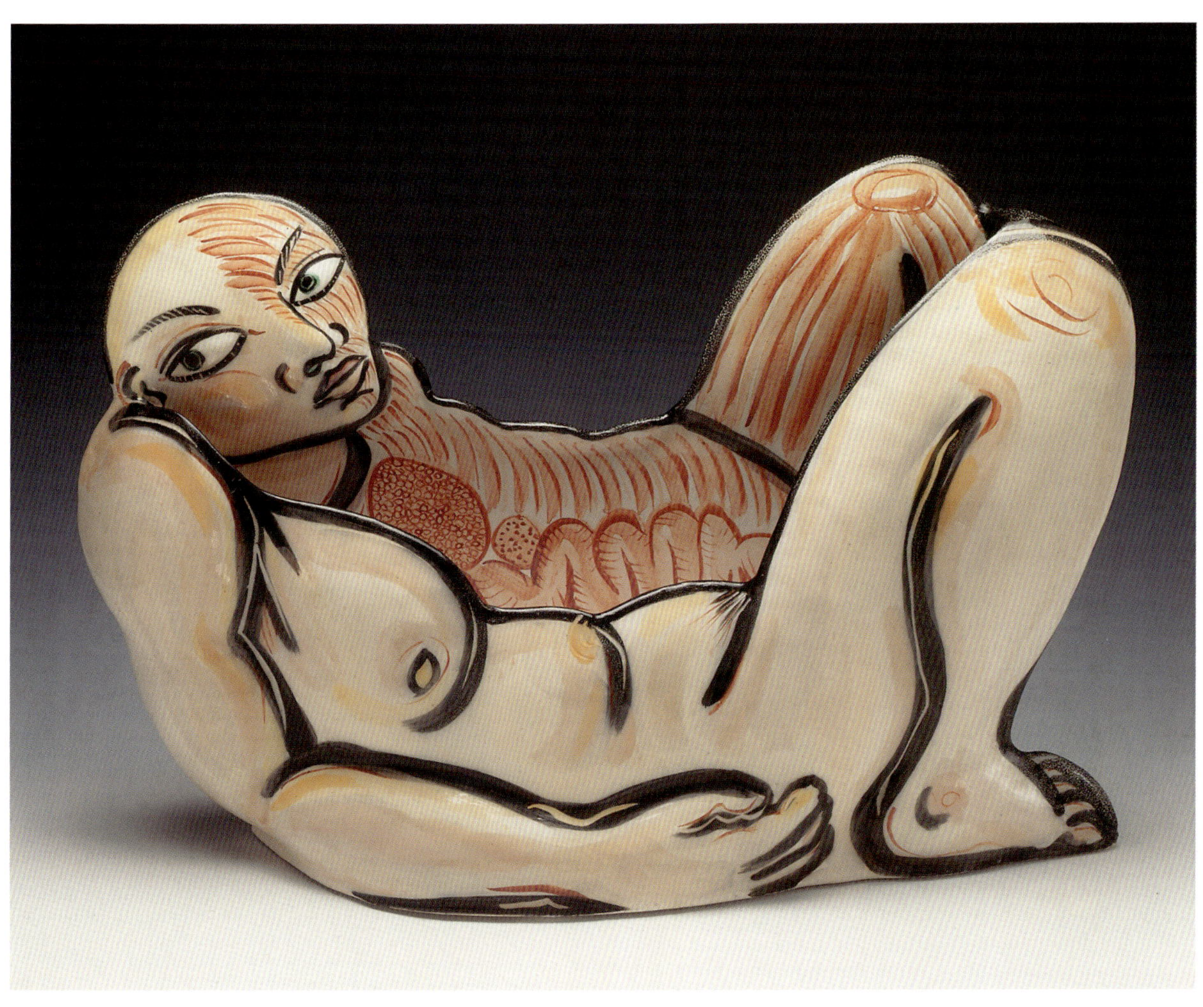

*Human,* 1987
17½ × 25 × 7 in.
Hand-built, porcelain, salt-fired
(cat. no. 11)

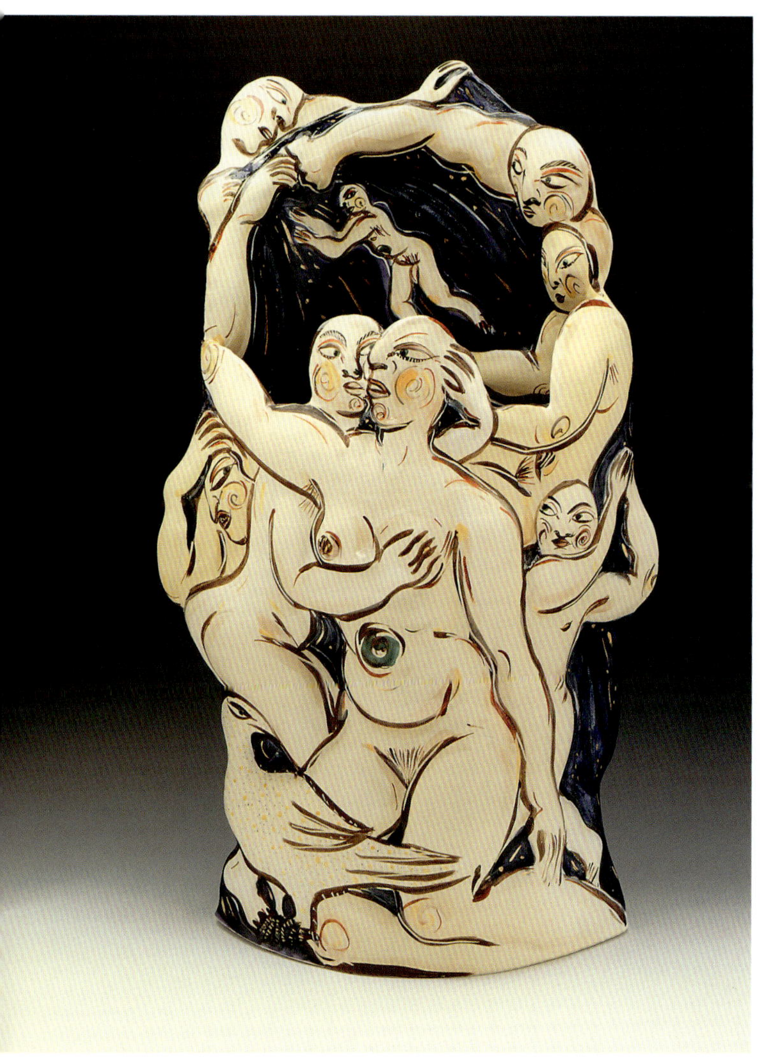

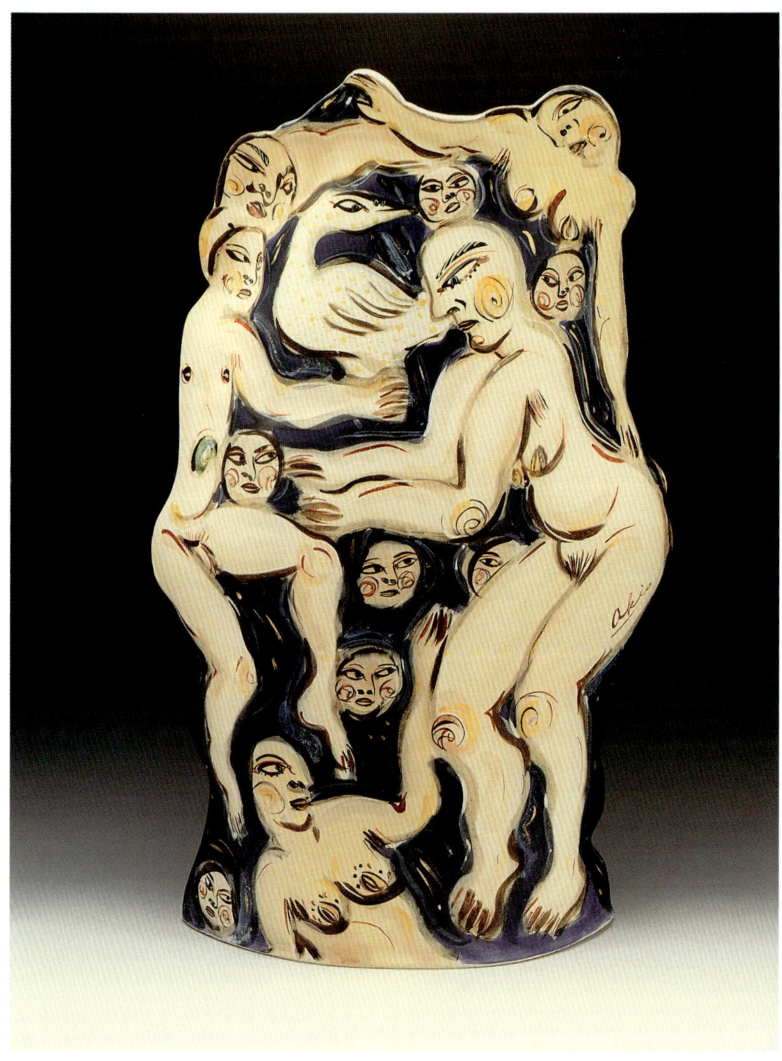

*Mother and Son: Homage to Bronzino*, 1987
32½ × 19½ × 9 in.
Hand-built, porcelain, salt-fired
(cat. no. 12)

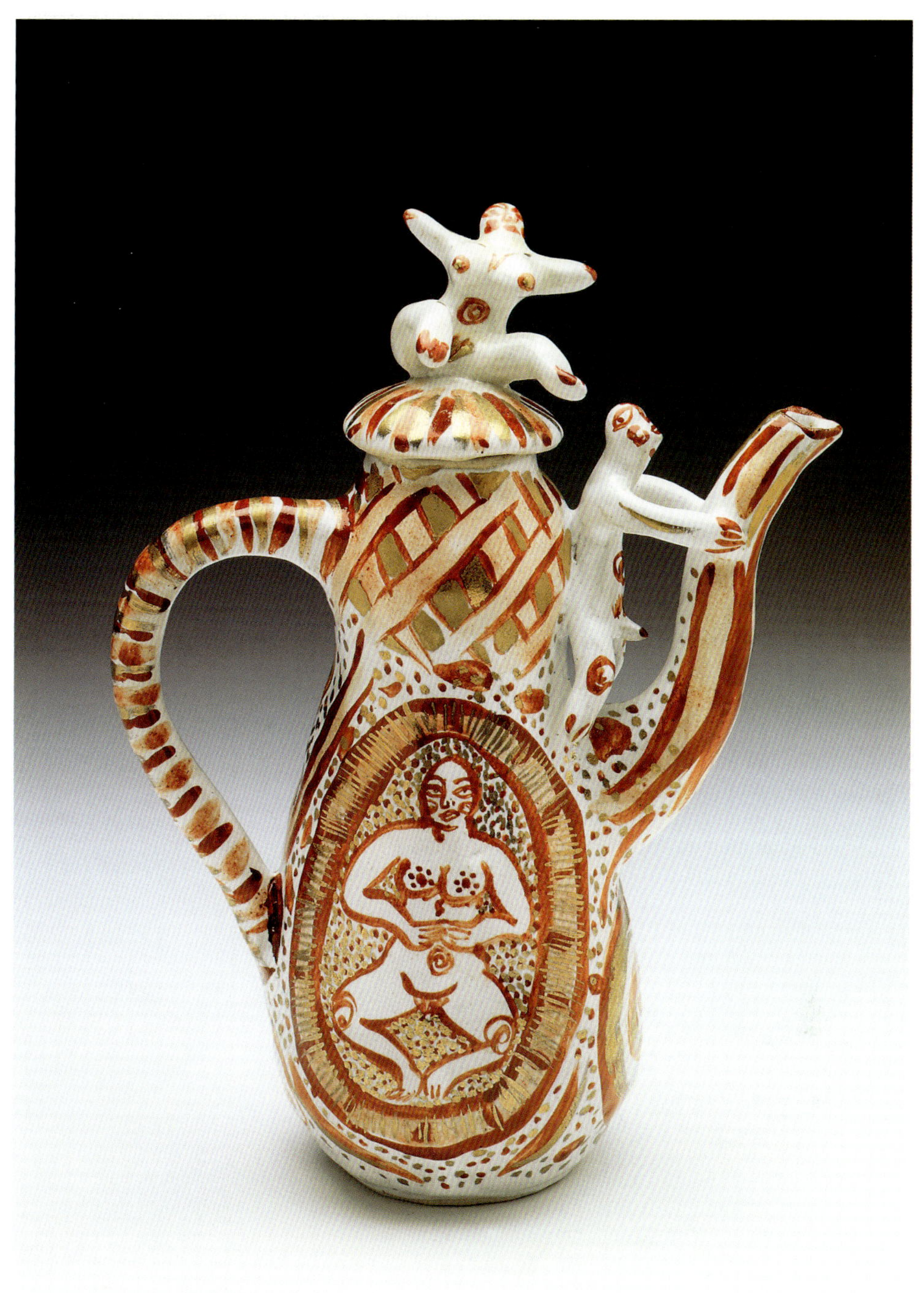

Untitled Teapot, 1987
8 × 5½ × 3 in.
Hand-built, porcelain
(cat. no. 13)

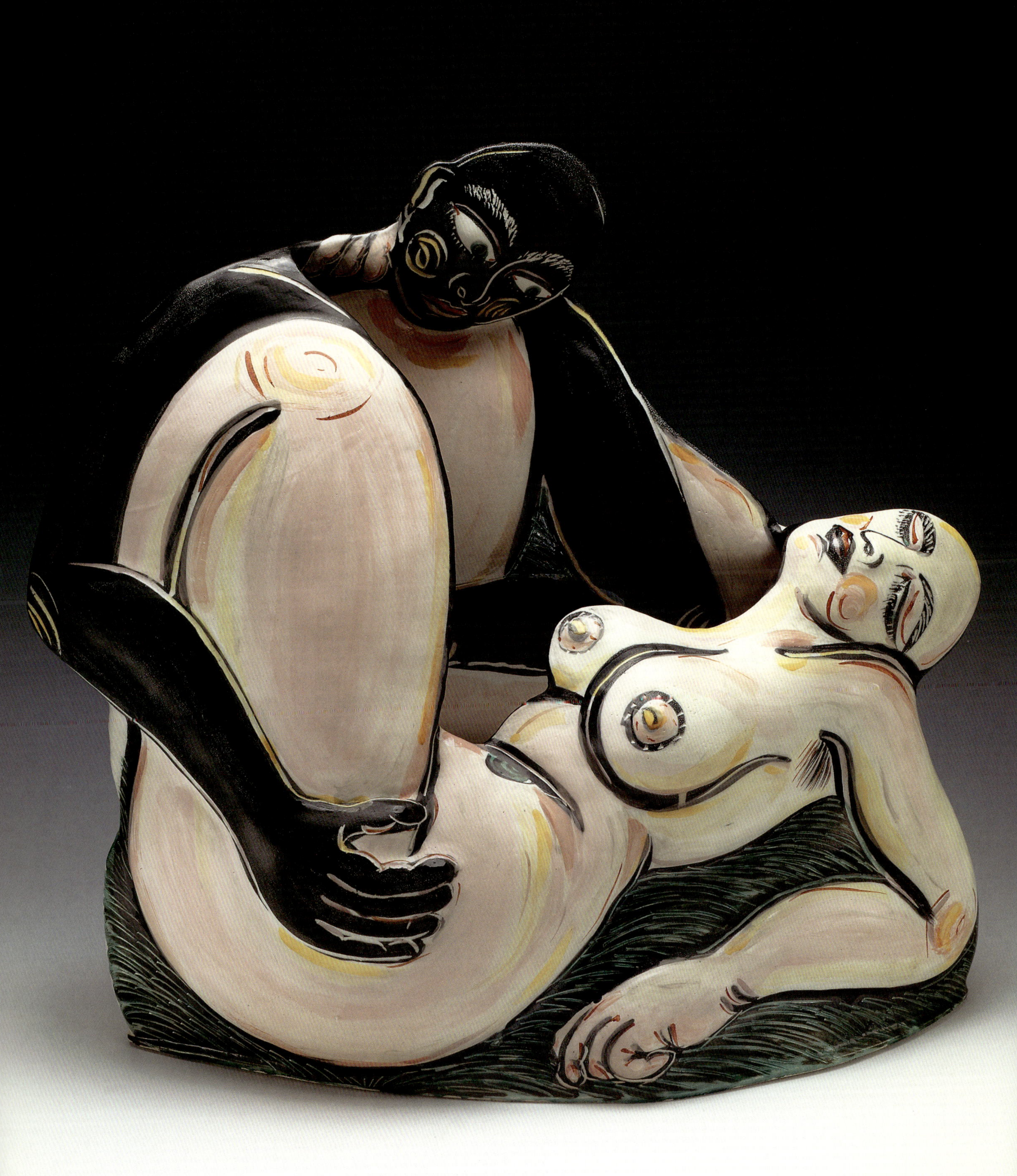

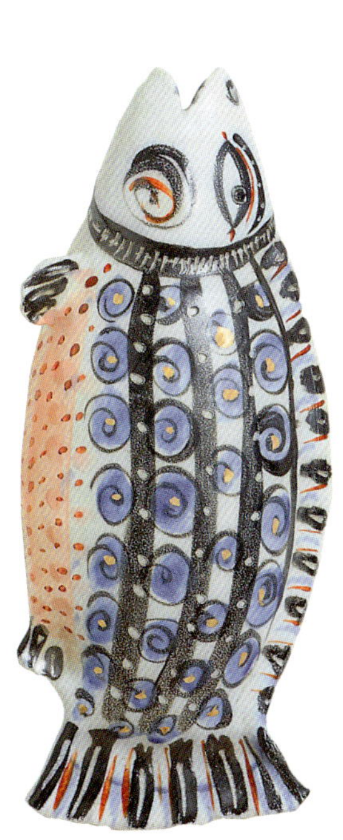

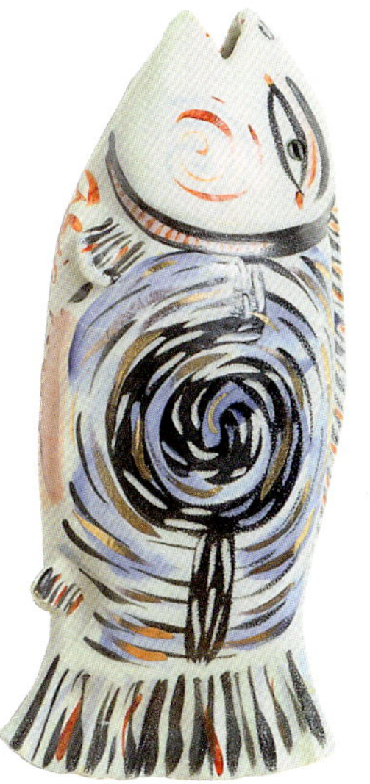

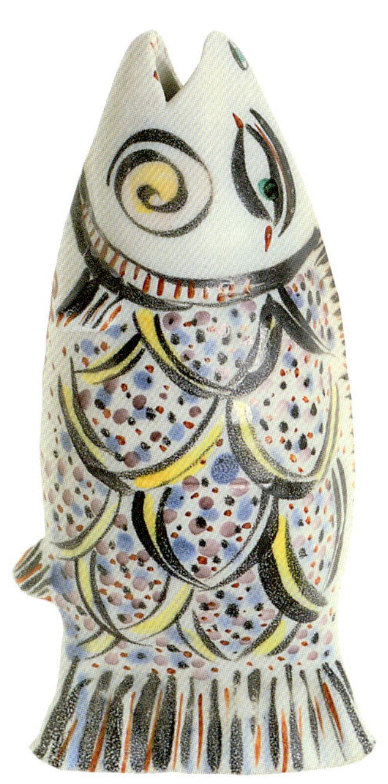

opposite
*Spring*, 1988
22 × 24 × 9½ in.
Hand-built, porcelain, salt-fired
(cat. no. 14)

*Two Fish*, ca. 1988
13 × 5 × 2½ in. and 11¼ × 5 × 2½ in.
Wheel-thrown and altered, porcelain, salt-fired
(cat. no. 16)

*Fish*, ca. 1988
9½ × 4½ × 2½ in.
Wheel-thrown and altered, porcelain, salt-fired
(cat. no. 15)

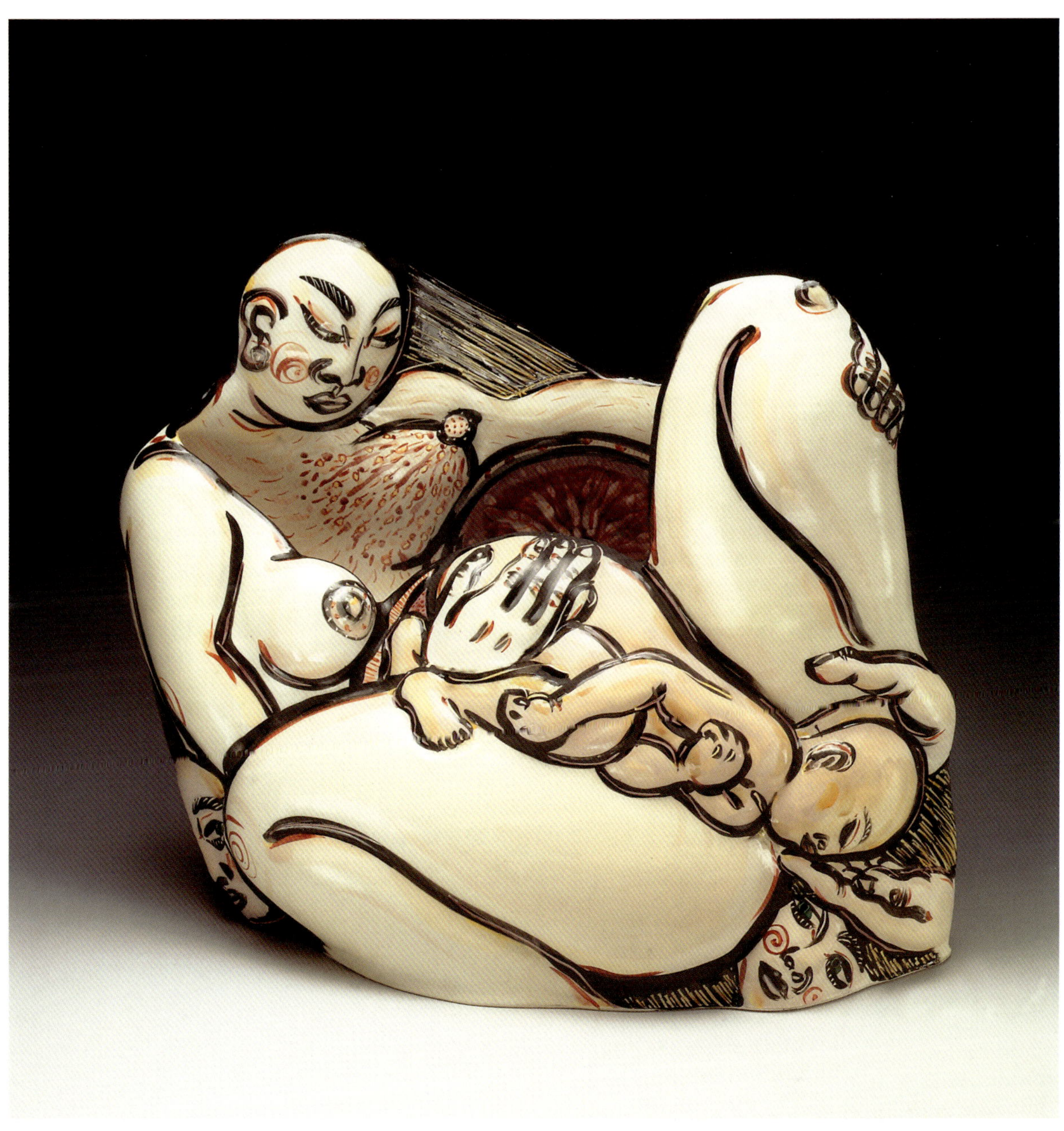

*Birth of Lena*, 1990
21 x 23 x 10 in.
Hand-built, porcelain, salt-fired
(cat. no. 17)

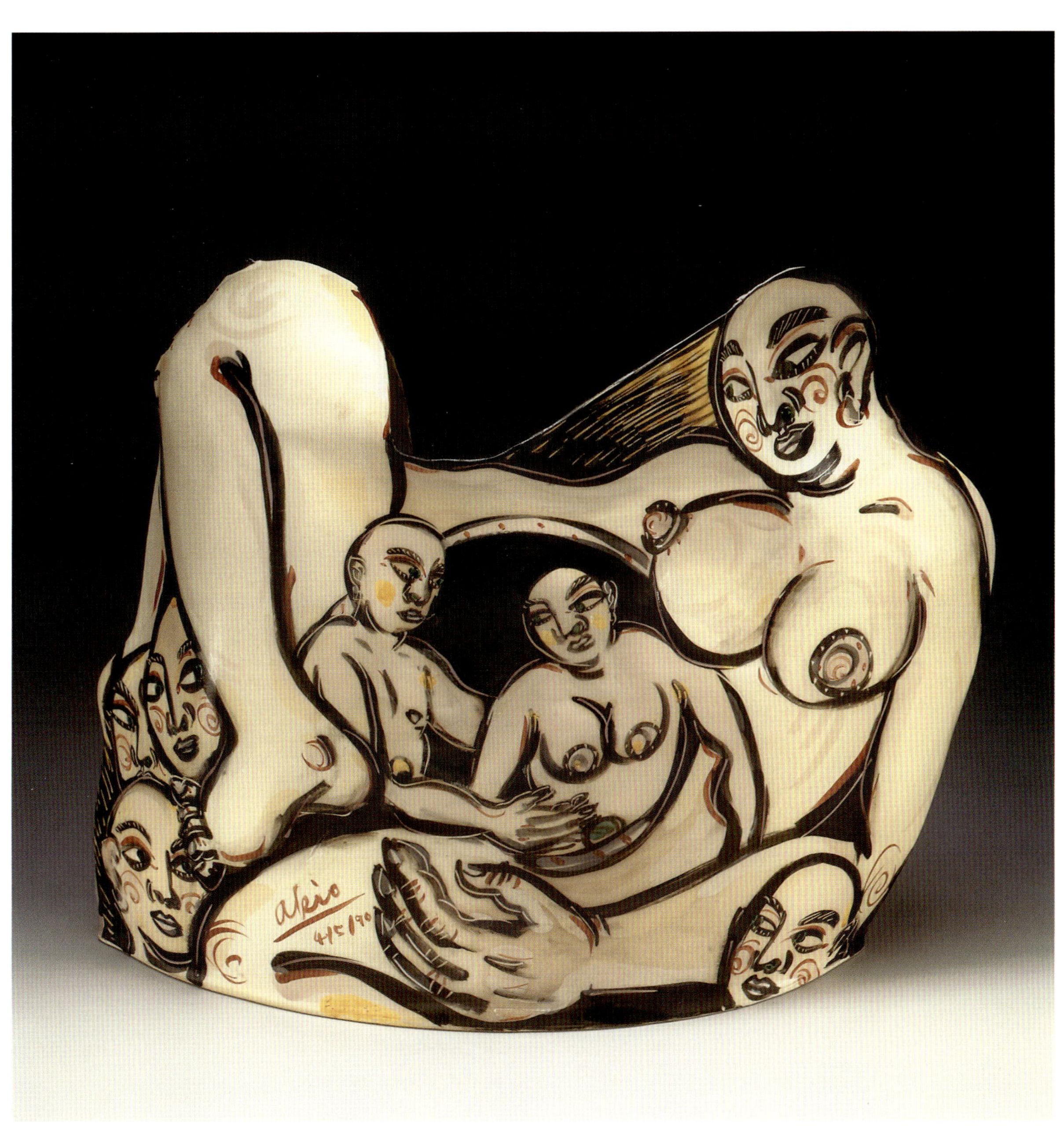
akio
4/5/90

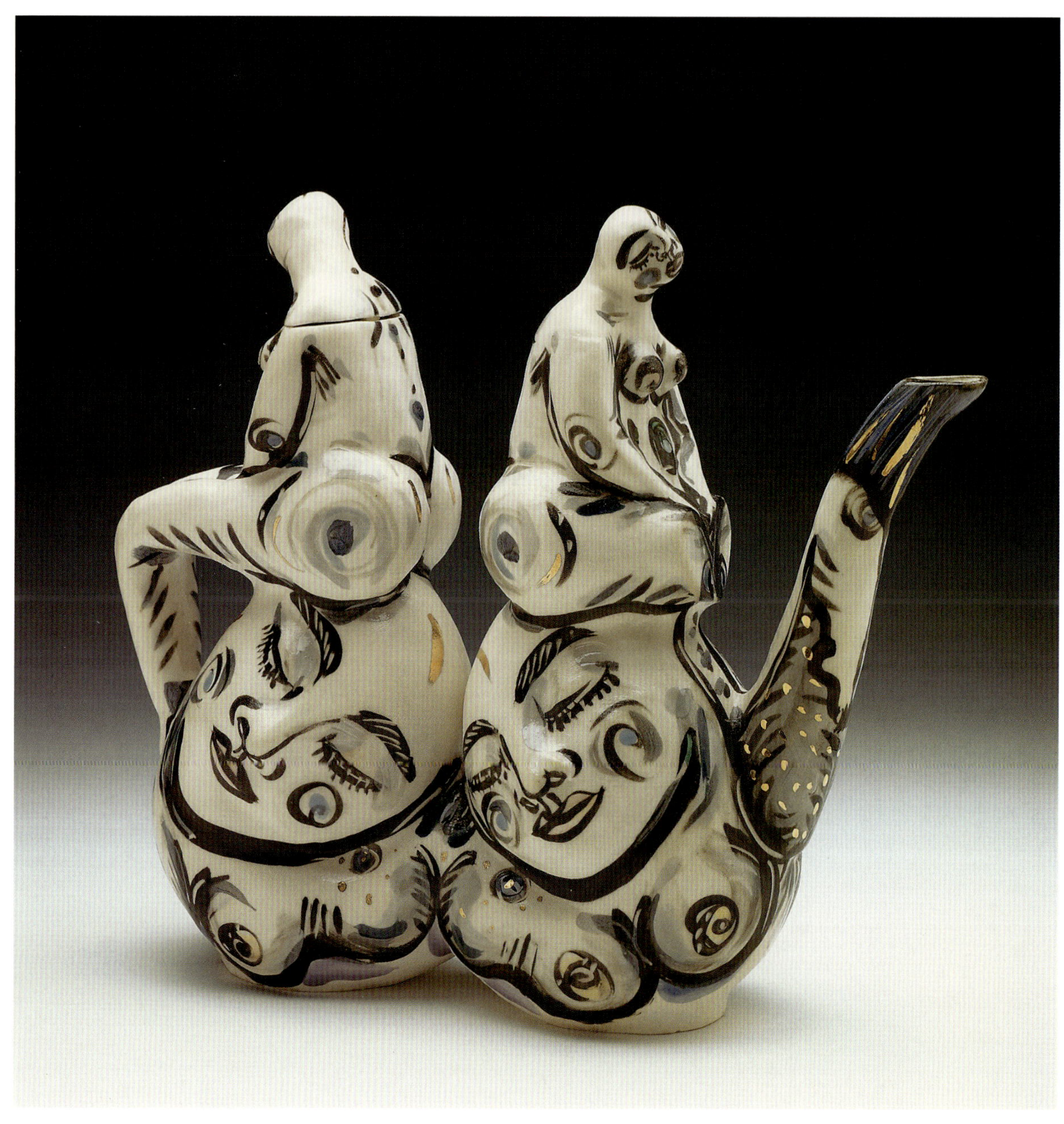

*Twin Sisters*, 1990
9½ × 10½ × 4 in.
Slip-cast, porcelain, salt-fired
(cat. no. 18)

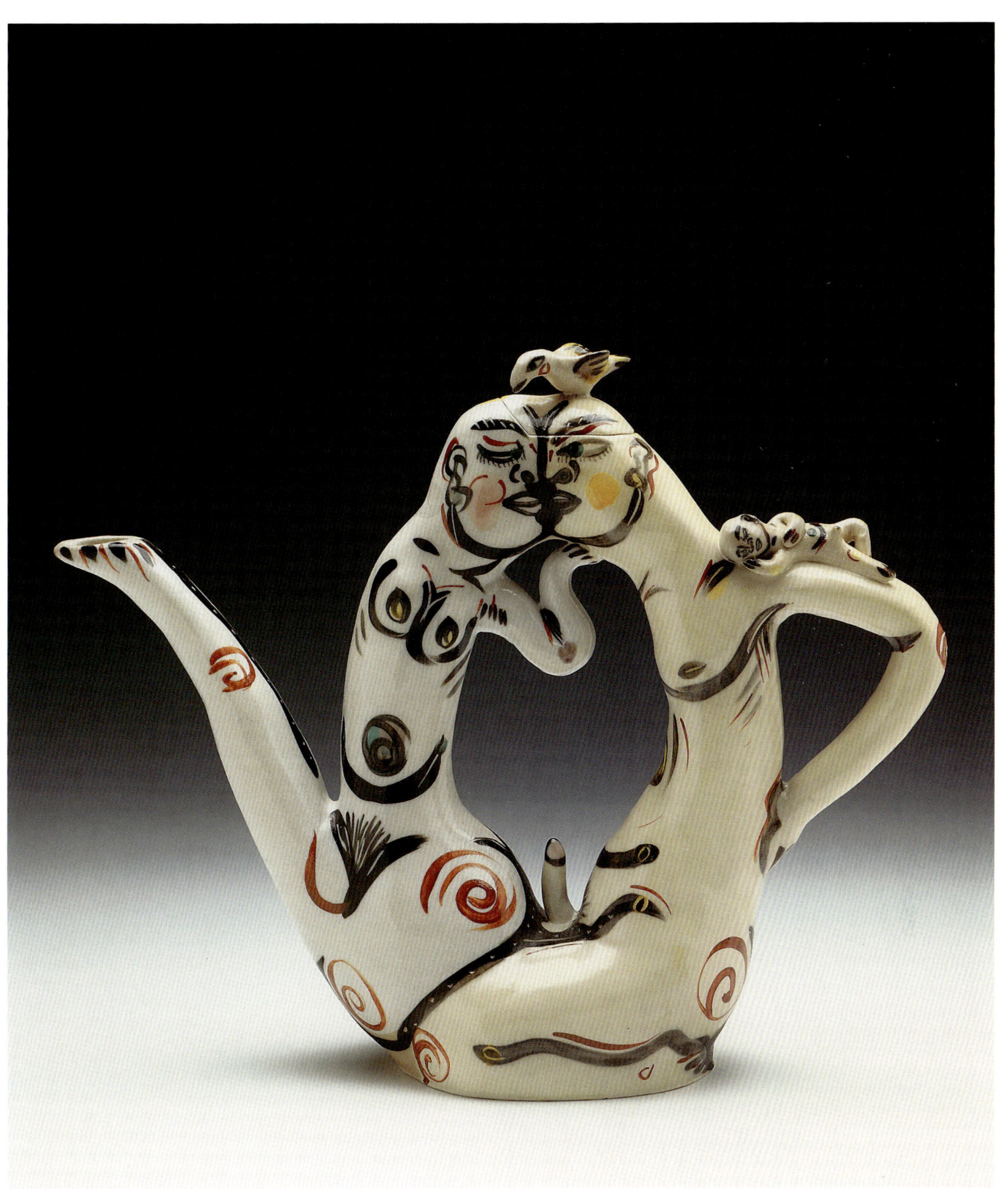

*Venus Disarming Mars (Lover's Teapot)*, ca. 1990
Slip-cast, porcelain, salt-fired
(cat. no. 19)

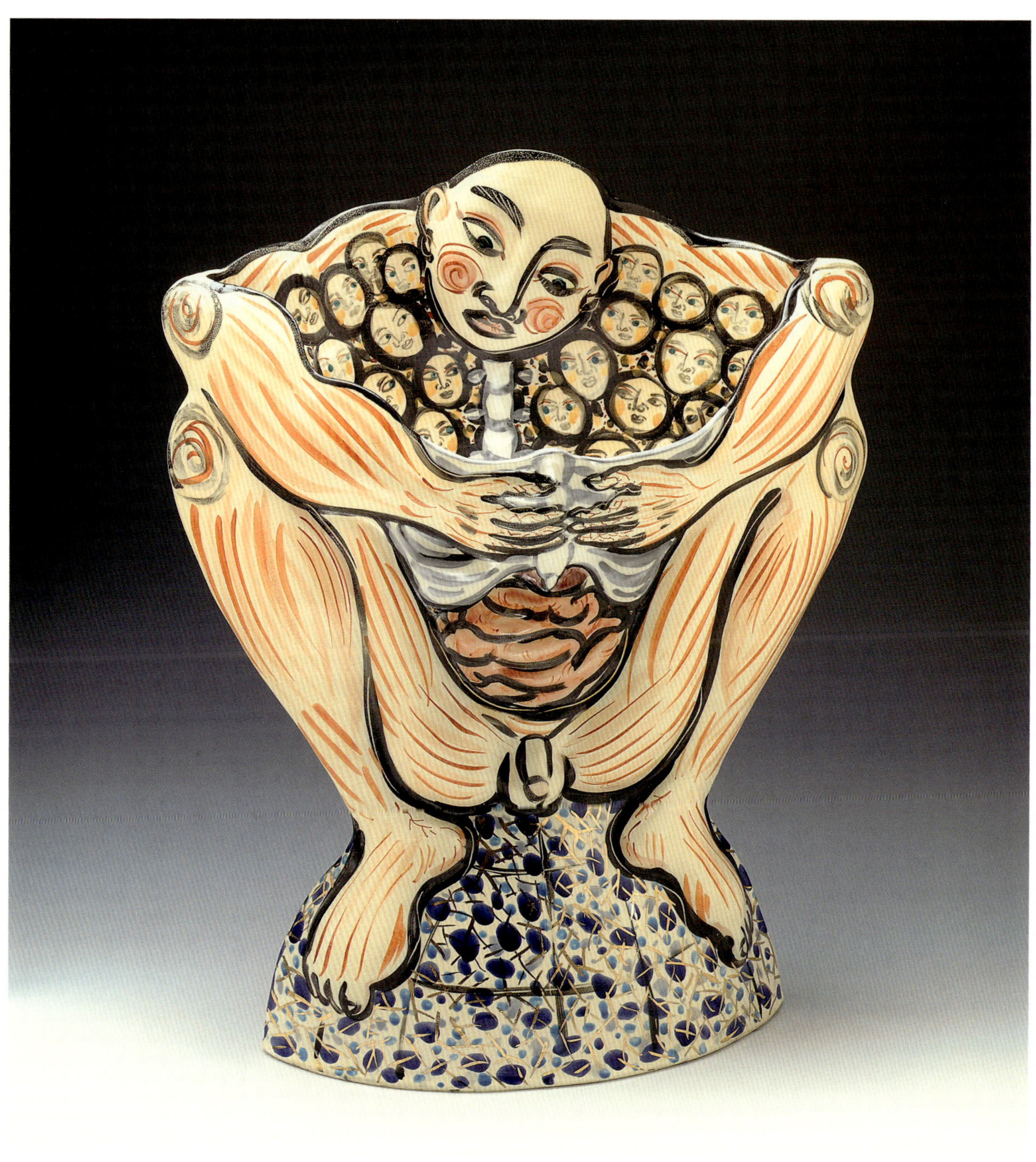

*Earth*, 1991
28 × 22 × 10 in.
Hand-built, porcelain, salt-fired
(cat. no. 20)

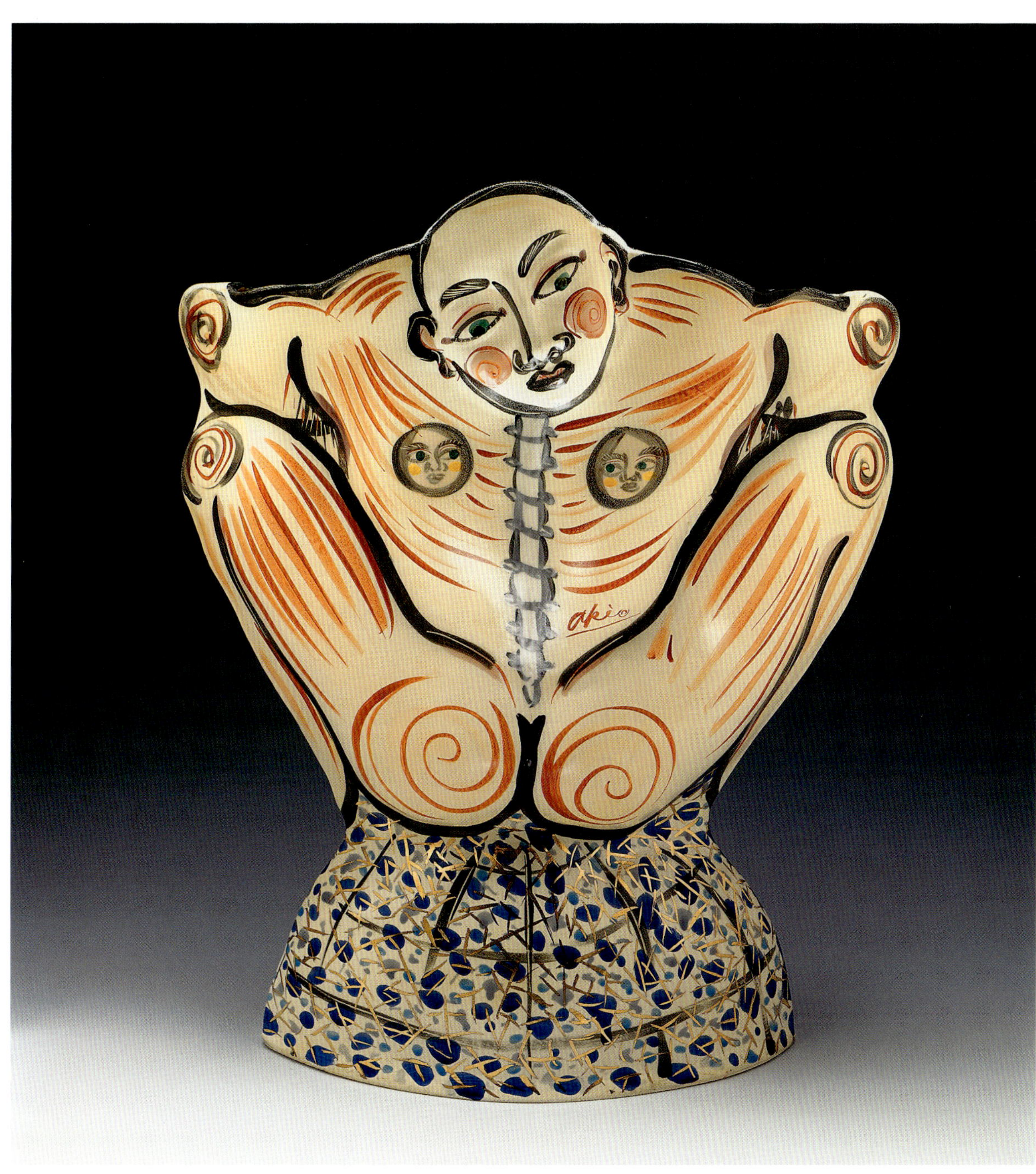
akio

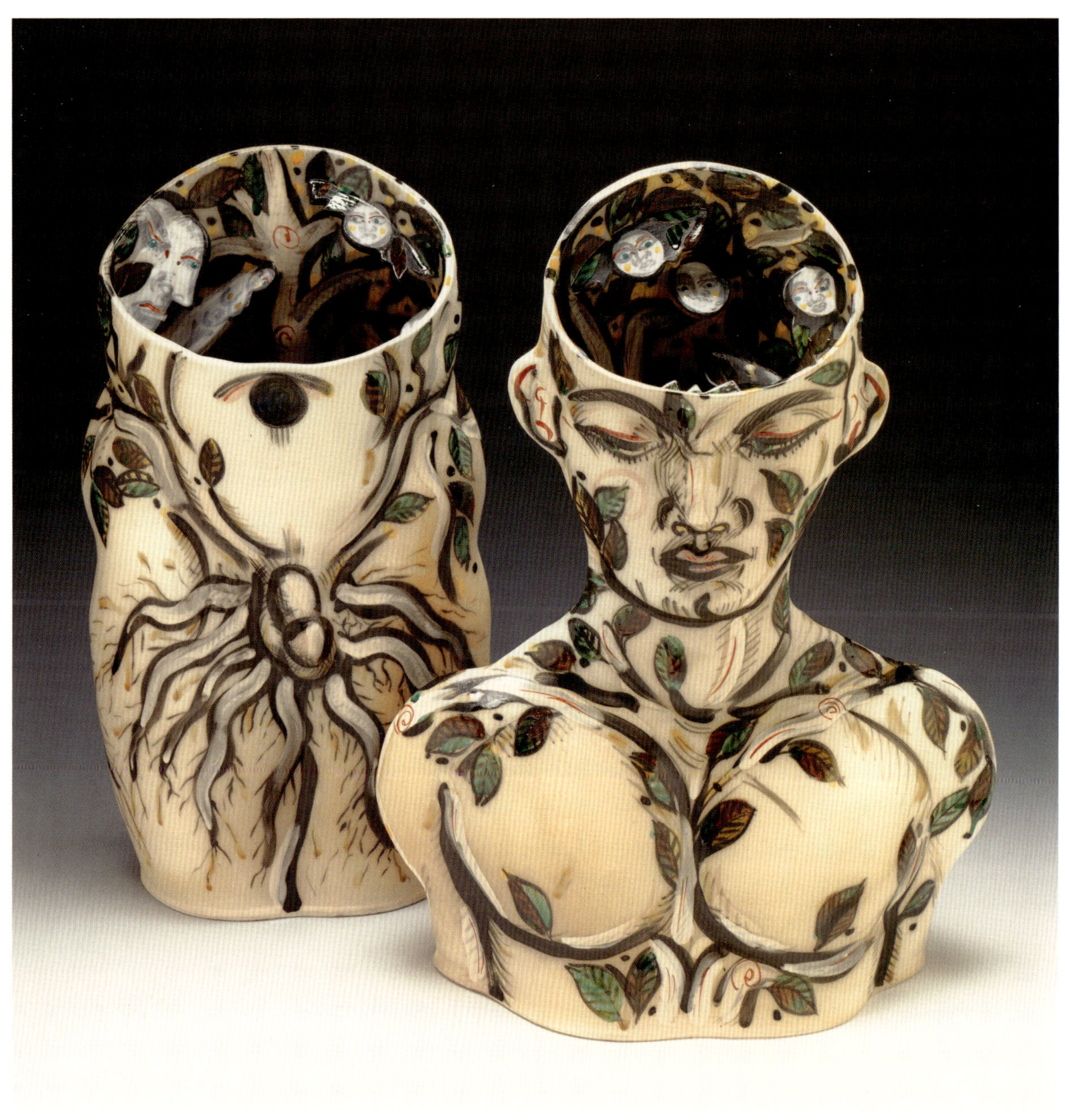

*Tree*, 1991
Lower torso: 20 × 11 × 6 in.
Upper torso: 21½ × 16 × 8 in.
Hand-built, porcelain, salt-fired
(cat. no. 21)

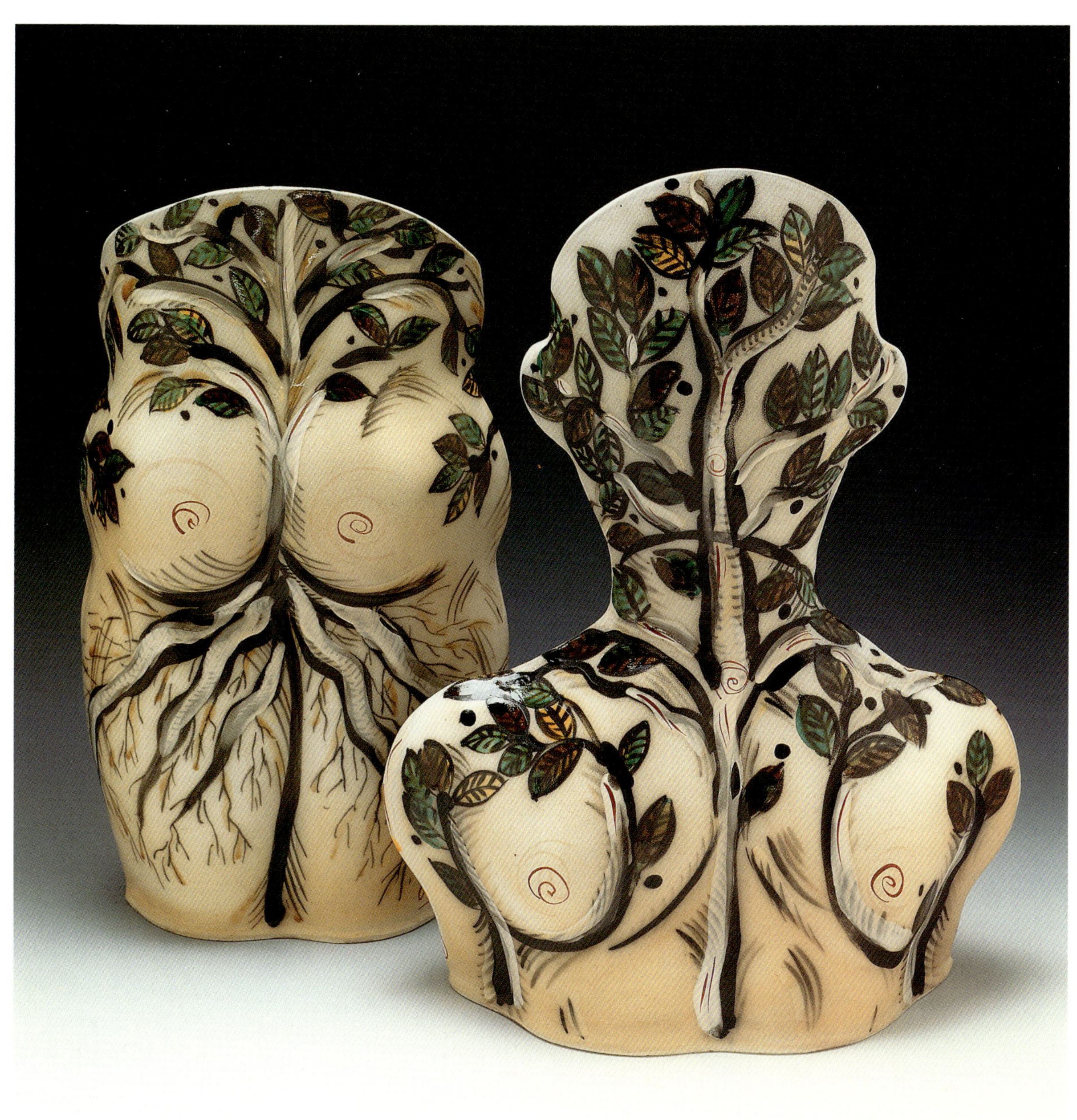

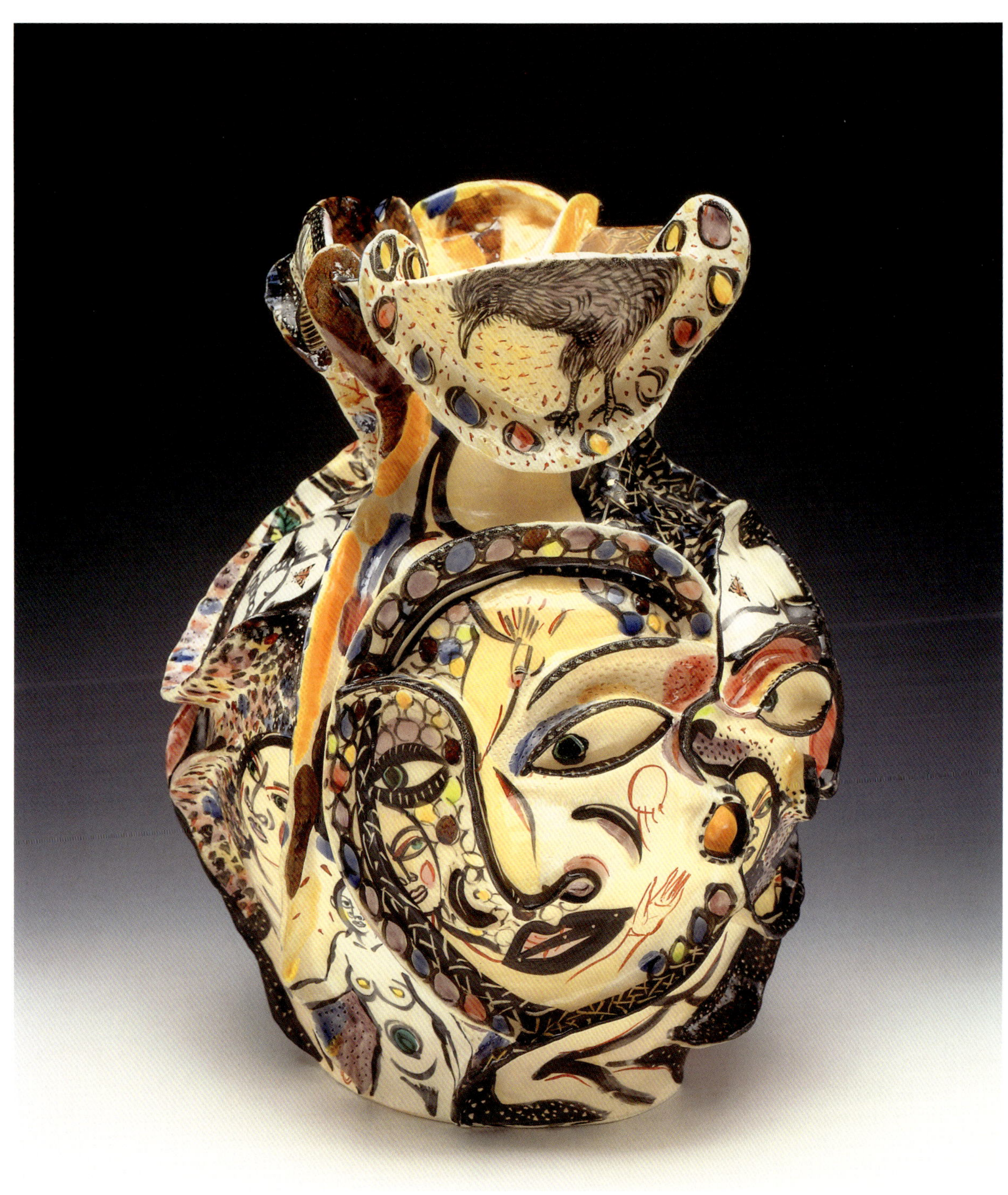

*Summer of '92 Vase*, 1992
16 × 9½ × 12 in.
Hand-built, porcelain, salt-fired
(cat. no. 22)

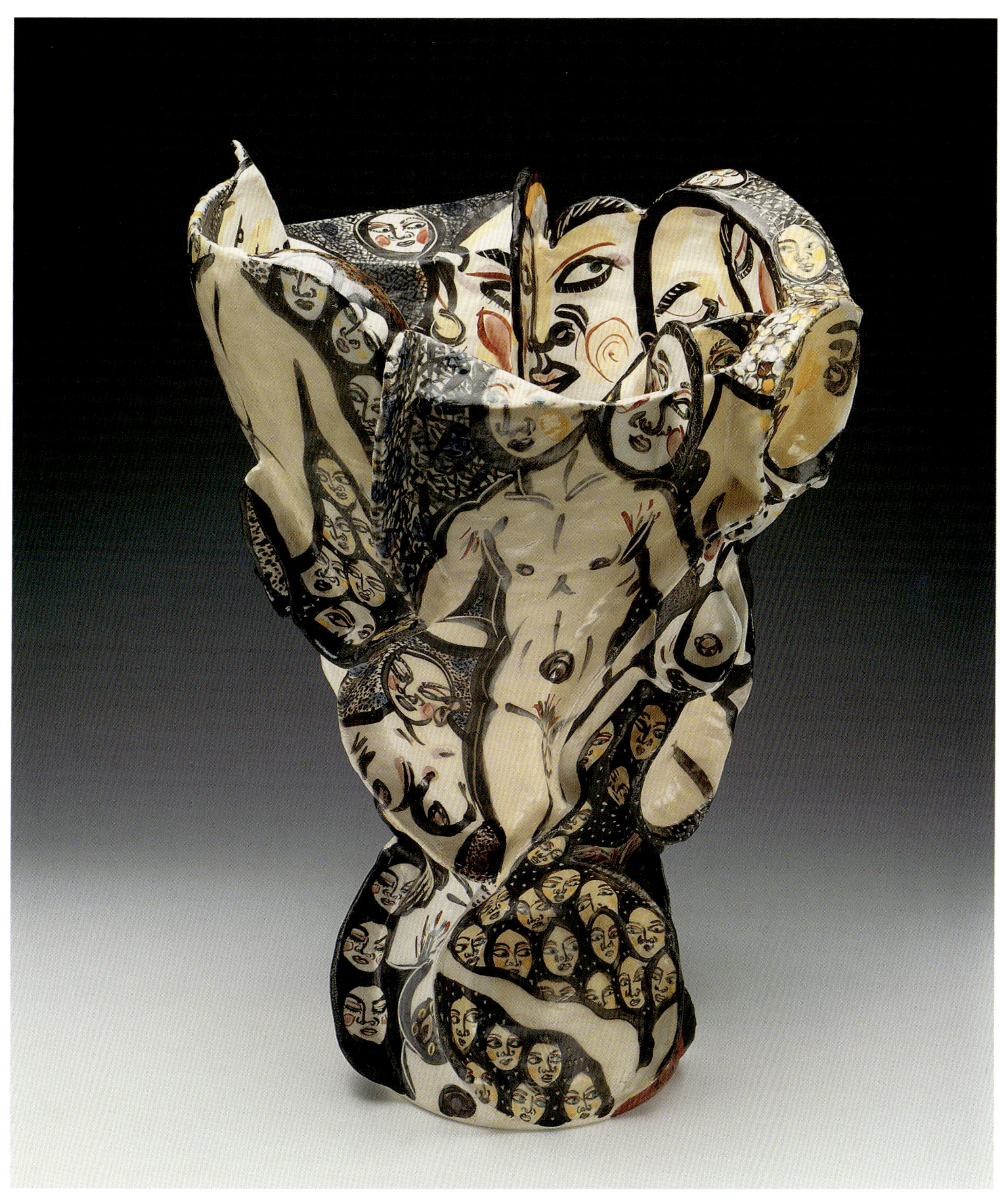

*Vase of Voyeur*, 1992
19 × 14 × 13 in.
Hand-built, porcelain, salt-fired
(cat. no. 23)

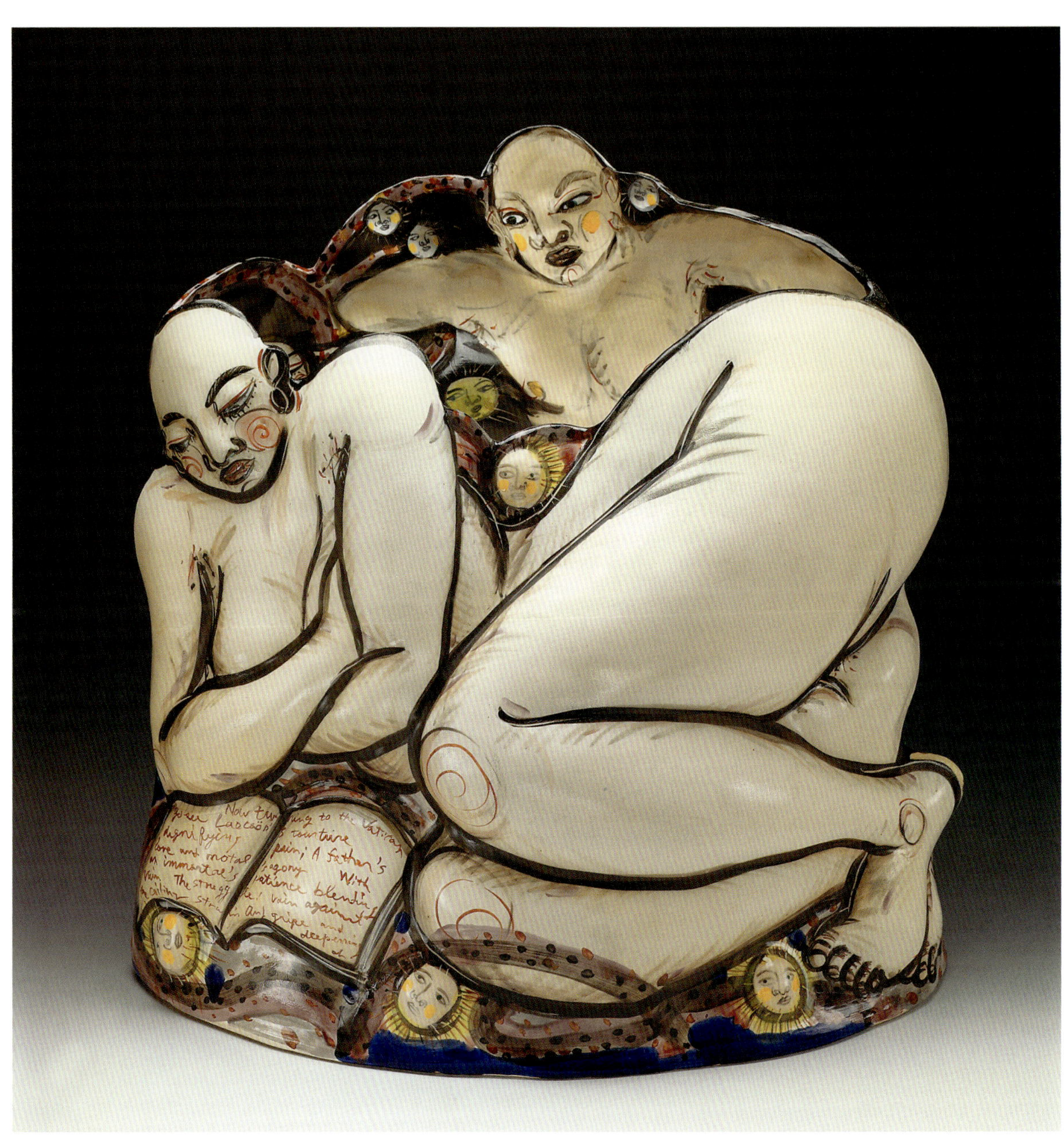

*Laocoön*, 1994
25 × 25 × 13 in.
Hand-built, porcelain, salt-fired
(cat. no. 24)

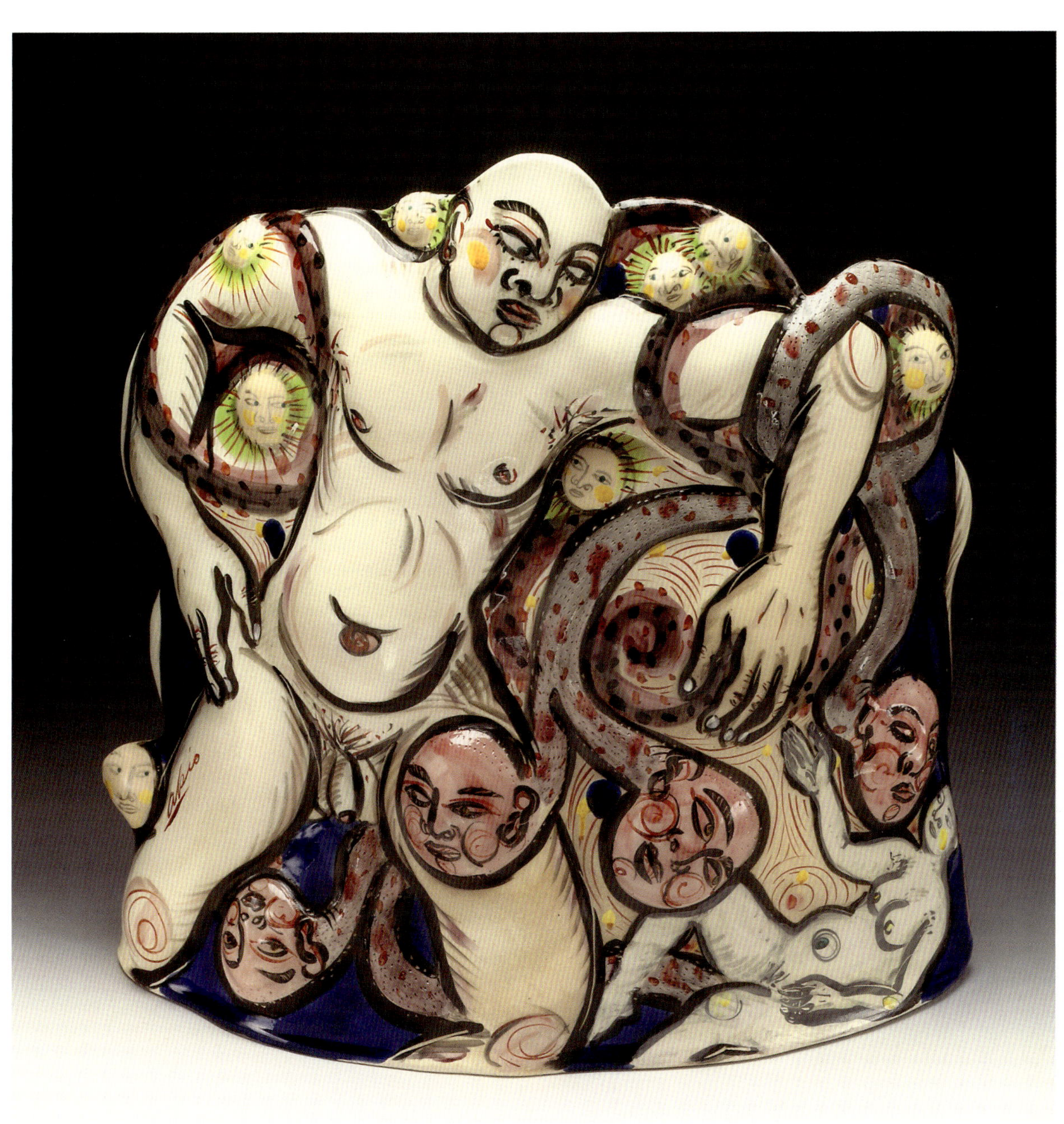

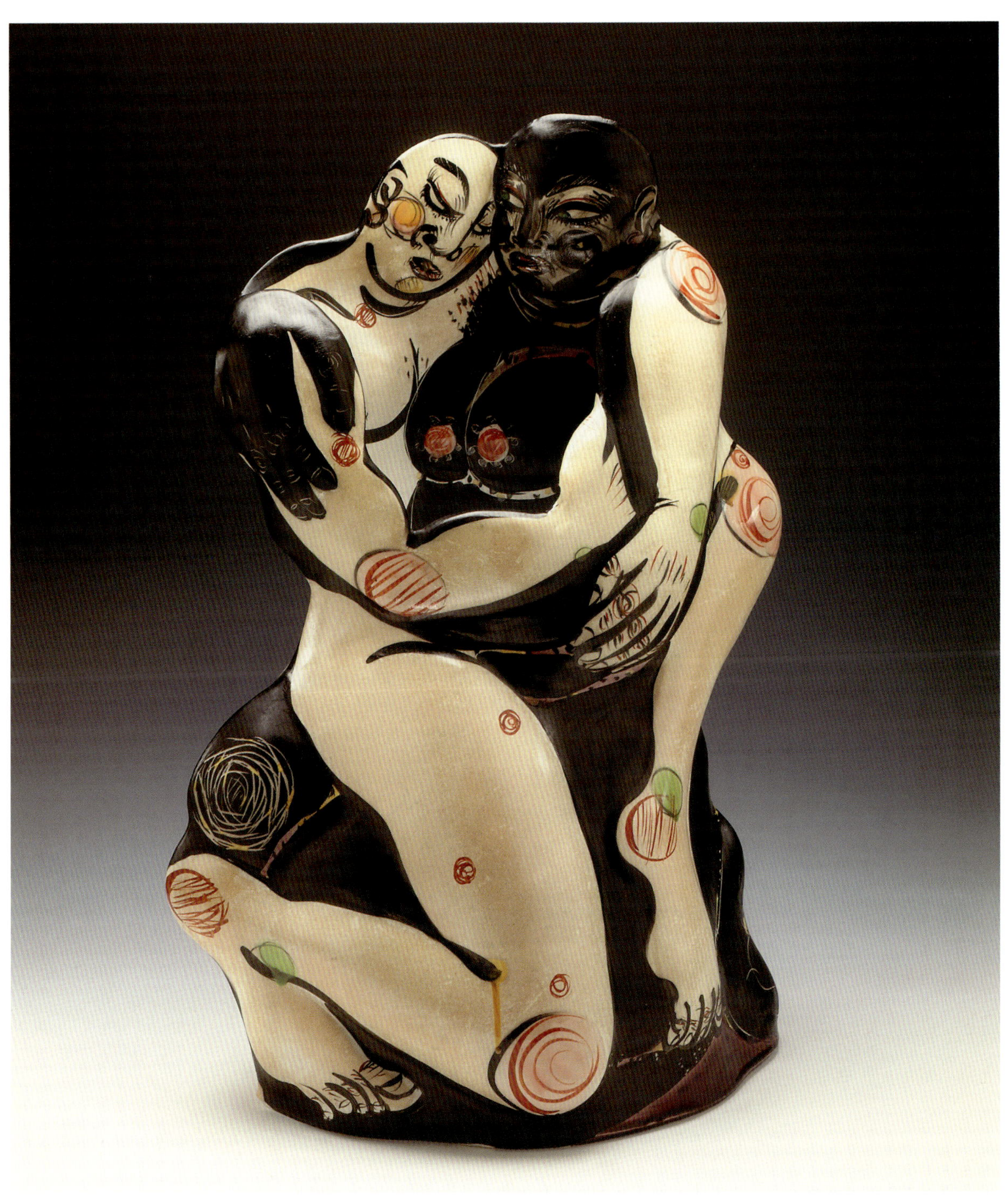

*Seduction*, 1995
24½ × 15 × 8 in.
Hand-built, porcelain, salt-fired
(cat. no. 25)

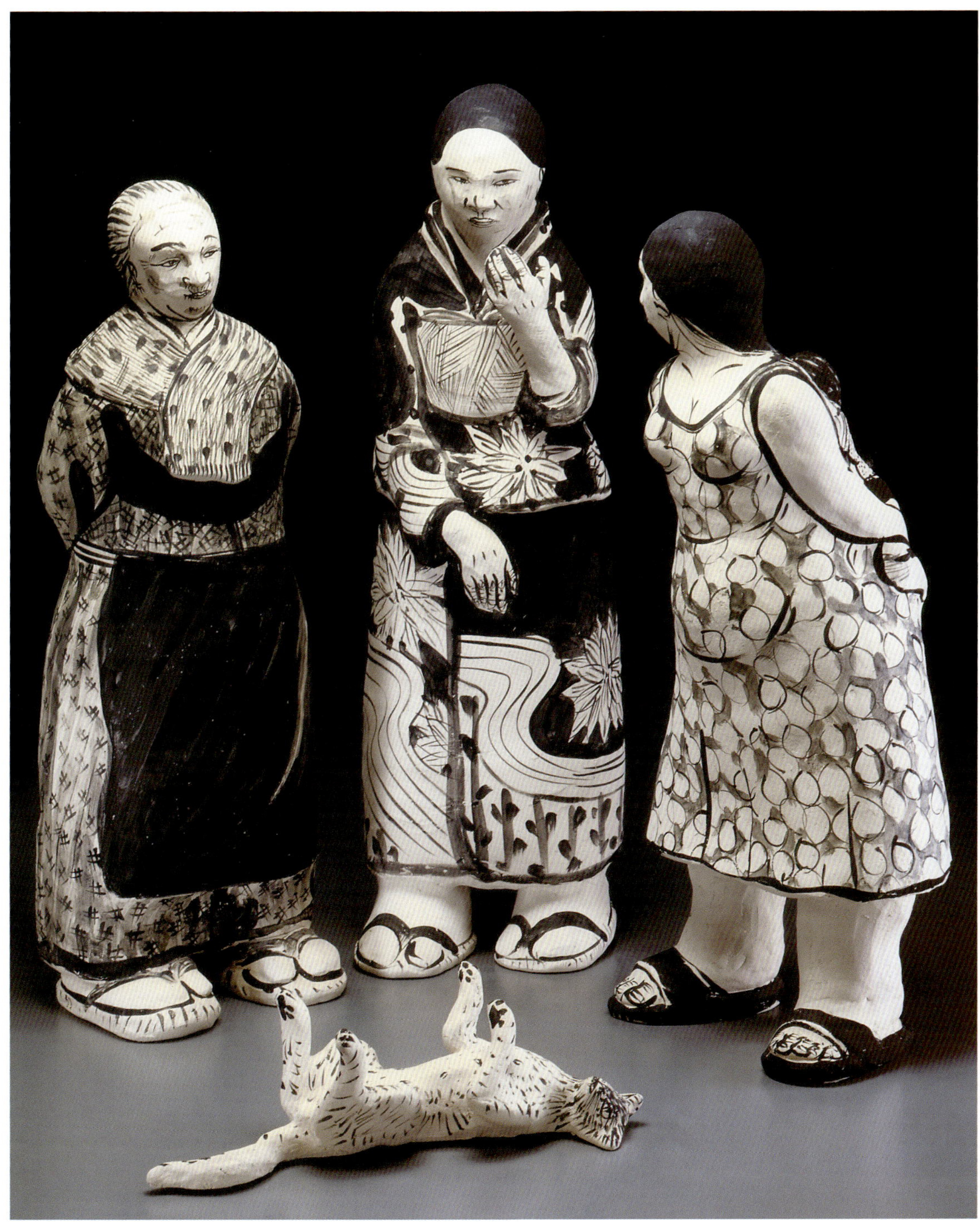

*Female Figure*, 1996
19 × 8 × 7 in.
Hand-built, stoneware
(cat. no. 28)

*Female Figure*, 1996
21 × 7 × 7 in.
Hand-built, stoneware
(cat. no. 27)

*Cat*, 1996
4 × 11 × 4 in.
Hand-built, stoneware
(cat. no. 26)

*Female Figure with Baby*, 1996
19 × 7 × 7 in.
Hand-built, stoneware
(cat. no. 29)

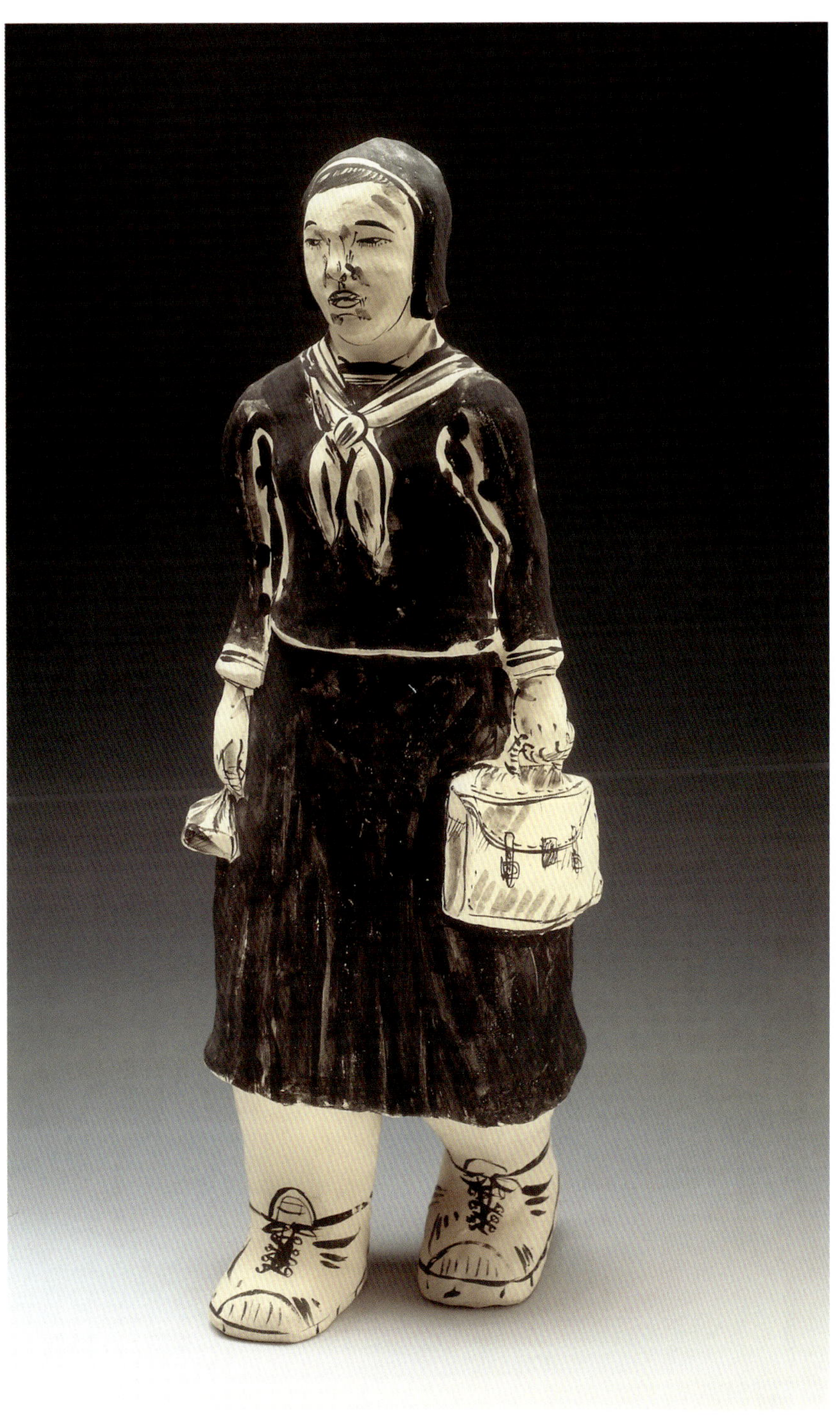

*Female Student*, 1996
22 × 7½ × 8 in.
Hand-built, stoneware
(cat. no. 30)

opposite
*Male Student*, 1996
34 × 11 × 12 in.
Hand-built, stoneware
(cat. no. 31)

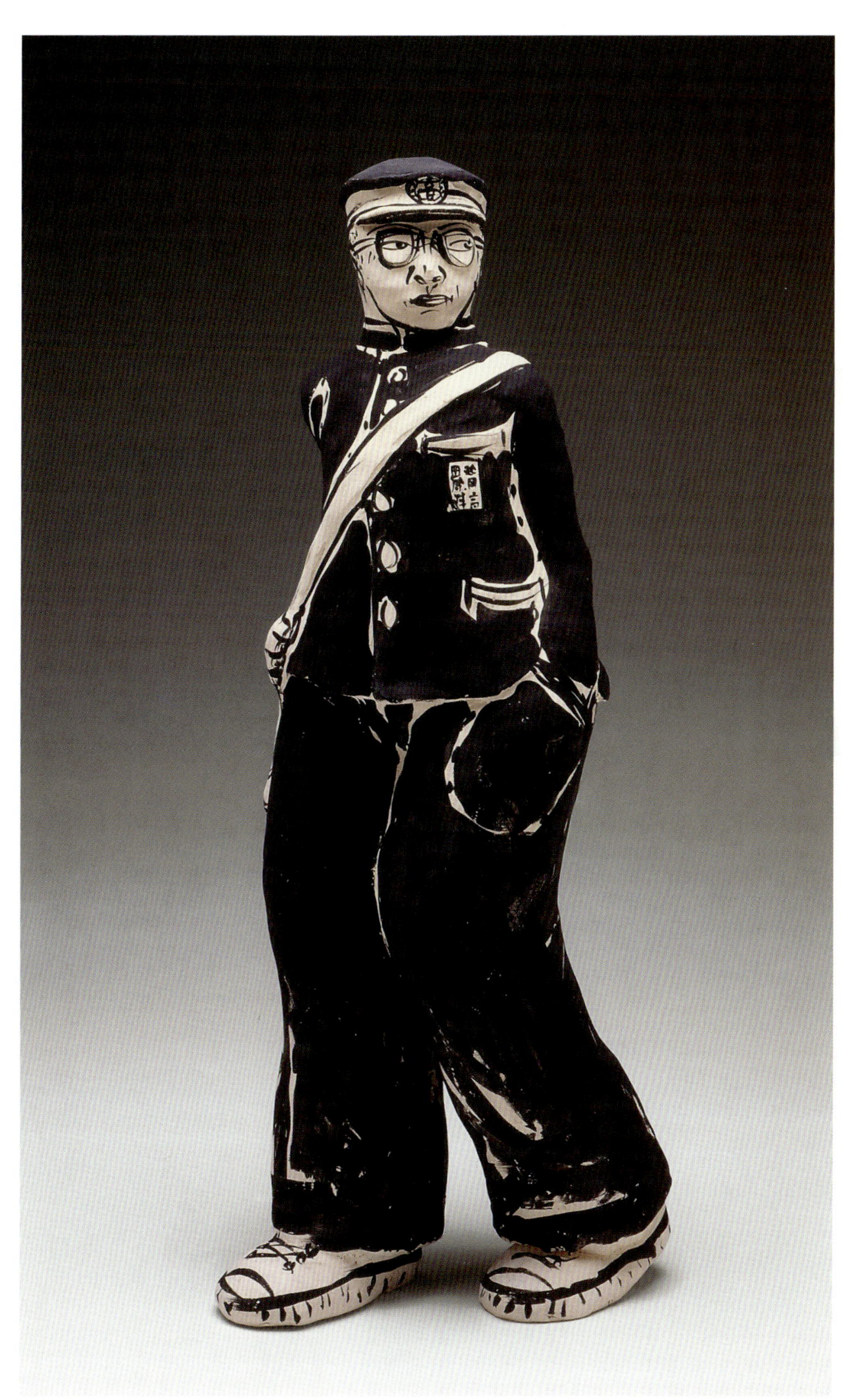

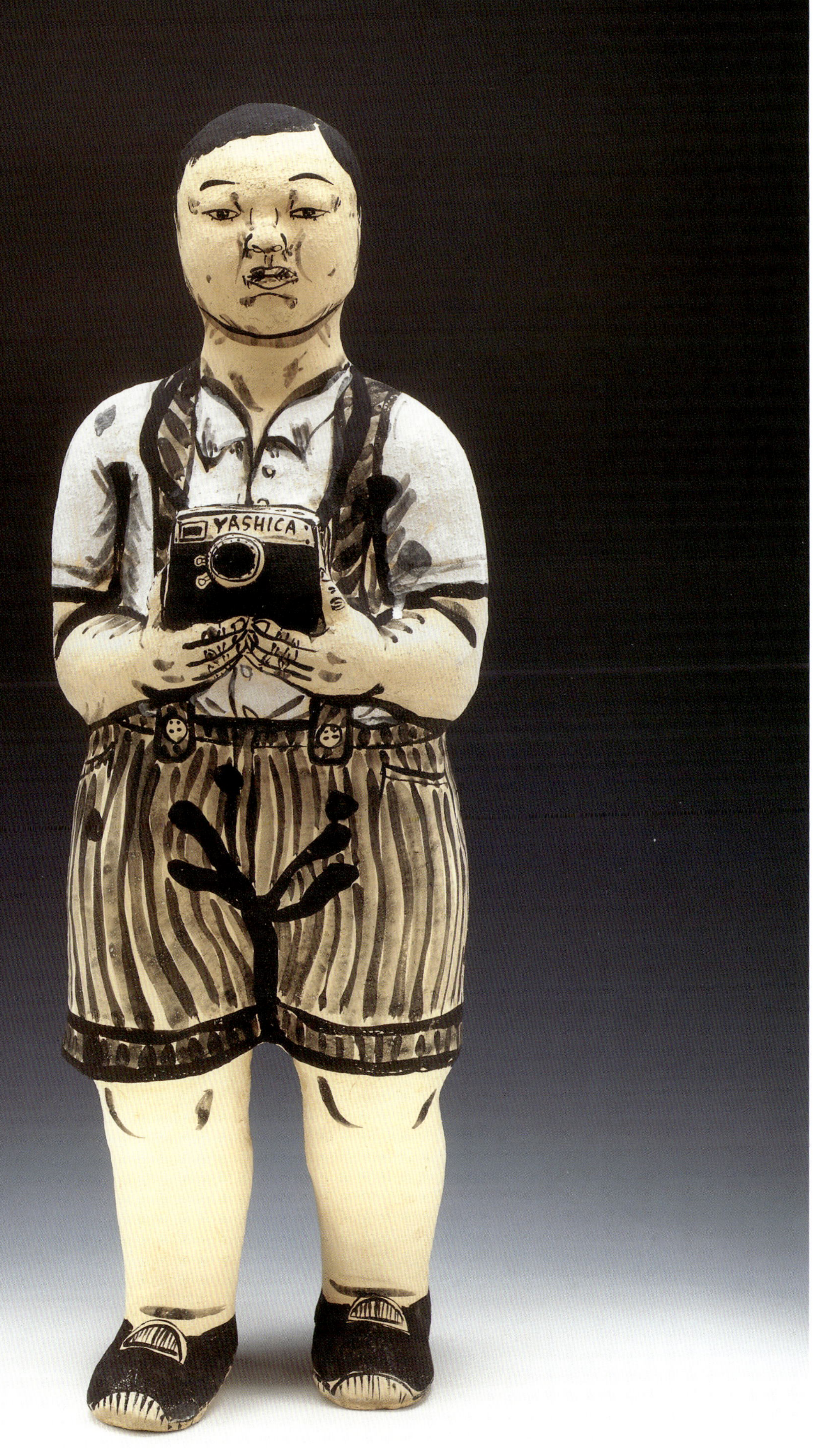
YASHICA

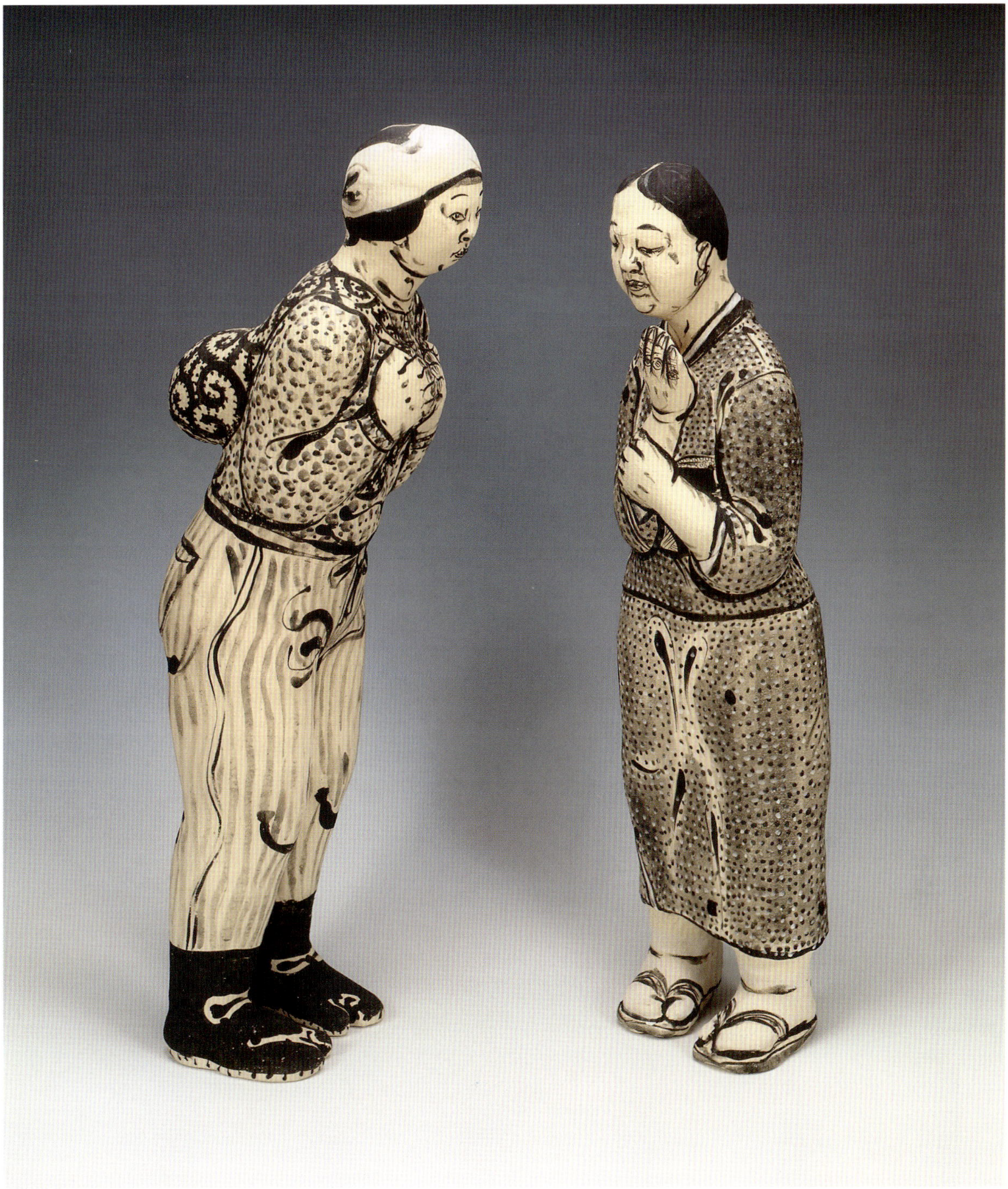

opposite
*Camera Boy*, 1998
31½ × 10 × 7½ in.
Hand-built, stoneware
(cat. no. 32)

*Greeters*, 1998
34½ × 10 × 7½ in.
33 × 8 × 6 in.
Hand-built, stoneware
(cat. no. 33)

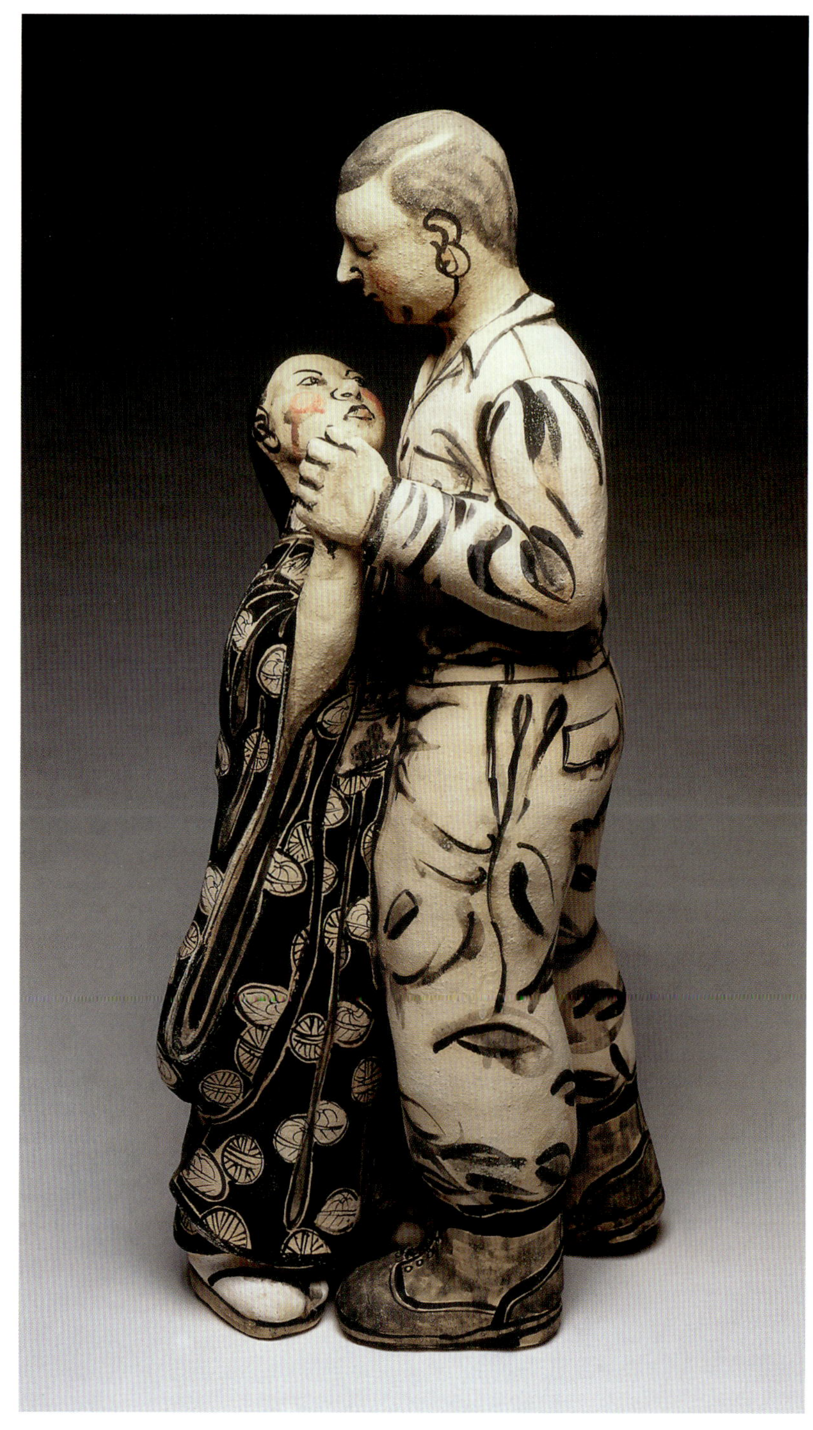

*Dance*, 2001
32 x 12 x 10 in.
Hand-built, stoneware
(cat. no. 35)

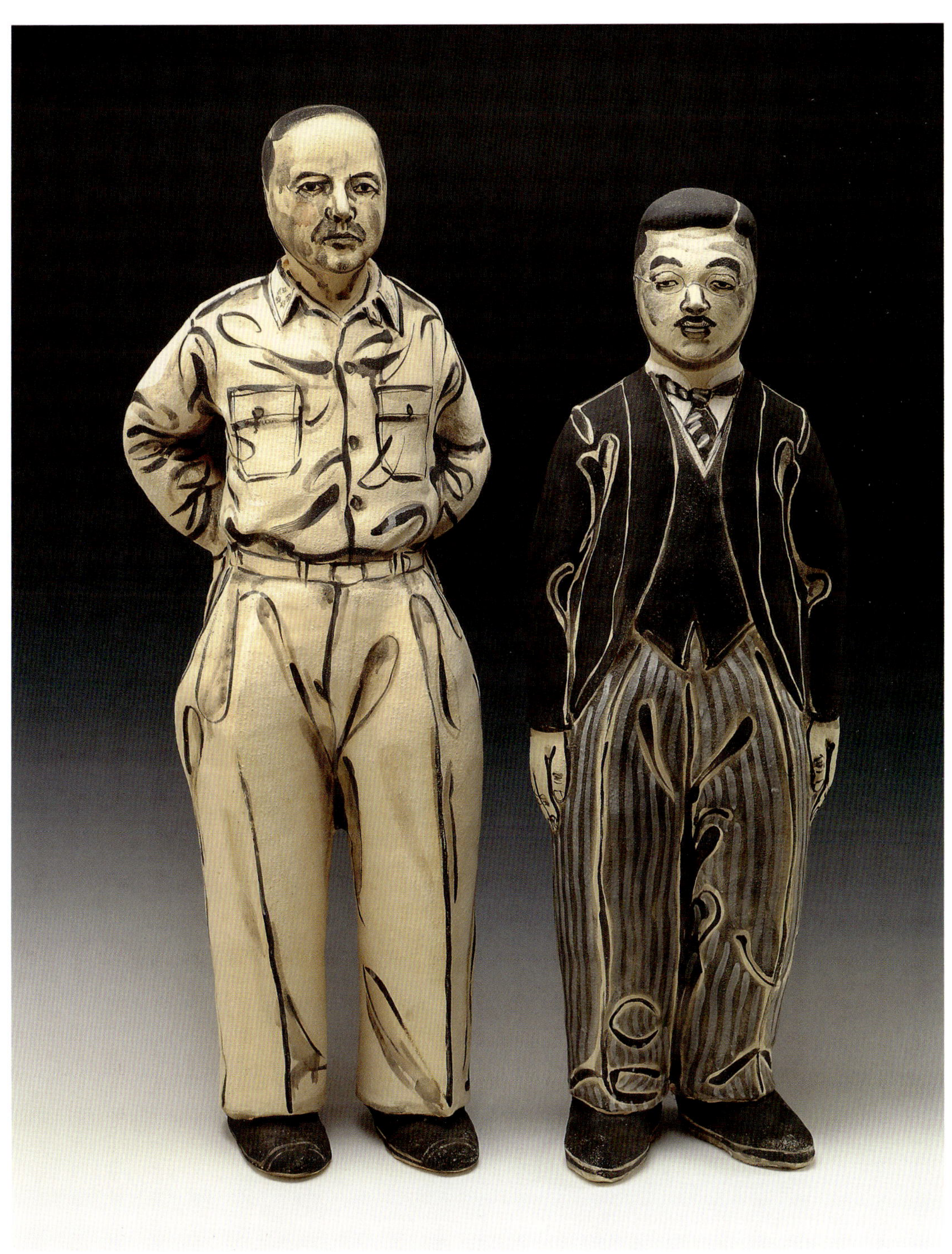

*General and Emperor,* 2001
38 × 11 × 8 in.
35 × 12 × 8 in.
Hand-built, stoneware
(cat. no. 36)

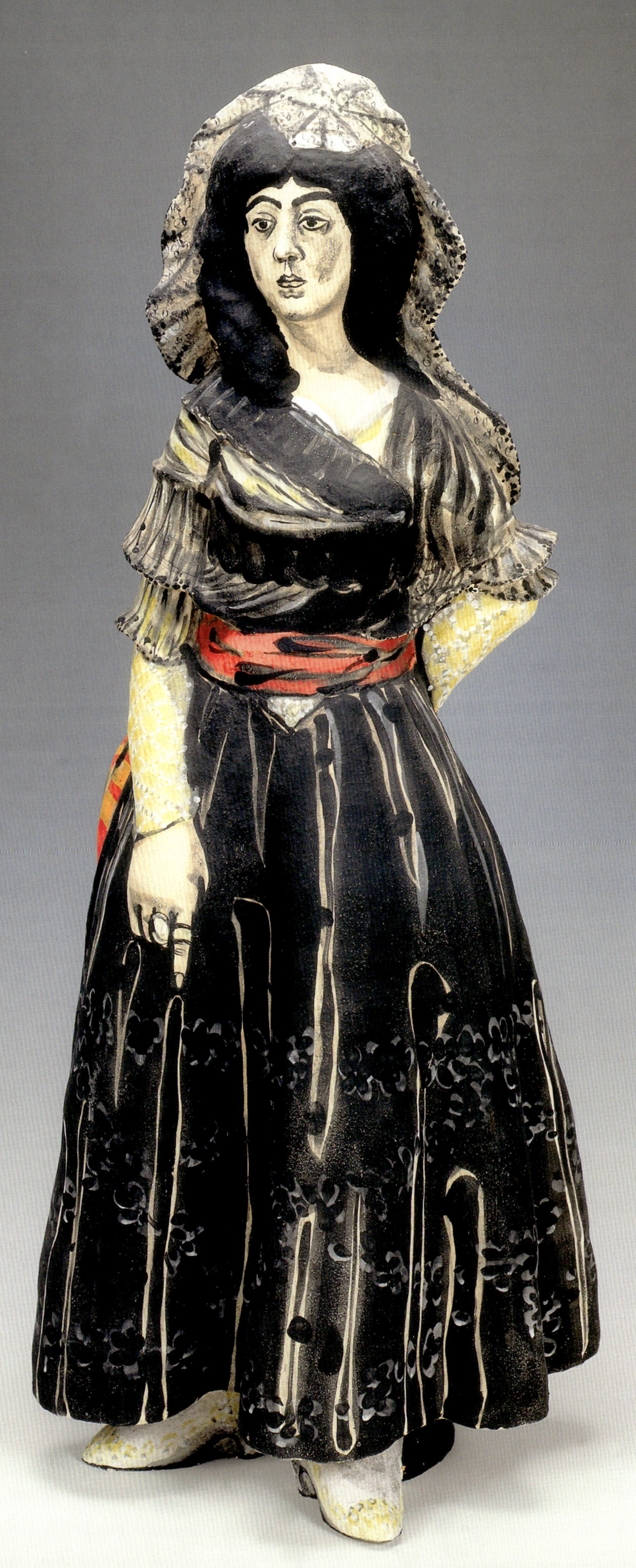

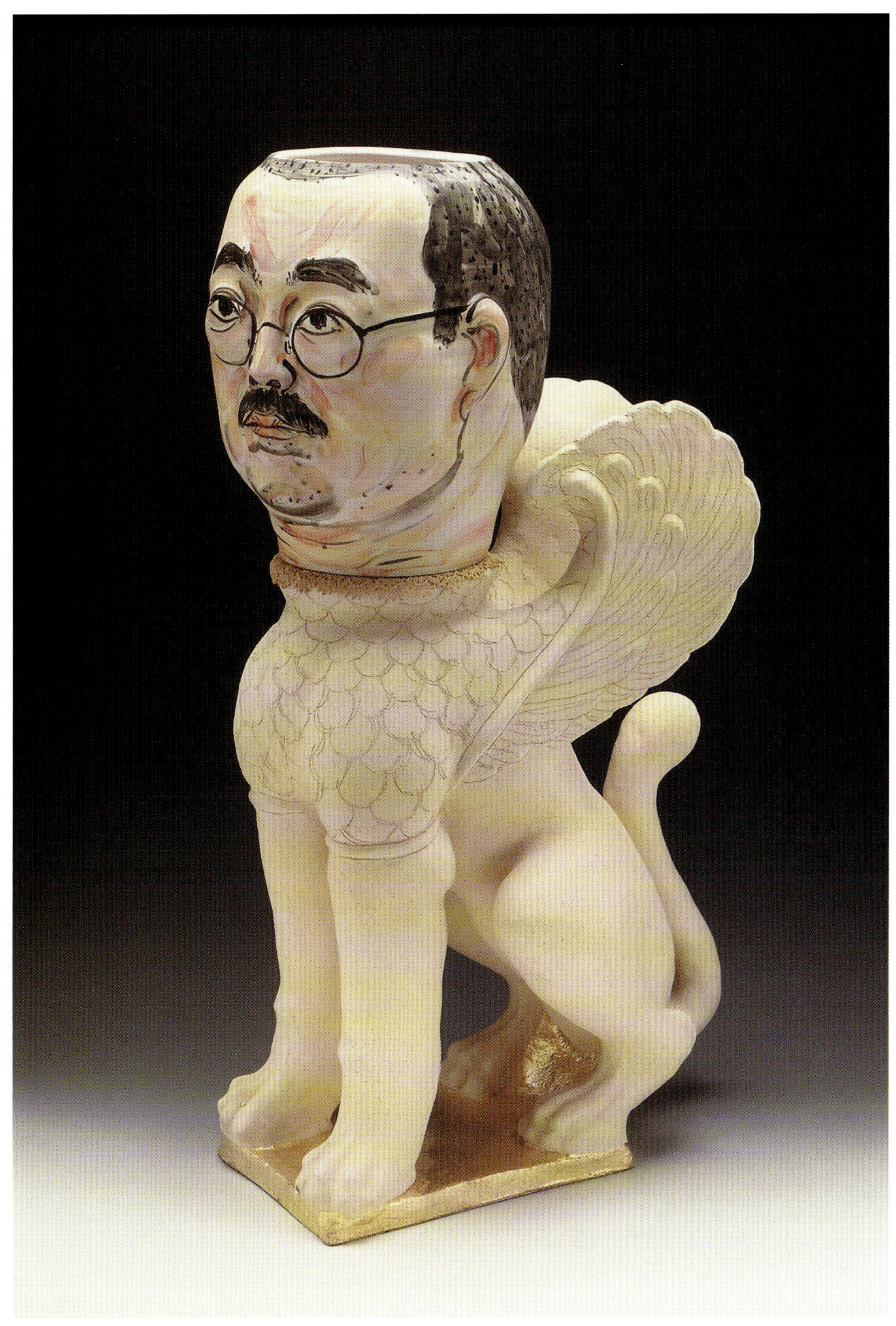

opposite
*Duchess*, 2000
42 × 16 × 14 in.
Hand-built, stoneware
(cat. no. 34)

*Sphinx*, 2002
30 × 6½ × 16 in.
Head: Wheel-thrown and altered porcelain, fabric
Base: Hand-built, stoneware
(cat. no. 37)

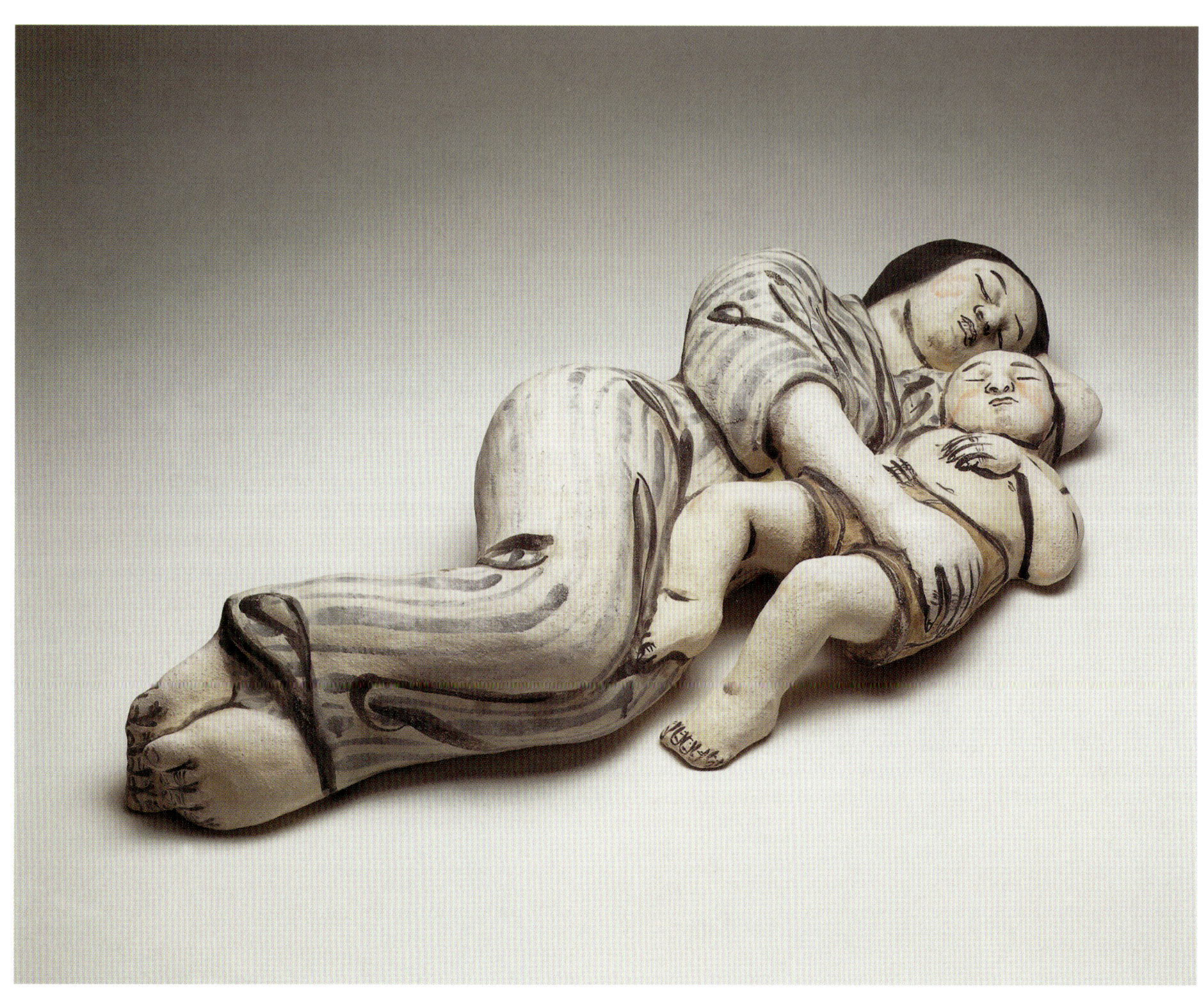

*Sleeping Woman and Child*, 2003
6 × 27 × 10½ in.
Hand-built, stoneware
(cat. no. 40)

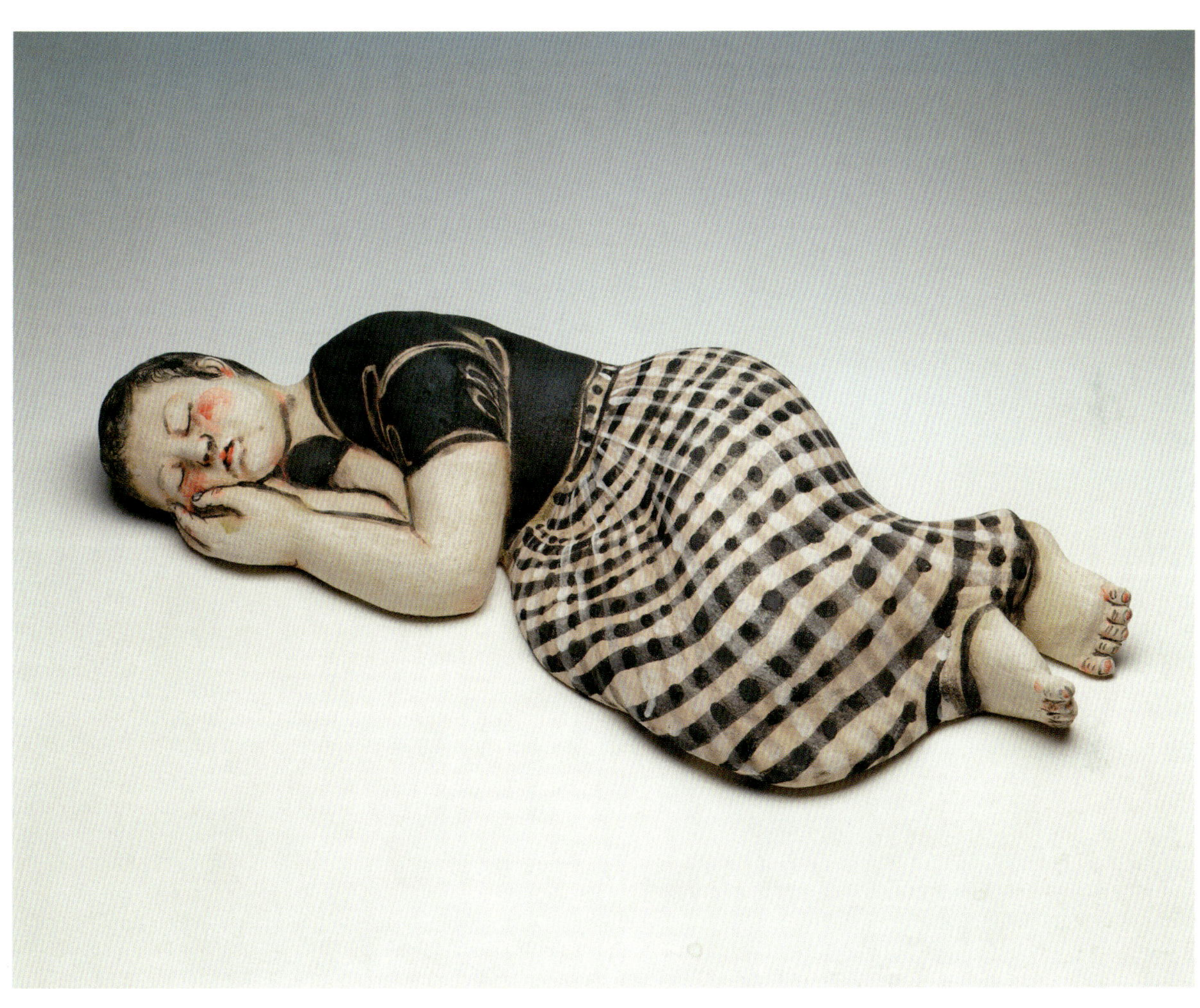

*Sleeping Woman in Checkered Skirt*, 2003
6 × 27 × 10½ in.
Hand-built, stoneware
(cat. no. 41)

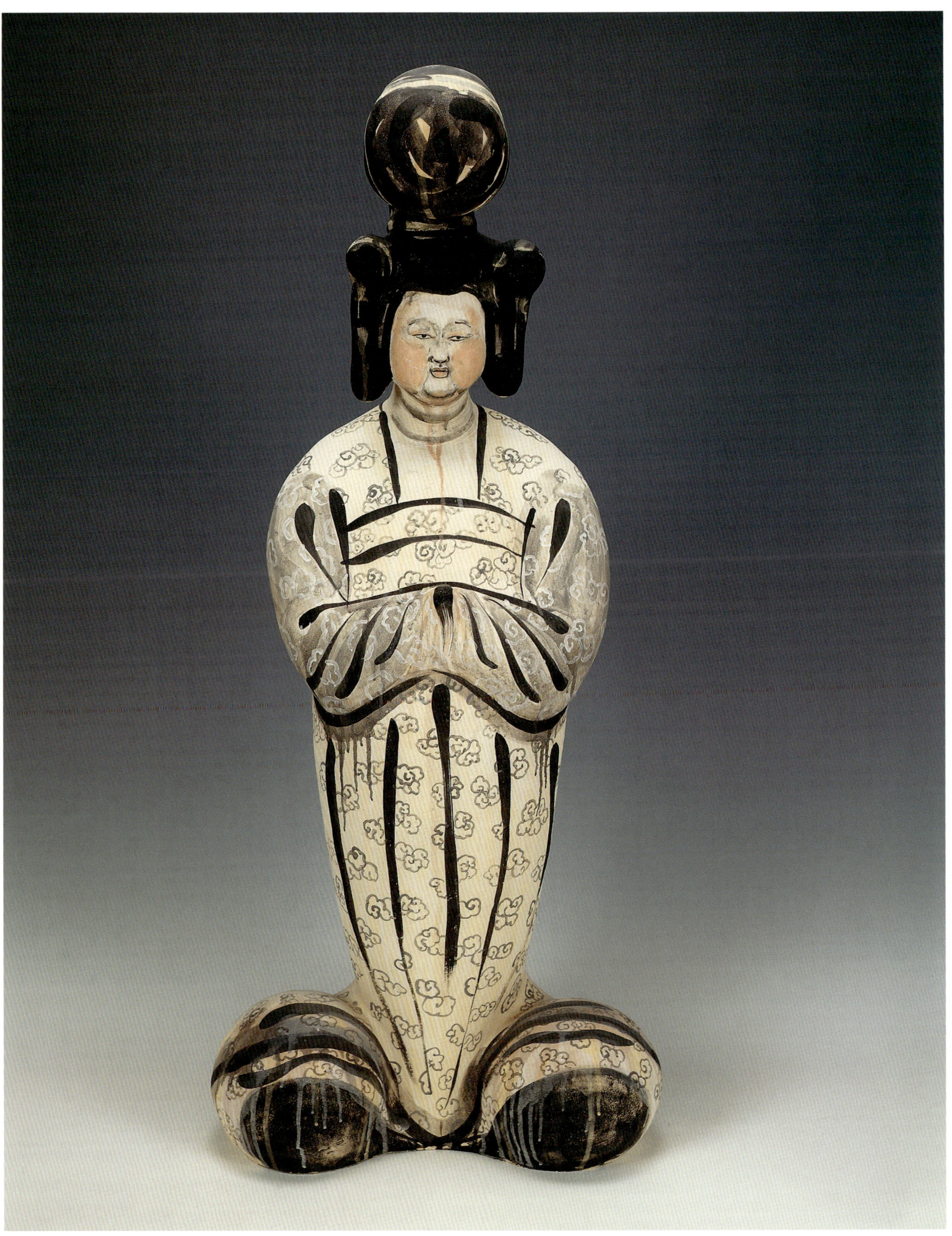

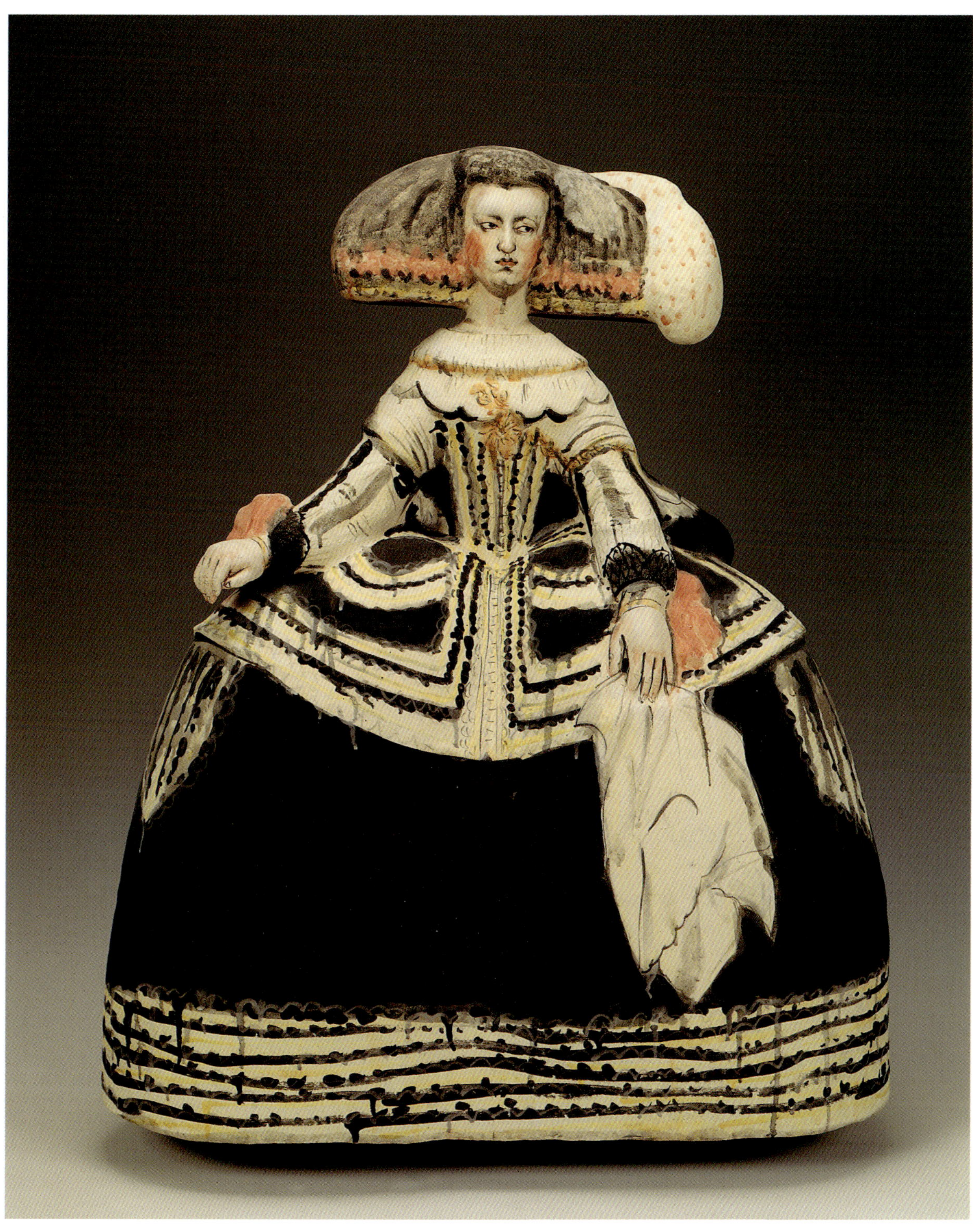

opposite
*Empress,* 2003
53 × 23 × 17 in.
Hand-built, stoneware
(cat. no. 38)

*Queen,* 2003
42 × 32 × 17 in.
Hand-built, stoneware
(cat. no. 39)

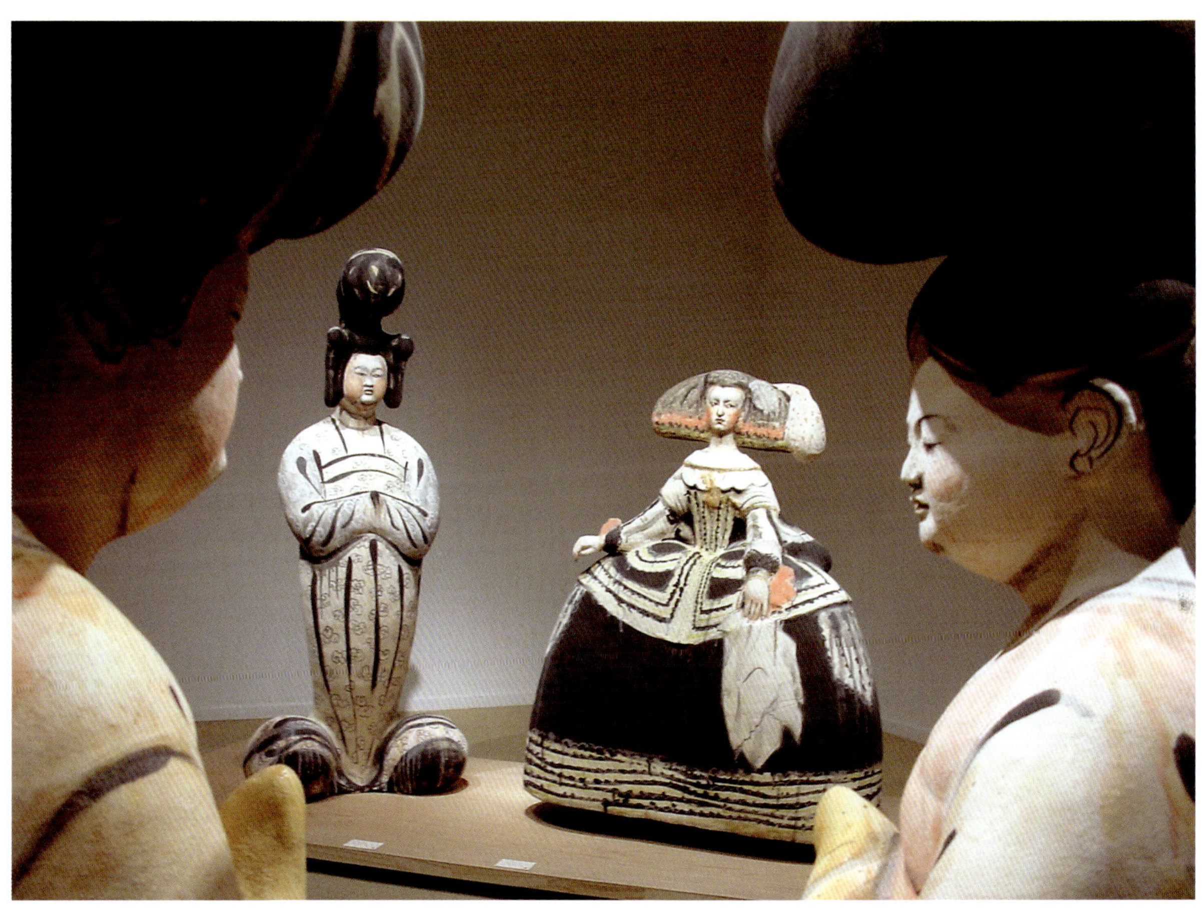

Installation view of *Omnipotent*, Garth Clark Gallery, New York, 2003. Photo: Osvaldo DaSilva

opposite
*Karako*, 2005
32 × 33 × 24 in.
Hand-built, stoneware
(cat. no. 42)

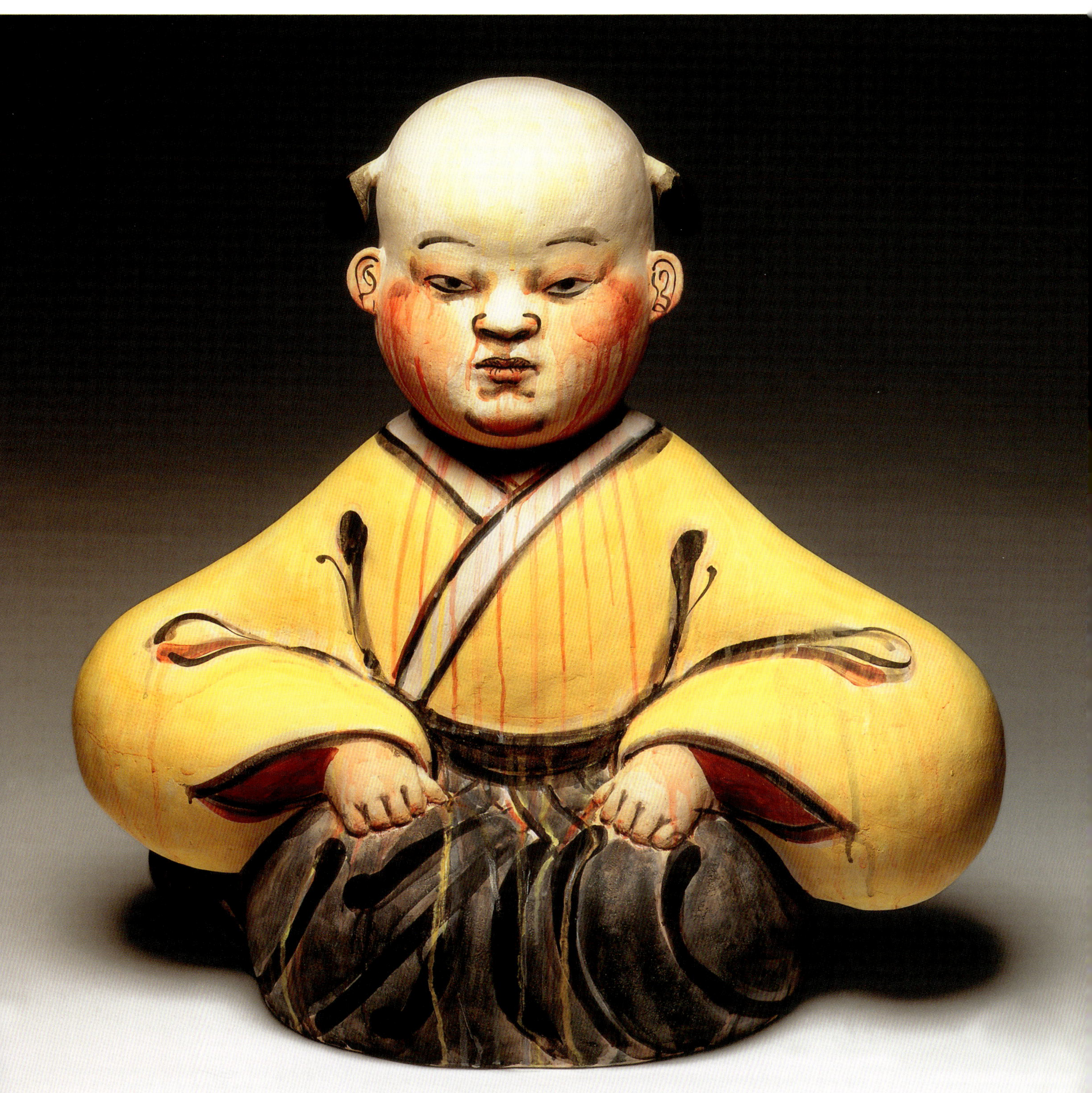

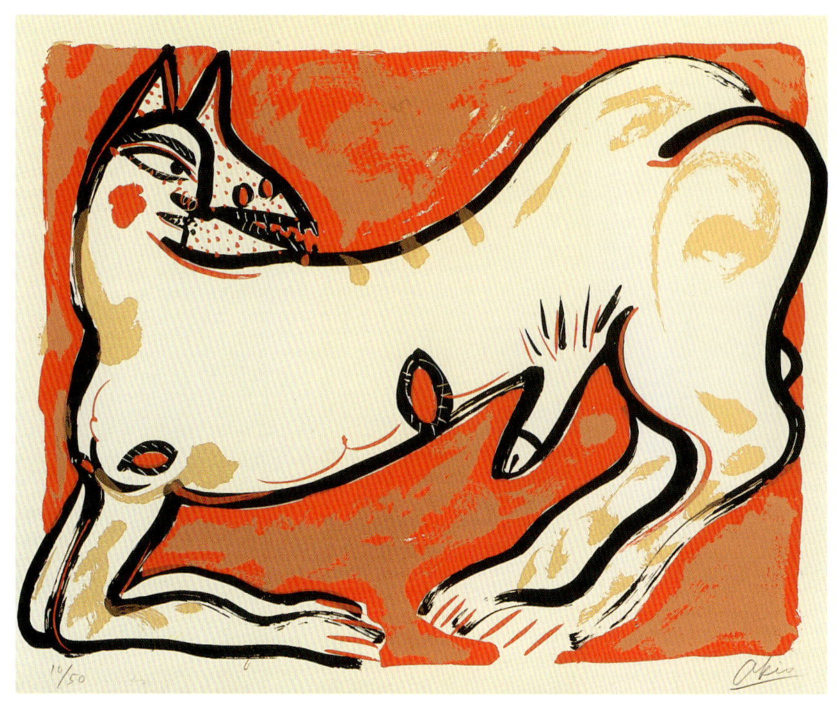



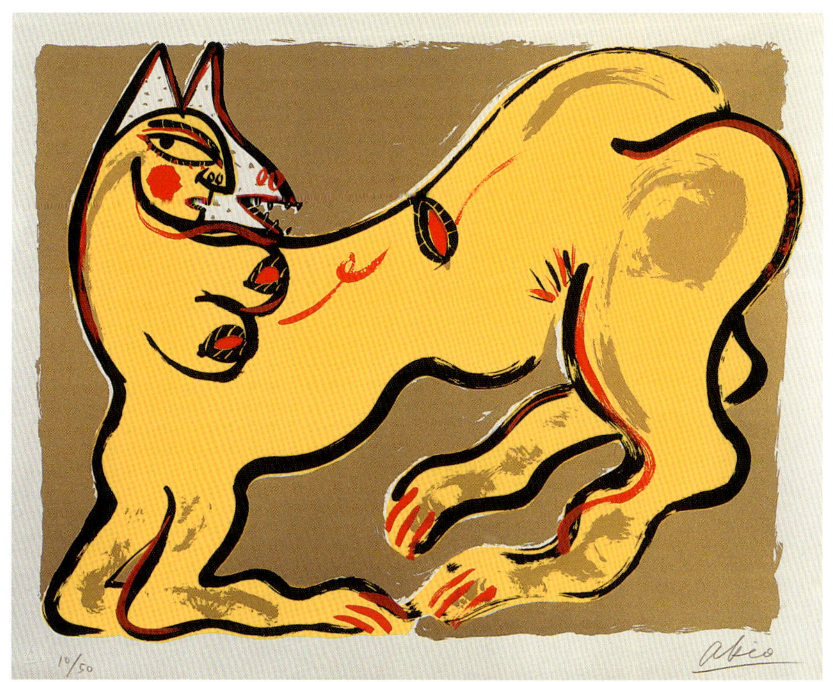



*Male Dog*, 1984
22¼ × 26¾ in. image size
Silkscreen on paper, ed. 10/50
(cat. no. 44)

*Female Dog*, 1984
22¼ × 26¾ in. image size
Silkscreen on paper, ed. 10/50
(cat. no. 43)

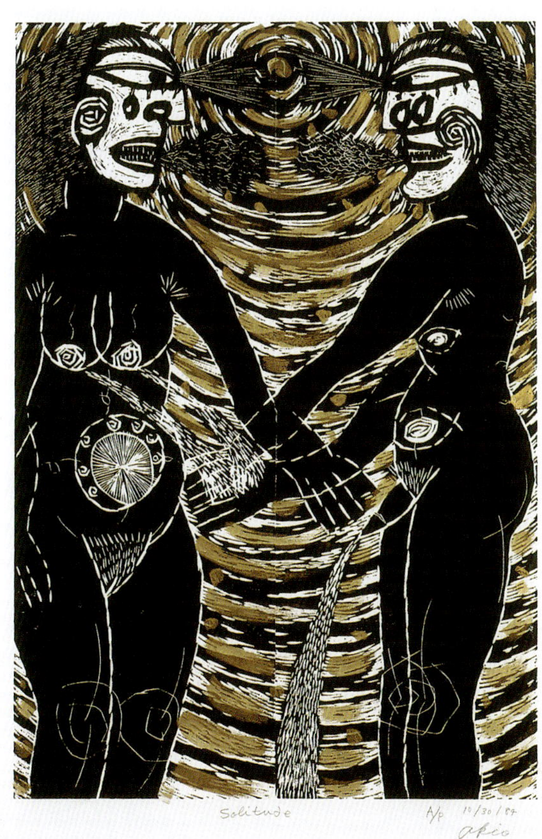

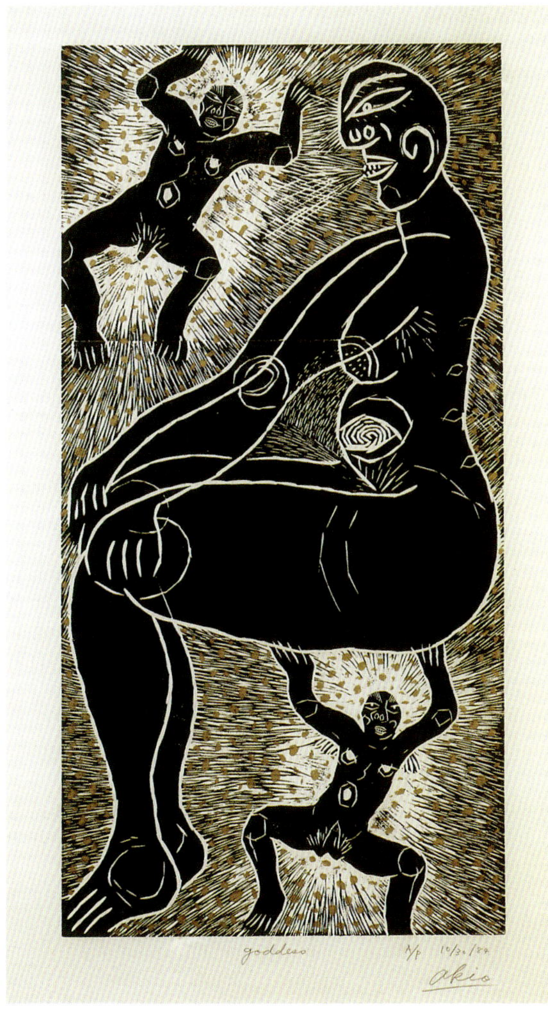

*Solitude*, 1989
35½ × 23½ in. image size
Woodblock on paper, artist's proof
(cat. no. 46)

*Goddess*, 1989
35½ × 17½ in. image size
Woodblock on paper, artist's proof
(cat. no. 45)

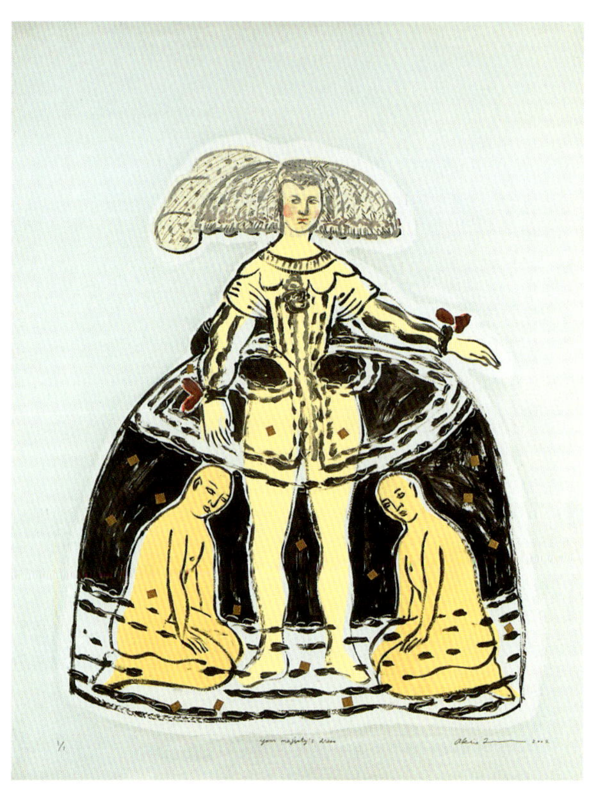

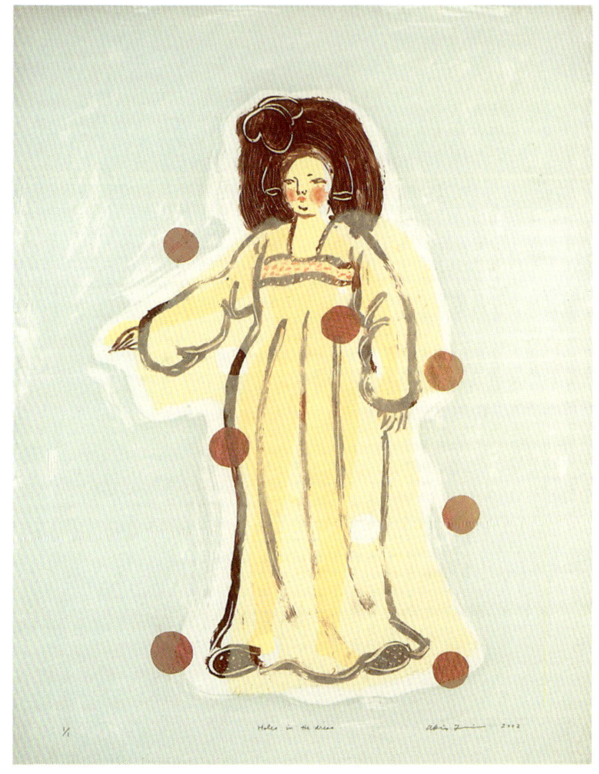

*Your Majesty's Dress*, 2002
28½ × 21½ in. image size
Monoprint, *chine collé*, etched glass
(cat. no. 51)

*Hole in the Dress*, 2002
28½ × 21½ in. image size
Monoprint, *chine collé*, etched glass
(cat. no. 49)

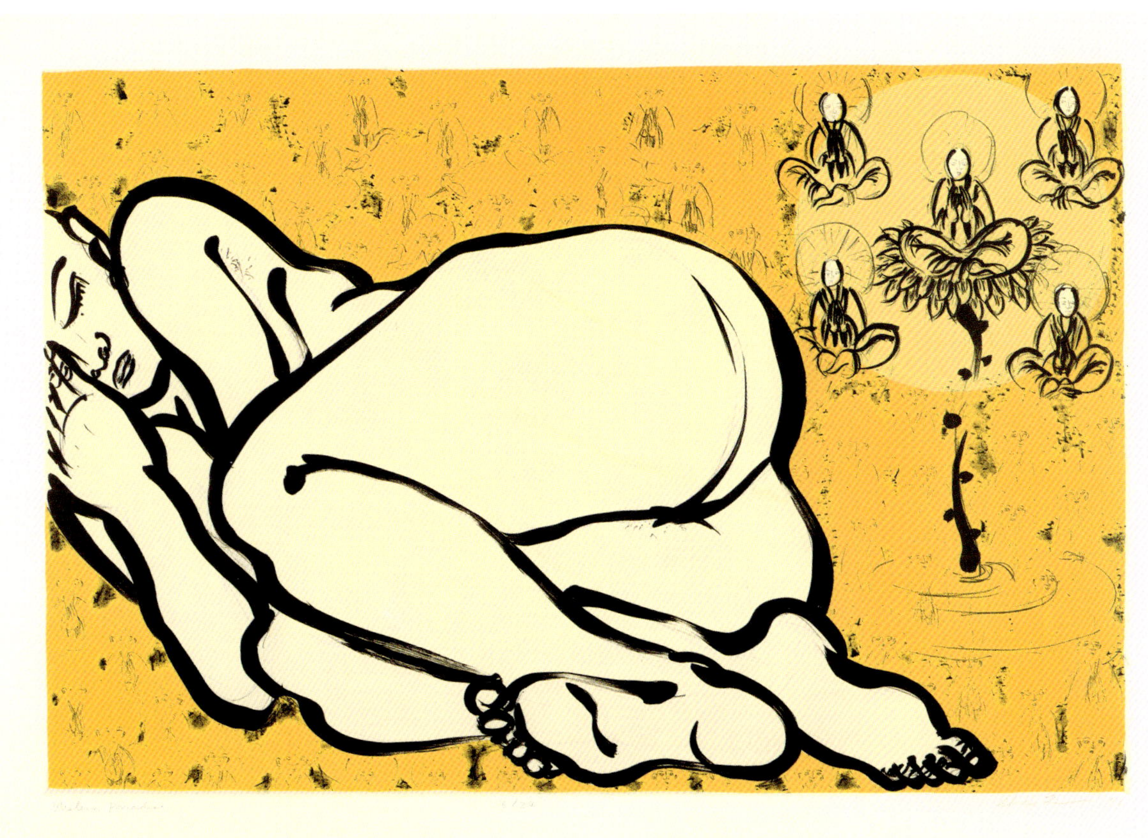

*Western Paradise*, 1996
20 × 30 in. image size
Lithograph on paper, ed. 16/24
(cat. no. 48)

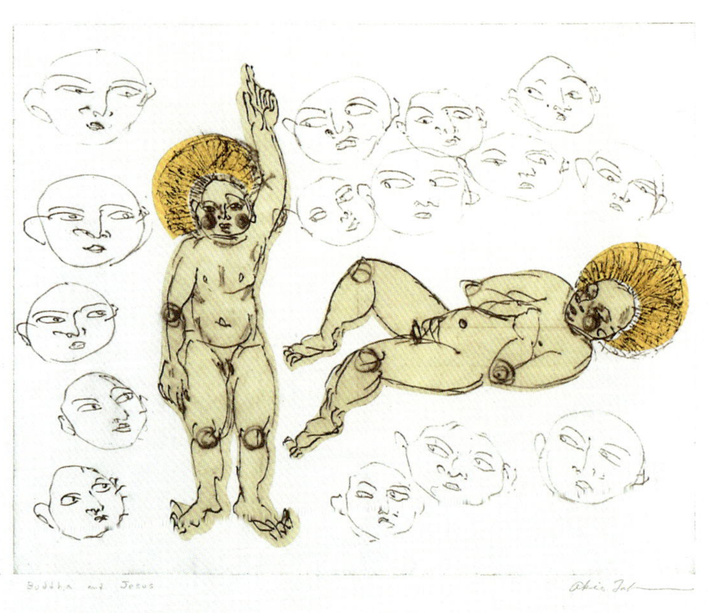

*Baby Jesus and Baby Buddha*, 1996
12½ × 16 in. image size
Monoprint, *chine collé* on paper
(cat. no. 47)

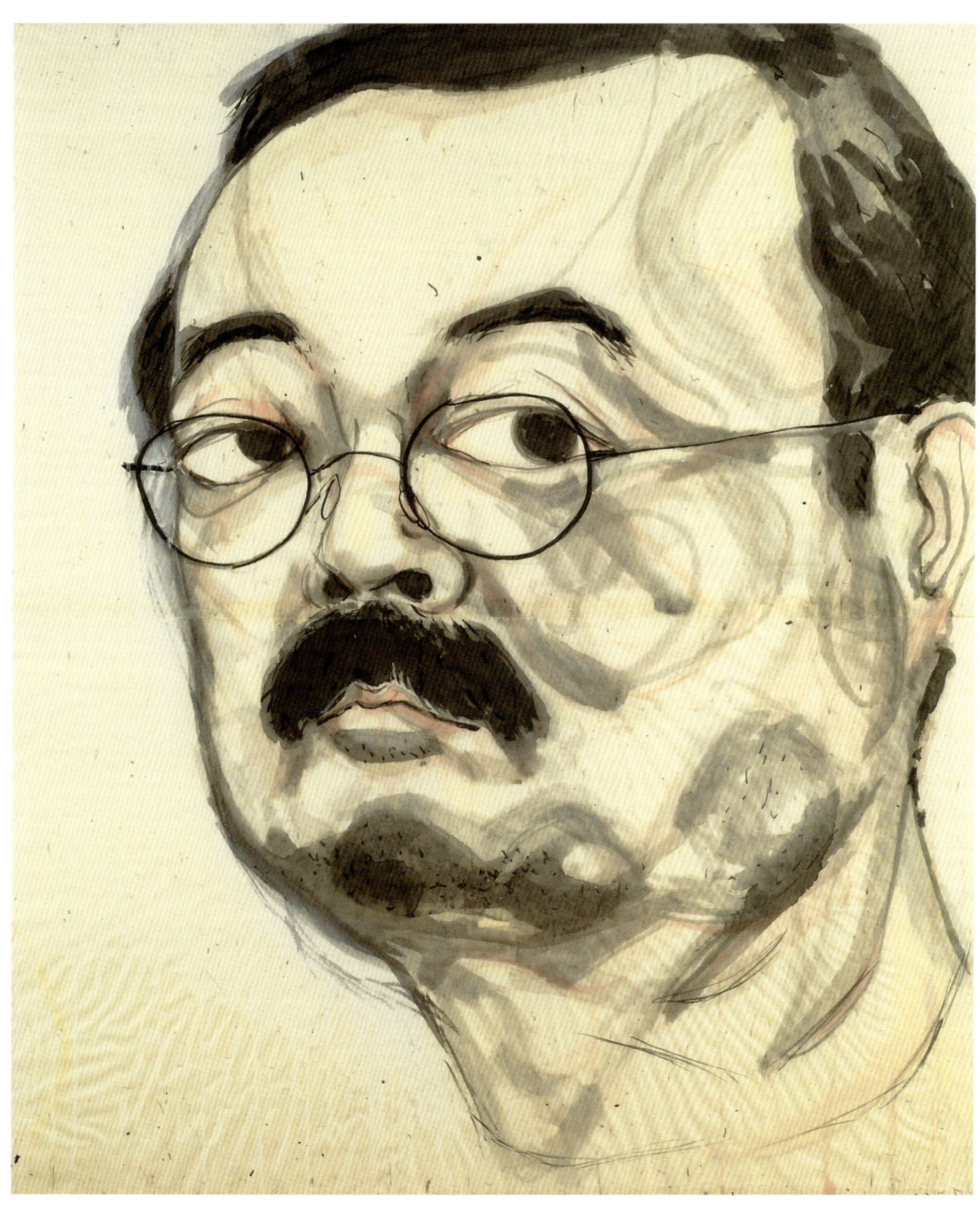

*Self-Portrait Drawing*, 2002
46¾ × 36 in. image size
Ink on paper
(cat. no. 50)

# Checklist of the Exhibition

Works are listed in chronological order; height precedes width precedes depth.
Unless otherwise noted, photography is by Anthony Cuñha.

## Ceramics

1. *Village,* 1976
12 × 57 × 35 in.
Hand-built, stoneware, raku-fired
Made at the Kansas City Art Institute, Kansas City, Missouri
Collection of the artist

2. *Couple,* 1980
12½ × 19½ × 6 in.
Hand-built, stoneware, salt-fired
Made at the Archie Bray Foundation for the Ceramic Arts, Helena, Montana
Collection of Ken Ferguson

3. *Leda and Swan,* 1982
13 × 17 × 6 in.
Hand-built, stoneware, salt-fired
Made at the Archie Bray Foundation for the Ceramic Arts, Helena, Montana
Collection of Nancy and Jean Paul Coupal

4. *Lovers with Onlookers,* 1982
14 × 19 × 7 in.
Hand-built, stoneware, salt-fired
Made at the Archie Bray Foundation for the Ceramic Arts, Helena, Montana
Collection of the artist

5. *Owl,* ca. 1982
9½ × 5½ × 6½ in.
Wheel-thrown and altered, porcelain, salt-fired
Collection of Garth Clark and Mark Del Vecchio

6. *Boy Holding Dog,* 1983
17½ × 25 × 7½ in.
Hand-built, stoneware, salt-fired
Made in Nagura, Japan
Collection of Dr. Michael and Audrey Landy

7. *Self-Portrait,* 1984
14 × 8 × 9 in.
Hand-built, earthenware
Made in Bozeman, Montana
Collection of Linda and Donald Schlenger
Photo by Katie Deits

8. *Portrait of Ms. M,* 1986
22 × 19 × 10 in.
Hand-built, porcelain
Made at the Archie Bray Foundation for the Ceramic Arts, Helena, Montana
Collection of Garth Clark and Mark Del Vecchio

9. *Portrait of Mr. W,* 1986
24 × 16 × 7 in
Hand-built, porcelain
Made at the Archie Bray Foundation for the Ceramic Arts, Helena, Montana
Collection of Garth Clark and Mark Del Vecchio

10. *Her Love,* 1987
21½ × 14½ × 7 in.
Hand-built, porcelain, salt-fired
Made at the Archie Bray Foundation for the Ceramic Arts, Helena, Montana
Collection of the Arizona State University Art Museum; Gift of Anne and Sam Davis

11. *Human,* 1987
17½ × 25 × 7 in.
Hand-built, porcelain, salt-fired
Made at the Archie Bray Foundation for the Ceramic Arts, Helena, Montana
Collection of the artist

12. *Mother and Son: Homage to Bronzino,* 1987
32½ × 19½ × 9 in.
Hand-built, porcelain, salt-fired
Made at the Archie Bray Foundation for the Ceramic Arts, Helena, Montana
Collection of Stéphane Janssen

13. Untitled Teapot, 1987
8 × 5½ × 3 in.
Hand-built, porcelain
Made at the Archie Bray Foundation for the Ceramic Arts, Helena, Montana
Collection of the Racine Art Museum Permanent Collection; Gift of Donna Moog

14. *Spring*, 1988
22 × 24 × 9½ in.
Hand-built, porcelain, salt-fired
Made in Vashon, Washington
Collection of Gretchen Adkins

15. *Fish*, ca. 1988
9½ × 4½ × 2½ in.
Wheel-thrown and altered, porcelain, salt-fired
Made in Vashon, Washington
Courtesy of Garth Clark Gallery, New York

16. *Two Fish*, ca. 1988
13 × 5 × 2½ in. and 11¼ × 5 × 2½ in.
Wheel-thrown and altered, porcelain, salt-fired
Made in Vashon, Washington
Collection of Stéphane Janssen

17. *Birth of Lena*, 1990
21 × 23 × 10 in.
Hand-built, porcelain, salt-fired
Made in Vashon, Washington
Collection of the Arizona State University Art Museum; Gift of Anne and Sam Davis

18. *Twin Sisters*, 1990
9½ × 10½ × 4 in.
Slip-cast, porcelain, salt-fired
Made in Vashon, Washington
Collection of Sonny and Gloria Kamm

19. *Venus Disarming Mars (Lover's Teapot)*, ca. 1990
Slip-cast, porcelain, salt-fired
Made in Vashon, Washington
Collection of the artist

20. *Earth*, 1991
28 × 22 × 10 in.
Hand-built, porcelain, salt-fired
Made in Vashon, Washington
Collection of Vicente Lim and Robert Tooey

21. *Tree*, 1991
Upper torso: 21½ × 16 × 8 in.
Lower torso: 20 × 11 × 6 in.
Hand-built, porcelain, salt-fired
Made in Vashon, Washington
Collection of Anne and Sam Davis

22. *Summer of '92 Vase*, 1992
16 × 9½ × 12 in.
Hand-built, porcelain, salt-fired
Made in Vashon, Washington
Collection of Barbara S. Rosenthal

23. *Vase of Voyeur*, 1992
19 × 14 × 13 in.
Hand-built, porcelain, salt-fired
Made in Vashon, Washington
Collection of Barbara S. Rosenthal

24. *Laocoön*, 1994
25 × 25 × 13 in.
Hand-built, porcelain, salt-fired
Made in Vashon, Washington
Collection of the Arizona State University Art Museum; Gift of Anne and Sam Davis

25. *Seduction*, 1995
24½ × 15 × 8 in.
Hand-built, porcelain, salt-fired
Made at the Archie Bray Foundation for the Ceramic Arts, Helena, Montana
Collection of Joanne Bussutil

26. *Cat*, 1996
4 × 11 × 4 in.
Hand-built, stoneware
Made at the European Ceramic Work Centre, 's Hertogenbosch, the Netherlands
Collection of Dale & Doug Anderson
Photo by Eva Heyd

27. *Female Figure*, 1996
21 × 7 × 7 in.
Hand-built, stoneware
Made at the European Ceramic Work Centre, 's Hertogenbosch, the Netherlands
Collection of Dale & Doug Anderson
Photo by Eva Heyd

28. *Female Figure,* 1996
19 × 8 × 7 in.
Hand-built, stoneware
Made at the European Ceramic Work Centre,
's Hertogenbosch, the Netherlands
Collection of Dale & Doug Anderson
Photo by Eva Heyd

29. *Female Figure with Baby,* 1996
19 × 7 × 7 in.
Hand-built, stoneware
Made at the European Ceramic Work Centre,
's Hertogenbosch, the Netherlands
Collection of Dale & Doug Anderson
Photo by Eva Heyd

30. *Female Student,* 1996
22 × 7½ × 8 in.
Hand-built, stoneware
Made at the European Ceramic Work Centre,
's Hertogenbosch, the Netherlands
Collection of Kenneth and Nancy Kranzberg

31. *Male Student,* 1996
34 × 11 × 12 in.
Hand-built, stoneware
Made at the European Ceramic Work Centre,
's Hertogenbosch, the Netherlands
Collection of the Mint Museum of Craft + Design,
Charlotte, North Carolina; Allan Chasanoff Ceramic
Collection, 2001.92.149
Photo by David H. Ramsey

32. *Camera Boy,* 1998
31½ × 10 × 7½ in.
Hand-built, stoneware
Made in Seattle, Washington
Collection of Devra Breslow

33. *Greeters,* 1998
34½ × 10 × 7½ in. and 33 × 8 × 6 in.
Hand-built, stoneware
Made in Seattle, Washington
Collection of Paul Schneider and Lauren Eulau

34. *Duchess,* 2000
42 × 16 × 14 in.
Hand-built, stoneware
Made in Seattle, Washington
Collection of Fay Jones

35. *Dance,* 2001
32 × 12 × 10 in.
Hand-built, stoneware
Made in Seattle, Washington
Collection of Jim and Marilyn Jonassen
Photo by Robert Vinnedge

36. *General and Emperor,* 2001
38 × 11 × 8 in. and 35 × 12 × 8 in.
Hand-built, stoneware
Made in Seattle, Washington
Collection of Maurice and Margery Katz
(Shown at ASU only)

37. *Sphinx,* 2002
30 × 6½ × 16 in.
Head: Wheel-thrown and altered porcelain, fabric
Base: Hand-built, stoneware
Made in Seattle, Washington
Collection of the Arizona State University Art Museum;
From the Collection of Diane and Sandy Besser

38. *Empress,* 2003
53 × 23 × 17 in.
Hand-built, stoneware
Made in Seattle, Washington
Collection of Sara and David Lieberman

39. *Queen,* 2003
42 × 32 × 17 in.
Hand-built, stoneware
Made in Seattle, Washington
Collection of Sara and David Lieberman

40. *Sleeping Woman and Child,* 2003
6 × 27 × 10½ in.
Hand-built, stoneware
Made in Seattle, Washington
Collection of Judith Davis and Michael Mickaliger

41. *Sleeping Woman in Checkered Skirt,* 2003
6 × 27 × 10½ in.
Hand-built, stoneware
Made in Seattle, Washington
Collection of Patricia and Michael Marcus

42. *Karako,* 2005
32 × 33 × 24 in.
Hand-built, stoneware
Made in Seattle, Washington
Collection of the artist
Photo by Robert Vinnedge

## Works on Paper

43. *Female Dog,* 1984
22¼ x 26¾ in. image size
Silkscreen on paper, ed. 10/50
Printed at the Sun Valley Art Center, Sun Valley, Idaho
Collection of the Arizona State University Art Museum;
Gift of James and Joanne Rapp

44. *Male Dog,* 1984
22¼ x 26¾ in. image size
Silkscreen on paper, ed. 10/50
Printed at the Sun Valley Art Center, Sun Valley, Idaho
Collection of the Arizona State University Art Museum;
Gift of James and Joanne Rapp

45. *Goddess,* 1989
35½ x 17½ in. image size
Woodblock on paper, artist's proof
Printed in Nagura, Japan
Collection of Mark R. Clark

46. *Solitude,* 1989
35½ x 23½ in. image size
Woodblock on paper, artist's proof
Printed in Nagura, Japan
Collection of Mark R. Clark

47. *Baby Jesus and Baby Buddha,* 1996
12½ x 16 in. image size
Monoprint, *chine collé* on paper
Printed at Armstrong-Prior, Inc., Phoenix, Arizona
Collection of Jim and Carol Young

48. *Western Paradise,* 1996
20 x 30 in. image size
Lithograph on paper, ed. 16/24
Printed at Lawrence Lithography, Kansas City, Missouri
Collection of the artist

49. *Hole in the Dress,* 2002
28½ x 21½ in. image size
Monoprint, *chine collé,* etched glass
Printed at the Pilchuck Glass School, Stanwood, Washington
Collection of the artist

50. *Self-Portrait Drawing,* 2002
46¾ x 36 in. image size
Ink on paper
Made in Seattle, Washington
Private collection

51. *Your Majesty's Dress,* 2002
28½ x 21½ in. image size
Monoprint, *chine collé,* etched glass
Printed at the Pilchuck Glass School, Stanwood, Washington
Collection of the artist

# Chronology

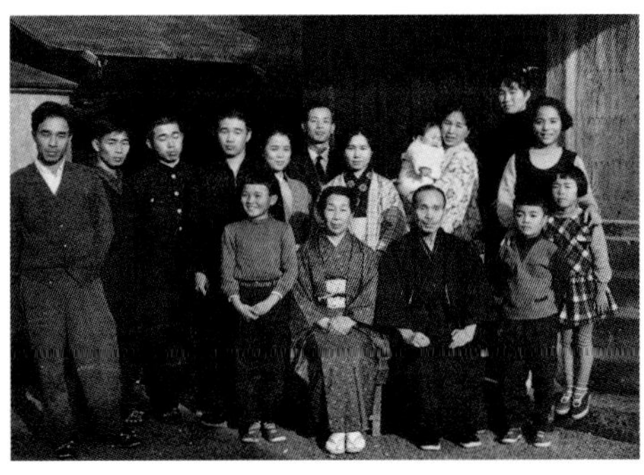

New Year's gathering in father's hometown of Yamage, Miyazaki, 1958. Photo courtesy of the artist

### 1950

Born in Nobeoka, Japan, Akio is the youngest of three children. Dr. Michio Takamori was a dermatologist and urologist who ran his own clinic, which was attached to the Takamori house. The nursing staff and other individuals needed to run the clinic were considered part of the extended family. At times, up to ten nurses, cooks, and housekeepers would live in the clinic dormitory. The household was filled with the daily drama of so many people living and working together. The artist's mother, Misako Takamori, supervised all the details of managing the home and the clinic.

### 1963

At the age of thirteen, moves to Miyazaki, about an hour away by local train, to live with his grandparents and attends Nishi Junior High School. Participates in the activities of the school's art club.

### 1969

Graduates from Oomiya High School in Miyazaki, where he had continued to pursue his interests in art.

### 1969–71

Attends Musashino Art University in Tokyo. Enrolls in the ceramics industrial design program, which places emphasis on Scandinavian modernism. Becomes active in the student movement and Vietnam War protests.

### 1971

Completes studies at Musashino Art University. Sees the exhibition *Contemporary Ceramic Art: Canada, U.S.A., Mexico, Japan* and is impressed by the works of Jim Melchert, Richard Shaw, Henry Takemoto, Peter Voulkos, and other Americans, especially their "antiauthoritarian" approach.

Takes his first trip outside of Japan to visit Europe, organized by the Osaka-based Japan Folk Art Museum. Visits museums in Denmark, England, France, Greece, Italy, Spain, and Portugal.

### 1972

Apprentices at the Kumao Oota Pottery, a family-run traditional domestic pottery located in Koishiwara, Fukuoka. Meets fellow apprentice Chris Holmquist, from Minnesota, and starts to learn English.

### 1973

American ceramic artist Ken Ferguson, professor of art at the Kansas City Art Institute, visits the Oota pottery while researching Japanese ceramics. Is Ferguson's tour guide for the day and expresses his interest

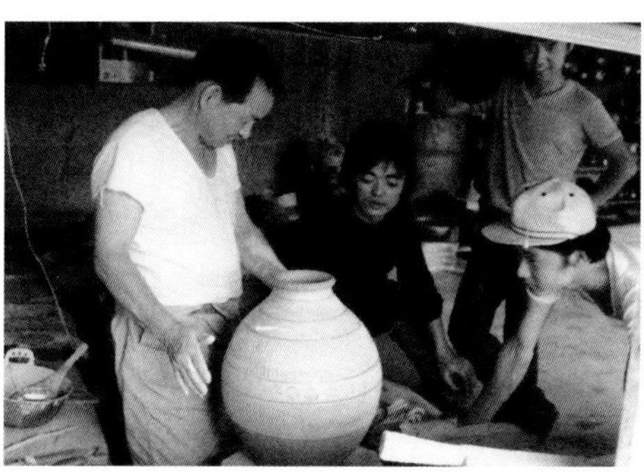

Kumao Oota demonstrating on the wheel for Takamori (second from left) and apprentices from Takatori pottery, 1972. Photo: Chris Holmquist

in American ceramics. Ferguson promises to send the artist an application to the Art Institute.

## 1974

Travels to the United States to visit Chris Holmquist in Minnesota and then to Chicago, where he enrolls in English-language courses at Loyola University. Sends a postcard to Ken Ferguson telling of his plans to learn English before applying to the Kansas City Art Institute. Ferguson tells him to come immediately, even though the fall semester has already started. Studies ceramics with Ferguson, Victor Babu, and George Timock. Moves from making functional pottery to producing small-scale, hand-built figurative work.

## 1975

During the summer, visits Jun Kaneko, a Japanese ceramist who is teaching at the Rhode Island School of Design.

## 1976

Completes junior and senior year at the Art Institute, graduating with a B.F.A. Fellow classmates include Barry Butler, Cate Elliot, Chris Gustin, Allan Winkler, and Arnold Zimmerman, among others. Meets Vicky Lidman, his future wife. Before graduating, finishes *Village,* based on childhood memories of his hometown.

## 1976–78

Attends the New York State College of Ceramics, Alfred University, in Alfred, New York. Studies under Val Cushing, Tony Hepburn, Wayne Higby, and Robert Turner. Fellow classmates include Bruce Cochrane, Cate Elliot, Judy Moonelis, Rina Peleg, Terry Rosenberg Stan Welsh, and Richard White, among others. Sees reproductions at the college library of Japanese artist Kitagawa Utamaro's woodblock prints, which will later influence the development of his envelope vessels.

## 1978

Graduates from Alfred University. Dissatisfied with the theory-based work he did there, deposits his entire M.F.A. thesis exhibition in the dumpster.

At the invitation of Kurt Weiser, newly hired Resident Director of the Archie Bray Foundation for the Ceramic Arts in Helena, Montana, heads west in his newly acquired 1963 blue Ford Mustang. Resident artist at the Bray for the summer. Spends time making functional thrown vessels with drawn figurative images on the surface. Fellow resident artists include Larry Bush, John and Andrea Gill, Wendy Mueller, and Allan Winkler, all alumni of the Kansas City Art Institute.

Selected to participate in the prestigious *Young Americans* exhibition at the American Craft Museum in New York.

Leaves Montana in August, drives to Seattle with the Gills, and flies back home to Nobeoka. In the fall, volunteers at a local kindergarten for disabled children. Visits Jun Kaneko at his home and studio in Nagura, Japan. Meets ceramist Suzuki Goro. Visits Seto, an important traditional ceramics center in Japan. Explores the possibility of setting up his own production pottery in Japan.

## 1979

Is invited to live and work in Kaneko's compound in Nagura. Works in the studio and is caretaker of the house while Kaneko is away teaching at Cranbrook Academy of Art in Bloomfield Hills, Michigan.

## 1980

Makes small-scale figurative pieces for his first solo exhibition at the Himawari Gallery in Miyazaki, Japan.

## 1981

Takes on several temporary teaching positions, the first in 1981 at the Nova Scotia College of Art and Design, Halifax, Canada, as the sabbatical replacement for Walter Ostrom. Later teaches summer school at Sheridan College of Applied Arts and Technology, Oakville, Ontario, Canada, for Bruce Cochrane, a former classmate at Alfred. Makes first slab-constructed sculpture based on Utamaro's print *The Lovers,* which he had seen as a graduate student at Alfred.

## 1982

On a visit to Cochrane's home, Garth Clark, a noted ceramics historian and dealer, sees Takamori's work. Is contacted by Clark and invited to show his work at Clark's recently opened Los Angeles gallery, beginning an enduring relationship that continues today.

Returns to the Archie Bray Foundation to begin work for his exhibition at Garth Clark Gallery.

Travels with Kurt Weiser, who is also represented by Garth Clark, to Los Angeles for Weiser's exhibition opening.

## 1983

First solo exhibition outside of Japan, titled *Archie Bray Series,* opens at Garth Clark Gallery in February. The works shown are slab-constructed and salt-fired (see *Leda and Swan,* cat. no. 3). Reaction to the work is extremely positive.

Also exhibits in *Ceramic Artists: Distinguished Alumni of the Kansas City Art Institute* at the Charlotte Crosby Kemper Gallery and in the huge survey exhibition *Ceramic Echoes: Historical References in Contemporary Ceramic Art* at the Nelson-Atkins Museum of Art, both in Kansas City.

Serves as a sabbatical replacement for Rick Pope at Montana State University, Bozeman. Makes work for a solo exhibition at the Morgan Gallery, Kansas City, Missouri. Uses Pope's office as his studio and salt-fires the work at the Archie Bray Foundation.

## 1984

Marries Vicky Lidman on July 21, in Denver, Colorado.

Has his first New York solo exhibition in January at the recently opened Garth Clark Gallery on 57th Street. Returns to Kaneko's Nagura studio to begin work on *Portraits,* an exhibition for Garth Clark Gallery, Los Angeles. Invited to make prints at the Sun Valley Center for the Arts and Humanities, Sun Valley, Idaho, which are exhibited in *Potters and Prints.*

## 1985

Once again returns to the Archie Bray Foundation. Looking to relocate, takes several trips to the Seattle area to look for a house and studio. Participates in eleven exhibitions, in Los Angeles, Philadelphia, Albuquerque, St. Louis, and other cities.

## 1986

Son, Peter, is born July 14.

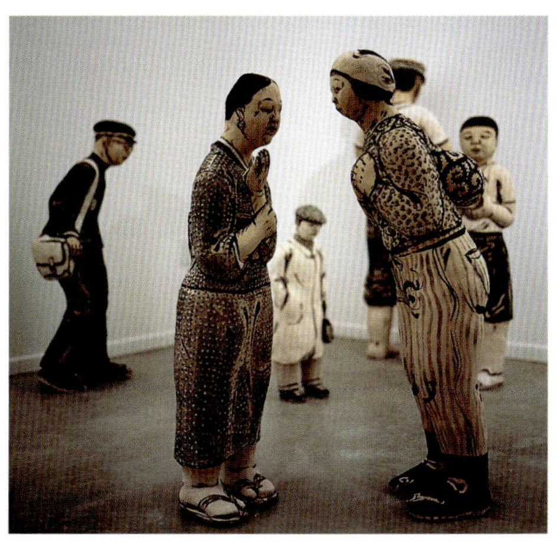

Studio view of work in progress, 1999. Photo: Ayumi Horie

Receives first National Endowment for the Arts Visual Artists Fellowship Grant. Exhibits in numerous group exhibitions, including *American Potters Today* at the Victoria & Albert Museum, London, and *International Ceramics Festival,* Mino, Japan.

The concept of eros begins to play an important role in the artist's imagery and is the featured topic of Andy Nasisse's article "The Battleground of Eros" (*American Ceramics* 5, no. 1 [1986]: 30–35). In it, the artist states, "We live between birth and death. Once a person is born, he cannot avoid death. The only energy that goes directly against death is what I call *eros.* It is a tremendous force to live, to reproduce, and to stave off death. I understand that sexuality is a very important positive energy for human life. We should set a proper value upon sexuality, which I think is one of the key components to a proper value upon humanity."

## 1987

Has a solo show at Garth Clark Gallery in New York and is included in eight group exhibitions.

## 1988

Moves to Vashon, Washington, an island in Puget Sound just a short distance from Seattle. Uses existing outbuilding as a studio and builds a propane-fueled salt kiln. Is invited to teach intermittently at the University of Washington in Seattle from 1988 to 1992. Receives a second NEA Visual Artists Fellowship Grant. Renovations to the new studio are completed.

## 1990

Daughter, Lena, is born April 5.

## 1992

Receives third NEA Visual Artists Fellowship Grant.

## 1993

Teaches at Alfred University in the winter. Spends the summer working at the European Ceramic Work Centre, an international ceramics residency program located in 's Hertogenbosch, the Netherlands. In the fall, is hired as an assistant professor in ceramics at the University of Washington. An assessment of his work by Martha Drexler Lynn is the cover feature in the June/July issue of *American Craft* magazine.

## 1994

Feeling isolated on Vashon Island and wanting to reduce commuting time, moves family to Seattle and uses the University of Washington ceramics department as a studio. Begins looking for a private studio space in the Seattle area.

## 1995

Last exhibition of the slab-constructed envelopes at the Garth Clark Gallery, Los Angeles.

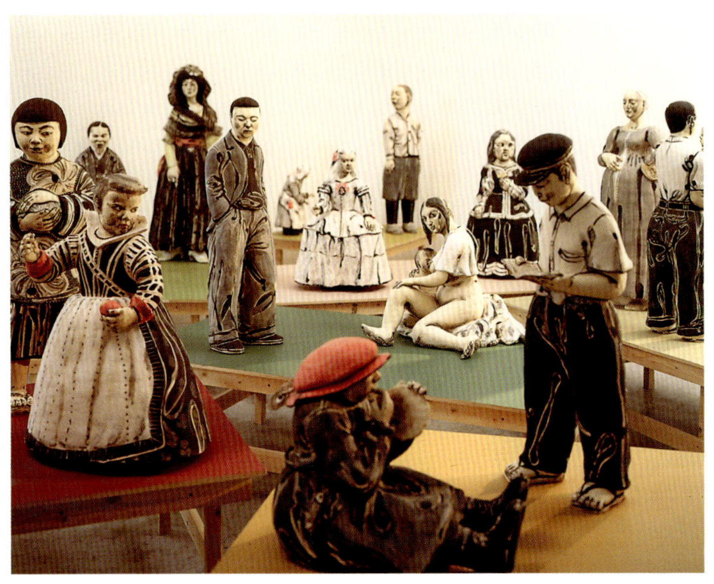

Studio view of *Ensemble*, 2000. Photo: Kate Preftakes

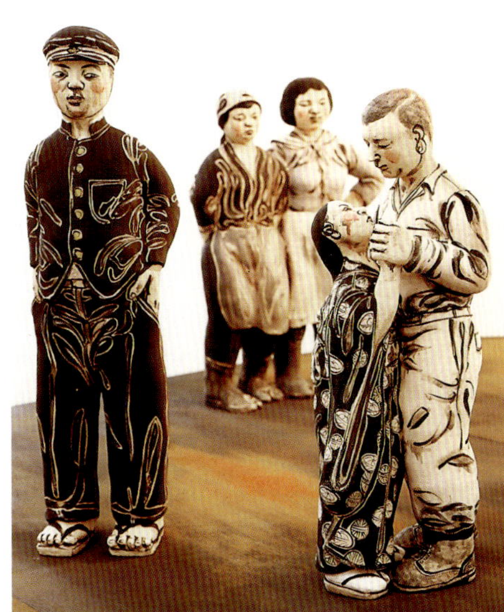

Installation view of the exhibition *Boat* at Frank Lloyd Gallery, Santa Monica, California, 2001. Photo: Kate Preftakes, courtesy of Frank Lloyd Gallery, Santa Monica

## 1996

Purchases property for a studio one mile from home. Promoted to Associate Professor.

In the summer, begins making his first free-standing figures at the European Ceramic Work Centre. *Master's Touch,* a solo exhibition, is presented at the Tempe Arts Center in Arizona.

## 1997

First solo exhibition of figural sculpture at Garth Clark Gallery, New York, in March. In recognition of the artist's edgy treatment of sexual subject matter, his work is included in *The Art of Desire: Erotic Treasures from the Collections of the Kinsey Institute,* at SoFA Gallery, Indiana University, School of Fine Art, Bloomington.

## 1998

Construction of studio is completed. Returns to the European Ceramic Work Centre in the summer.

First solo exhibition with the Frank Lloyd Gallery, Santa Monica, California.

## 1999

First solo exhibition with the Grover/Thurston Gallery, Seattle.

## 2000

Solo exhibition *Ensemble* opens at the Grover/Thurston Gallery, Seattle; the artist borrows freely from Old Master paintings by Brueghel, Goya, and Velázquez (see *Duchess,* cat. no. 34), with size and scale frequently reversed. His intention was to place people from different epochs and racial, social, and cultural backgrounds on an equal plane.

## 2001

Awarded first-place prize for the Virginia A. Groot Foundation Grant competition.

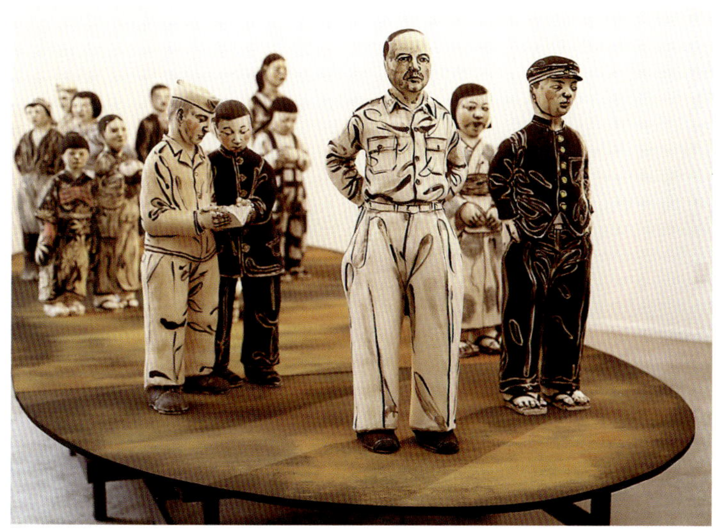

Installation view of the exhibition *Boat* at Frank Lloyd Gallery, Santa Monica, California, 2001. Photo: Kate Preftakes, courtesy of Frank Lloyd Gallery, Santa Monica

Solo exhibition *Boat* opens at the Frank Lloyd Gallery. Based on the defeat of Japan in the Second World War, the show consists of groupings of American and Japanese figures (see *Dance* and *General and Emperor,* cat. nos. 35, 36). The work is installed on a raised platform to simulate a rusted steel boat deck; General MacArthur is positioned on the bow, Emperor Hirohito on the stern.

## 2002

Solo exhibition *Others and Self* opens at the Grover/Thurston Gallery in Seattle, in which he approaches self-portraiture with irony and humor. Works reference historical objects, including Mesopotamian stone sculpture, Grecian terra-cotta figures, Han and Tang Dynasty imagery, and nineteenth-century decorative art objects (see *Sphinx,* cat. no. 37). The exhibition also includes a number of self-portrait drawings (see *Self-Portrait Drawing,* cat. no. 50).

## 2003

Awarded Seattle Collects 2003 Purchase Award, City of Seattle, and the Hermine Pruzan Faculty Fellowship Appointment from the University of Washington. Work is included in the book *Sex Pots: Eroticism in Ceramics,* by Paul Mathieu.

## 2004

Promoted to full Professor of Art at the University of Washington. Receives the Flintridge Foundation Visual Artists Award.

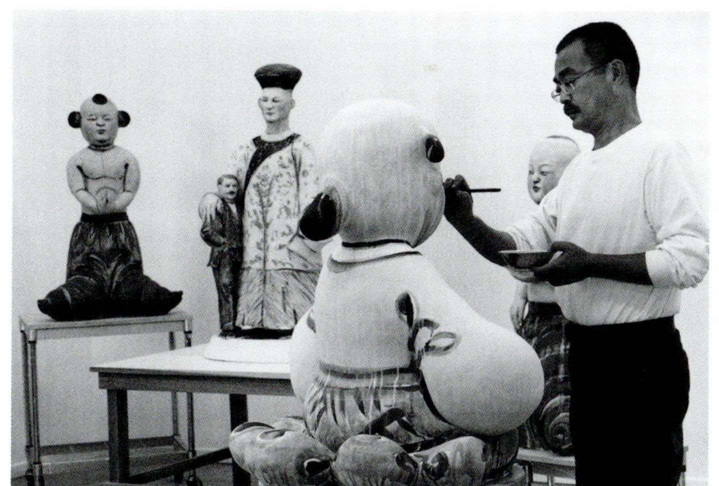

Takamori working in his Seattle studio, 2004. Photo: Vicky Takamori

# Biography and Selected Exhibition History

## Akio Takamori

Born Nobeoka, Miyazaki, Japan, 1950

### Education

**1976–78** M.F.A., New York State College of Ceramics, Alfred University, Alfred, New York

**1974–76** B.F.A., Kansas City Art Institute, Kansas City, Missouri

**1972–74** Apprentice in traditional domestic pottery, Koishiwara, Fukuoka, Japan

**1969–71** Musashino Art University, Tokyo, Japan

### Studios

**1995 to present** Maintains a studio in Seattle, Washington

**1988–94** Maintained a studio in Vashon, Washington

**1979–85** Maintained a ceramics studio in Nagura, Aichi, Japan

### Selected Artist Residencies

**2002** Pilchuck Glass School, Stanwood, Washington

**2000** Yeoju Institute of Technology, Yeoju, South Korea

**1996** European Ceramic Work Centre, 's Hertogenbosch, the Netherlands

**1995** Archie Bray Foundation for the Ceramic Arts, Helena, Montana

**1993** European Ceramic Work Centre, 's Hertogenbosch, the Netherlands

**1985–88** Archie Bray Foundation for the Ceramic Arts, Helena, Montana

**1982** Archie Bray Foundation for the Ceramic Arts, Helena, Montana

**1978** Archie Bray Foundation for the Ceramic Arts, Helena, Montana

### Awards

**2004** Visual Artists Award, Flintridge Foundation

**2003** Hermine Pruzan Faculty Fellowship Appointment, University of Washington

Seattle Collects 2003 Purchase Award, City of Seattle, Office of Arts and Cultural Affairs

**2002** Corporate Council for the Arts, Seattle, Washington

**2001** First Place, Virginia A. Groot Foundation Grant, Evanston, Illinois

**1998** Finalist, Public Art in the Pike Place Market project/Japanese American Citizens League, Seattle, Washington

**1996** Fellowship, European Ceramic Work Centre, 's Hertogenbosch, the Netherlands

**1993** Fellowship, European Ceramic Work Centre, 's Hertogenbosch, the Netherlands

**1992** Visual Artists Fellowship Grant, National Endowment for the Arts, Washington, DC

1988 Visual Artists Fellowship Grant, National Endowment for the Arts, Washington, DC

1986 The Artist Trust / Washington State Arts Commission Fellowship, Seattle, Washington

Visual Artists Fellowship Grant, National Endowment for the Arts, Washington, DC

## Selected One-Person Exhibitions

* catalogue published

2005 Garth Clark Gallery, New York

2004 *Sleeping Figures,* Frank Lloyd Gallery, Santa Monica, California

*Akio Takamori: New Work,* Grover/ Thurston Gallery, Seattle, Washington

2003 *Omnipotent,* Garth Clark Gallery, New York

*Akio Takamori,* The Jacob Lawrence Gallery, University of Washington, Seattle, Washington

2002 *Others and Self,* Grover/Thurston Gallery, Seattle, Washington

2001 *Boat,* Frank Lloyd Gallery, Santa Monica, California

2000 *Akio Takamori: Ceramic Sculpture,* Garth Clark Gallery, New York*

*Ensemble,* Grover/Thurston Gallery, Seattle, Washington

1999 *New Work: Akio Takamori,* Grover/ Thurston Gallery, Seattle, Washington

1998 Frank Lloyd Gallery, Santa Monica, California

1997 *New Work: European Ceramic Work Centre,* Garth Clark Gallery, New York

*Women in Memories,* Cohen/Berkowitz Gallery, Kansas City, Missouri

Trax Gallery, Berkeley, California

1996 *Master's Touch: Akio Takamori,* Tempe Arts Center, Tempe, Arizona

European Ceramic Work Centre, 's Hertogenbosch, the Netherlands

1995 Habitat/Shaw Gallery, Pontiac, Michigan

Garth Clark Gallery, Los Angeles, California

1994 Garth Clark Gallery, Los Angeles, California

Garth Clark Gallery, Kansas City, Missouri

1993 European Ceramic Work Centre, 's Hertogenbosch, the Netherlands

Garth Clark Gallery, New York

1992 Garth Clark Gallery, Los Angeles, California

1991 Garth Clark Gallery, New York

1990 *Blue and White,* Garth Clark Gallery, Los Angeles, California

1989 Garth Clark Gallery, New York

Garth Clark Gallery, Kansas City, Missouri

1988 *Akio Takamori,* Garth Clark Gallery, Los Angeles, California

1987 *Akio Takamori,* Garth Clark Gallery, New York

1986 *New Works: The Montana Suite,* Garth Clark Gallery, New York

Esther Saks Gallery, Chicago, Illinois

1985 *Portraits,* Garth Clark Gallery, Los Angeles, California

1984 Garth Clark Gallery, New York

Morgan Gallery, Kansas City, Missouri

1983 *Archie Bray Series,* Garth Clark Gallery, Los Angeles, California

1980 Himawari Gallery, Miyazaki, Japan

## Selected Group Exhibitions

* catalogue published

**2004** *Double Vision,* Northern Clay Center, Minneapolis, Minnesota*

**2003** *Clay Body: New Work by Claudia Fitch, Akio Takamori, and Patti Warashina,* Bellevue Art Museum, Bellevue, Washington*

*Now & Now: World Ceramic Biennale 2003,* Inchon, South Korea (traveling)*

*Home/Land: Artist, Immigration, and Identity,* Society for Contemporary Craft, Pittsburgh, Pennsylvania*

*Building Tradition: Gifts in Honor of the Northwest Art Collection,* Tacoma Art Museum, Tacoma, Washington*

*Panopticon: An Art Spectacular,* Carnegie Museum of Art, Pittsburgh, Pennsylvania

*The Artful Teapot: 20th Century Expressions from the Kamm Collection,* curated by Garth Clark, organized and circulated by Exhibitions International, New York (traveling)*

*Shared Passion: Sara and David Lieberman Collection of Contemporary Ceramics and Craft,* Arizona State University Art Museum, Ceramics Research Center, Tempe, Arizona*

*Ceramic Artists of the Archie Bray Foundation,* Gallery Materia, Scottsdale, Arizona

**2002** *A Public Trust: Recent Acquisitions at the Museum of Art,* University of Arizona Museum of Art, Tucson, Arizona

*Teapots and Opium,* Garth Clark Gallery, New York

*Small Is Beautiful,* Frank Lloyd Gallery, Santa Monica, California

*Clay Body Rhetoric: Ceramic Figures of Speech,* Beach Museum of Art, Kansas State University, Manhattan, Kansas*

*The Erotic Life of Clay: A Group Exhibition of Contemporary and Historical Ceramics,* San Francisco State University Fine Art Gallery, San Francisco, California

*The Perception of Appearance: A Decade of Contemporary American Figure Drawing,* Frye Art Museum, Seattle, Washington*

*Visual Perspectives: Fourteen Years of the Virginia A. Groot Awards,* Groot Foundation Space and SOFA at Navy Pier, Chicago, Illinois*

*The Figure in Ceramics,* Gallery of Contemporary Art, Lewis & Clark College, Portland, Oregon*

*Identities: Contemporary Portraiture,* New Jersey Center for Visual Arts, Summit, New Jersey*

*Figuration in Clay: A Collection,* McMaster Gallery, University of South Carolina, Columbia, South Carolina*

**2001** *A Ceramic Continuum: Fifty Years of the Archie Bray Influence,* Holter Museum of Art, Helena, Montana (traveling)*

*Taking Measure: American Ceramic Art at the New Millennium,* World Ceramic Exposition, Yeoju, South Korea*

*Poetics of Clay: An International Perspective,* Museum of Art and Design/ Taideteollisuusmuseo, Helsinki, Finland (traveling)*

**2000** *Color and Fire: Defining Moments in Studio Ceramics, 1950–2000,* Los Angeles County Museum of Art, Los Angeles, California (traveling)*

*Ceramic National 2000: The 30th Ceramic National Exhibition,* Everson Museum of Art, Syracuse, New York (traveling)*

*Allan Chasanoff Ceramic Collection,* Mint Museum of Craft + Design, Charlotte, North Carolina*

**1999** *'99 Cups,* Mesa Arts Center, Mesa, Arizona

*Born of Clay 3,* Garth Clark Gallery, New York

*Works on Paper,* Pewabic Pottery, Detroit, Michigan

*Anne and Sam Davis Collection,* Arizona State University Art Museum, Tempe, Arizona*

*Crack Pots from the Collection of Donna Moog,* Forum for Contemporary Art, St. Louis, Missouri

**1998** *Fire for Ceramics: Contemporary Art from the Daniel Jacobs and Derek Mason Collection,* Hand Workshop Art Center, Richmond, Virginia*

**1997** *Wit and Wisdom: Mind Meets Matter,* Kirkland Arts Center, Kirkland, Washington

*The Art of Desire: Erotic Treasures from the Collections of the Kinsey Institute,* Indiana University, School of Fine Art, SoFA Gallery, Bloomington, Indiana*

*The Contemporary Teapot: Keramikmuseet Grimmerhus,* The Grimmerhus Museum of Ceramic Art, Middlefart, Denmark

**1996** *The Nude in Clay,* The Charles A. Wustum Museum of Fine Art, Racine, Wisconsin*

*Clay: The University of Washington Ceramics Department Faculty,* William Traver Gallery, Seattle, Washington

*Beyond the Rock Garden: Craft Forms for a New World,* Wing Luke Asian Museum, Seattle, Washington

**1995** *Clay Works: Ceramic New Arrivals,* Arizona State University Art Museum, Tempe, Arizona

*Keepers of the Flame: Ken Ferguson's Circle,* Kemper Museum of Contemporary Art and Design, Kansas City, Missouri

*50th Anniversary Faculty Invitational Exhibition,* Arrowmont School of Arts and Crafts, Gatlinburg, Tennessee

**1994** *Working in Other Dimensions: Objects and Drawings II,* Arkansas Arts Center Decorative Arts Museum, Little Rock, Arkansas*

*Émigrés: Cultural References in Contemporary Clay,* New Orleans Museum of Art, New Orleans, Louisiana*

*Aha Hana Lima: Gathering of Craftsmen,* The Contemporary Museum, Honolulu, Hawaii

*The Archie Bray Foundation: Selected Clay Works,* Joanne Rapp Gallery/Hand and the Spirit, Scottsdale, Arizona

*The Collector's Eye: Contemporary Ceramics, American, Canadian, and British from the Collection of Aaron Milrad,* Koffler Centre of the Arts, Toronto, Canada*

**1993** *The Anne Davis Collection: Contemporary British and American Clay,* El Paso Museum of Art, El Paso, Texas*

*The Legacy of the Archie Bray Foundation: Four Decades of Tradition and Innovation in American Ceramic Art,* Archie Bray Foundation, Helena, Montana, and the Bellevue Art Museum, Bellevue, Washington*

*The Moderns: 20th Century Art from the Permanent Collection,* Museum of Art, Rhode Island School of Design, Providence, Rhode Island

**1992** American Craft Museum, New York

*Contemporary Ceramic Art,* Museum of Contemporary Ceramic Art, Shigaraki, Japan

Pro Art Gallery, St. Louis, Missouri

*7th Annual San Angelo National Ceramic Competition,* San Angelo Museum of Fine Art, San Angelo, Texas

*The 1992 International Invitational Exhibition of Contemporary Ceramic Art,* National Museum of History, Taipei, Taiwan

**1991** *The Narrative Vessel,* John Michael Kohler Art Center, Sheboygan, Wisconsin

*Archie Bray Foundation: Benefit Exhibition,* Helen Drutt Gallery, New York

*The Figurine: High and Low,* Jane Hartsook Gallery, Greenwich House Pottery, New York

**1990** *American Ceramics,* Gallery Koyanagi, Tokyo, Japan

*Ceramic Sculpture,* National Museum of Ceramic Art, Baltimore, Maryland

Louisiana State University, Baton Rouge, Louisiana

*Beverly/LaBrea Expressions,* Garth Clark Gallery, Los Angeles, California

**1989** *The Alfred Show,* Dorothy Weiss Gallery, San Francisco, California

*Form and Surface,* National Museum of Ceramic Art, Baltimore, Maryland*

*Kansas City Collects Contemporary Ceramics,* Nelson-Atkins Museum of Art, Kansas City, Missouri*

*The Vessel: Studies in Form and Media,* Craft and Folk Art Museum, Los Angeles, California

**1988** *Cultural Currents,* San Diego Museum of Art, San Diego, California

*Northwest Clay,* Littman Gallery, Portland State University, Portland, Oregon

*A Fine Place to Work: The Legacy of the Archie Bray Foundation,* Arkansas Arts Center Decorative Arts Museum, Little Rock, Arkansas*

*The Teapot as Metaphor,* Pasadena State College, Pasadena, California

*The Figure and Clay,* Pewabic Pottery, Detroit, Michigan*

**1987** *Northwest Ceramics Today,* Boise State University, Boise, Idaho (traveling)*

*Drawn to the Surface: Artists in Clay and Glass,* Pittsburgh Center of the Arts, Pittsburgh, Pennsylvania*

*The Smits Collection,* Los Angeles County Museum of Art, Los Angeles, California

*Figurative Clay,* Southern Illinois University at Edwardsville, Edwardsville, Illinois

*National Craft Invitational,* Arkansas Arts Center Decorative Arts Museum, Little Rock, Arkansas*

*Rituals of Tea,* Garth Clark Gallery, Los Angeles, California

**1986** *First International Ceramics Festival '86,* Mino, Japan*

*American Potters Today,* Victoria & Albert Museum, London, England*

*Painted Volumes,* Chrysler Museum, Norfolk, Virginia

*Ceramics Works,* Charlotte Crosby Kemper Gallery, Kansas City Art Institute, Kansas City, Missouri

*New Clay: Contemporary Ceramic Art Selected by Garth Clark,* University Art Gallery, California State University, San Bernardino, California

*International Contemporary Ceramics Salon,* Garth Clark Gallery in association with Smith's Galleries, London, England

**1985** *Teapots: Sanford M. Besser Collection of Contemporary Ceramic Teapots,* Arkansas Arts Center Decorative Arts Museum, Little Rock, Arkansas*

*Recent Ceramic Sculpture,* University Art Museum, University of New Mexico, Albuquerque, New Mexico

*Architectural Ceramics: Eight Concepts,* Washington University Gallery of Art, St. Louis, Missouri (traveling)*

*Rituals of Tea,* Garth Clark Gallery, Los Angeles, California

**1984** *Potters and Prints,* Sun Valley Center for the Arts and Humanities, Sun Valley, Idaho (traveling)*

*Personal Imagery Clay,* Suzanne Lemberg Usdan Gallery, Bennington College, Bennington, Vermont

**1983** *Ceramic Echoes: Historical References in Contemporary Ceramics,* Nelson-Atkins Museum of Art, Kansas City, Missouri*

*Ceramic Artists: Distinguished Alumni of the Kansas City Art Institute,* Charlotte Crosby Kemper Gallery, Kansas City Art Institute, Kansas City, Missouri*

*Teapots: Poetry in Mass and Line,* Garth Clark Gallery, Los Angeles, California

*Faculty Exhibition,* Montana State University School of Art, Bozeman, Montana

**1982** *Two-Person Show: Archambeau and Takamori,* Ginza Corner, Ogikubo, Tokyo, Japan

**1981** *12 from Kansas City + 1: Ken Ferguson and Students,* Surrounding, New York

**1978** *The Young Americans Show,* Contemporary Craft Museum, New York (traveling)*

**1976** *The Super Mud Student Show,* Niagara Falls Craft Museum, Niagara, New York

# Selected Public and Corporate Collections

Archie Bray Foundation for the Ceramic Arts, Helena, Montana
Arizona State University Art Museum, Ceramics Research Center, Tempe, Arizona
Arkansas Arts Center Decorative Arts Museum, Little Rock, Arkansas
Boise Art Museum, Boise, Idaho
Carnegie Institute Art Museum, Pittsburgh, Pennsylvania
City of Seattle, Seattle, Washington
George Gardiner Museum of Ceramic Art, Toronto, Canada
Hallmark Art Collection, Kansas City, Missouri
Jundt Art Museum, Gonzaga University, Spokane, Washington
Kansas City Art Institute, Kansas City, Missouri
Kinsey Institute, Bloomington, Indiana
Kruithuis Museum, 's Hertogenbosch, the Netherlands
Long Beach Museum of Art, Long Beach, California
Los Angeles County Museum, Los Angeles, California
Microsoft Corporation, Redmond, Washington
Mint Museum of Craft + Design, Charlotte, North Carolina
Museum of Arts and Design, New York
Museum of Contemporary Ceramic Art, Shigaraki, Japan
National Museum of History, Taipei, Taiwan
Racine Art Museum, Racine, Wisconsin
Rhode Island School of Design, Providence, Rhode Island
Schein-Joseph International Museum of Ceramic Art, Alfred, New York
Tacoma Art Museum, Tacoma, Washington
Taipei Fine Arts Museum, Taipei, Taiwan
University of Washington, School of Law, Seattle, Washington
Victoria & Albert Museum, London, England

# Selected Bibliography

## Books and Catalogues

Biskeborn, Susan. *Artists at Work: Twenty-five Northwest Glassmakers, Ceramists, and Jewelers.* Seattle: Alaska Northwest Books, 1990, pp. 68–73.

Bloemink, Barbara. *Keepers of the Flame: Ken Ferguson's Circle.* Kansas City, Mo.: Kemper Museum of Contemporary Art and Design, 1995, pp. 40–41.

Briggs, Peter. *Émigrés: Cultural References in Contemporary Clay.* New Orleans: New Orleans Museum of Art, in association with the National Council on Education for the Ceramic Arts, 1994, p. 28.

Brown, Glen R. *Clay Body Rhetoric: Ceramic Figures of Speech.* Manhattan, Kans.: Marianna Kistler Beach Museum of Art, Kansas State University, 2002, p. 18.

Carney, Margaret. *Visual Perspectives: Fourteen Years of the Virginia A. Groot Awards.* Chicago: Virginia A. Groot Foundation, 2002, pp. 156–59.

Chen, Kang-Shuen. *The 1992 International Invitational Exhibition of Contemporary Ceramic Art.* Taipei: National Museum of History, 1992, p. 31.

Clark, Garth. *Akio Takamori: Ceramic Sculpture.* New York: Garth Clark Gallery, 2000, pp. 1–28.

———. *American Ceramics: 1876 to the Present.* New York: Abbeville Press, 1987, pp. 219, 222.

———. *The Artful Teapot.* New York: Watson-Guptill, 2001, pp. 121, 156, 226, 247.

———. *The Book of Cups.* New York: Abbeville Press, 1990, p. 76.

———. *Ceramic Echoes: Historical References in Contemporary Ceramics.* Kansas City, Mo.: Nelson-Atkins Museum of Art, 1983, pp. 73, 97, 116.

———. *The Eccentric Teapot.* New York: Abbeville Press, 1989, pp. 10, 99.

Clark, Garth, and Oliver Watson. *American Potters Today.* London: Victoria & Albert Museum, 1986, p. 50.

Clowes, Jody, and Bruce Pepich. *The Nude in Clay.* Chicago: Perimeter Gallery; Racine, Wisc.: Charles A. Wustum Museum of Fine Arts, 1996, pp. 9, 29.

Del Vecchio, Mark. *Postmodern Ceramics.* New York: Thames & Hudson, 2001, pp. 138, 140, 141, 163, 217.

Dietz, Ulysses Grant. *Great Pots: Contemporary Ceramics from Function to Form.* Madison, Wisc.: Guild Publishing, [2003], pp. 148–49.

Douglas, Diane, and Frances Senska. *The Legacy of the Archie Bray Foundation: Four Decades of Tradition and Innovation in American Ceramic Art.* Helena, Mont.: Archie Bray Foundation, 1993.

Douglas, Mary F. *Allan Chasanoff Ceramic Collection.* Charlotte, N.C.: Mint Museum of Craft + Design, 2000, pp. 78, 205.

Ferrin, Leslie. *Teapots Transformed: Exploration of an Object.* Madison, Wisc.: Guild Publishing, 2000, p. 89.

Gregersen, Thomas. *Japanese-American Craft Invitational.* Delray Beach, Fla.: Morikami Museum and the Boca Raton Museum of Art, 1987.

Guido, Jeff. *The Figure and Clay.* Detroit: The Pewabic Society, 1988, pp. 26–27.

Hammel, Lisa. *Drawn to the Surface: Artists in Clay and Glass.* Pittsburgh: Pittsburgh Center for the Arts, 1987, p. 20.

Hartman, Bruce. *American Clay: 1960 to 1985.* Canyon, Tex.: Panhandle-Plains Historical Museum, 1985.

Held, Peter, and Susan Peterson. *Shared Passion: Sara and David Lieberman Collection of Contemporary Ceramics and Craft.* Tempe: Arizona State University Art Museum, 2003, pp. 10, 26.

Held, Peter, et al. *A Ceramic Continuum: Fifty Years of the Archie Bray Influence.* Seattle: University of Washington Press, 2001, pp. 54, 55, 57, 71, 126, 132.

Herman, Lloyd. *The Collector's Eye: Contemporary Ceramics American, Canadian, and British from the Collection of Aaron Milrad.* Toronto, Canada: Koffler Center of the Arts, 1994, p. 50.

———. *Northwest Ceramics Today.* Boise, Idaho: Boise State University, 1987, p. 44.

Johnston, Phillip M. *Kansas City Collects Contemporary Ceramics.* Kansas City, Mo.: Nelson-Atkins Museum of Art, 1989, p. 23.

Kangas, Matthew. *Material Vision: Image and Object.* Charleston, Ill.: Tarble Art Center, 1993, pp. 52–53.

Kato, Naoki. *First International Ceramics Festival '86.* Mino, Japan: Tajimi City Special Exhibition Hall, 1986.

Koyanagi, Atsuko. *Ceramic Art: Seven Individuals.* Tokyo: Kyoto Shoin International, 1990.

Lauria, Jo. *Color and Fire: Defining Moments in Studio Ceramics, 1950–2000.* Los Angeles: Los Angeles County Museum of Art in association with Rizzoli International Publications, 2000, pp. 178, 184–87.

Levin, Elaine. *The History of American Ceramics.* New York: Harry N. Abrams, 1988, p. 232.

Lynn, Martha Drexler. *Clay Today, Contemporary Ceramists and Their Work.* Los Angeles: Los Angeles County Museum of Art, 1990, pp. 184–85.

Mathieu, Paul. *Sex Pots: Eroticism in Ceramics.* Piscataway, N.J.: Rutgers University Press, 2003.

McTwigan, Michael. *In the Eye of the Beholder: A Portrait of Our Time.* New York: State University of New York at New Paltz, College Art Gallery, 1985, pp. 12–13.

———. *Surface and Form: A Union of Polarities in Contemporary Ceramics.* Baltimore: National Museum of Ceramic Art, 1989, p. 31.

Ming, Bai. *Overseas Contemporary Ceramic Art Classics.* Xinjang, China: Xinjang Fine Art Publishing House, 2002, pp. 64–67.

Peterson, Susan. *Contemporary Ceramics.* New York: Watson-Guptill Publications, 2000, p. 74.

———. *The Craft and Art of Clay.* Woodstock, N.Y.: Overlook Press, 2000, pp. 265, 321.

Piche, Thomas, Jr. *Everson Ceramic National 2000.* Syracuse, N.Y.: Everson Museum of Art, 2000, pp. 68–69.

Rinder, Lawrence. *Awards for Visual Artists: Flintridge Foundation 2003/04.* Pasadena, Calif.: Flintridge Foundation, 2004, pp. 34–35.

Rubin, Michael G. *Architectural Ceramics: Eight Concepts.* St. Louis, Mo.: Gallery of Art, Washington University, 1985, pp. 22–23.

Stirrat, Betsy, and Sarah Burns. *The Art of Desire: Erotic Treasures from the Kinsey Institute.* Bloomington, Ind.: SoFA Gallery, Bloomington Fine Arts Gallery, Indiana University, 1997, pp. 18–19.

Troy, Jack. *American Clay Artists: Philadelphia '85.* Philadelphia: Port of History Museum, 1985, p. 22.

Waller, Jane. *The Human Form in Clay.* Marlborough, England: Crowood Press, 2001, pp. 82–85.

Wolfe, Townsend. *National Craft Invitational.* Little Rock, Ark.: Arkansas Arts Center Decorative Arts Museum, 1987, p. 40.

———. *Working in Other Dimensions: Objects and Drawings II.* Little Rock, Ark.: Arkansas Arts Center Decorative Arts Museum, 1994, p. 51.

## Periodicals and Reviews

"Akio Takamori." *Ceramics Monthly* 31 (September 1983): 37.

"Akio Takamori." *Craft New Zealand,* no. 40 (Winter 1992): 37.

"Architectural Ceramics: Eight Concepts." *Antiques & Collectibles,* April 1985.

Bonansinga, Kate. "Theater of Memory." *Ceramics Monthly* 48, no. 2 (February 2000): 55–57.

Brown, Glen. "Figura y fondo." *Ceramica,* no. 74 (2000): 36–39.

———. "Multiplicity, Ambivalence, and Ceramic Installation Art." *Ceramics: Art and Perception,* no. 54 (2003): 3–8.

Brunner, Astrid. "4th International Ceramics Symposium." *American Craft,* February/March 1986.

"Ceramic Review." *Crafts,* no. 165 (May–June 1997).

Chattopadhyay, Collette. "Akio Takamori at Frank Lloyd Gallery." *World Sculpture News* 4, no. 2 (Spring 1998): 55.

Clark, Garth. "Akio Takamori's Villagers." *Kerameiki Techni: International Ceramic Art Review,* no. 35 (August 2000): 4–8.

———. "The Pictorialisation of the Vessel." *Crafts* (May/June 1986): 40–47.

Davis, Karen. "Akio." *The Independent Record,* January 14, 1987.

Davis, Margi. "Akio Takamori: La Terre Vivante." *La Revue de la Céramique et du Verre,* no. 50 (January/February 1990): 36–38.

Doherty, Jack. "Head, Heart, and Hand." *Ceramic Review,* no. 171 (May/June 1998).

Dorsey, John. "New Show Highlights Ceramic Sculpture, Enamels." *The Sun,* September 28, 1990.

Downey, Roger. "Face Time." *Seattle Weekly,* July 25, 2002.

"Edges." *Ceramics Monthly* (March 1986).

Failing, Patricia. "Seizing the Moment." *Artnews* 101, no. 3 (March 2002): 76, 78–79.

Farr, Sheila. "Figures Explore Multicultural Life." *Seattle Times,* October 22, 2004.

———. "Takamori Looks Upward and Inward for Ceramic Inspiration." *Seattle Times,* March 15, 2002.

"Galleries: 57th Street." *New York Times,* November 14, 2003.

"Gallery Notes." *Center Magazine: Arvada Center for the Arts and Humanities,* September/October 1986.

Giambruni, Helen. "Review: Akio Takamori." *Crafts International* (April 1986): 43.

Glowen, Ron. "Craftiness with Clay Often Breaks Mold." *Herald,* September 24, 1993.

Glueck, Grace. "Art: Using Ceramics to Adorn Architecture." *New York Times,* July 7, 1985.

Hackett, Regina. "Art Review: Takamori's Heavily Built Figures Are Adrift in Clouds of Memory." *Seattle Post-Intelligencer,* March 18, 1999.

Hedger, Leigh. "The Art of Desire/Kinsey Institute Today." *Research and Creative Activity* (September 1997): 34–35.

Hurlburt, Roger. "Museums Gather Works of Japanese-Americans." *Sun-Sentinel,* May 13, 1987.

Iwano, Elaine. "Sculptors Takamori and Warashina Share Personal Histories." *International Examiner,* September 17–30, 2003.

Jefferies, Sue. "Recent Acquisitions." *Potpourri: The Gardiner Museum of Ceramic Art* 15 (Fall 2001): 6.

Jensen, Robert. "Architectural Ceramics, Eight Concepts." *American Craft* (June/July 1985): 46–51.

Johnson, Ken. "From the Neck Up." *New York Times,* August 8, 2003.

Kangas, Matthew. "Akio Takamori: Global Village People." *Sculpture* 20, no. 5 (June 2001): 12–13.

———. "Exhibits Feature Work of Ceramic Sculptors." *Seattle Times,* October 20, 2000.

———. "Feats of Clay, Thanks to the Folks at Bray." *Seattle Times,* September 29, 1993.

Kelley, Jeff. "Potters and Prints." *American Ceramics* 4, no. 1 (1985): 52–59.

Kinzer, Stephen. "In North Carolina, the Superstars Are Potters." *New York Times,* April 10, 2001.

Lange, Peter. "Encounters with Clay: The 16th Fletcher Challenge Ceramic Award 1992." *Ceramic Review,* no. 139 (January/February 1993): 16–20.

Lauria, Jo. "The Vessel's the Thing." *Art Week,* February 21, 1991, p. 21.

Lebow, Edward. "A Crock." *New Times* (Phoenix), February 25, 1999.

Luecking, Stephen. "Stories Seldom Told." *American Ceramics* 10, no. 1 (Spring 1992): 38–45.

Lynn, Martha Drexler. "Akio Takamori, Piquant Contemporary Observations, Time-honored Means." *American Craft* 53, no. 3 (June/July 1993): 52–55.

Marshall, Will Levi. "Head, Heart and Hand." *Ceramic Review,* no. 171 (May/June 1998): 34–35.

McTwigan, Michael. "A Passionate Vision: The Collector Daniel Jacobs." *American Ceramics* 3, no. 2 (1984): 20–29.

Miller, Donald. "Collective Approach Energizes Galleries." *Pittsburgh Post-Gazette,* September 21, 1987.

Nakane, Kazuko. "Akio's World." *International Examiner* 26, no. 6 (March 17–April 7, 1999).

Nasisse, Andy. "The Battleground of Eros: Akio Takamori." *American Ceramics* 5, no. 1 (1986): 30–35.

Newby, Rick. "Out of the Box: The Graphic Art of Akio Takamori." *American Ceramics* 14, no. 1 (2002): 34–37.

———. "To Stave Off Death: Akio Takamori's Life Studies." *Ceramics: Art and Perception,* no. 8 (1992): 33–37.

Ohaus, Thomas. "The Ceramic Art of Akio Takamori." *International Examiner* 28, no. 10 (May 16–June 5, 2001).

Ollman, Leah. "Different Worlds Intersect as They Set Sail Together in Takamori's Boat." *Los Angeles Times,* June 1, 2001.

Roberts-Pullen, Paulette. "Ceramics Make a Comeback at the Hand Workshop." *Style Weekly,* March 10, 2004.

Ross, Jeanette. "Out of the Basic Clay." *Art Week,* October 24, 1987, 6.

Ruiz, Cristina. "The Art Behind the Science." *Collections, International Magazine of Art and Culture* 6, no. 1 (2001).

Shank, Will. "The Erotic Life of Clay." *Ceramics Monthly* 51, no. 4 (April 2003): 16, 18.

Shimabukuro, Betty. "Potters Throw an Exhibit." *The Sun,* October 8, 1986.

Silver, Joanne. "Sparkling, Sexy Ceramics Brighten Show Full of Humorous Slices of Life." *Boston Herald,* December 28, 1993.

Sperry, Robert. "Potters Making Prints." *Ceramics Monthly* 33, no. 5 (May 1985): 38–40.

Takamori, Akio. "The Figure Erotic." *Studio Potter* 16, no. 1 (December 1987): 10–12.

———. "Impression of Travel." *Yukan Daily* (Japan), December 4 and 16, 1990.

———. "My God Images." *Monthly to Magazine* (Japan), September 1982.

———. "Out of the Cage." *Studio Potter* 21, no. 1 (December 1992): 54–55.

Takamori, Akio, and Peter Ferris. "Vessel Concepts." *Ceramics Monthly* 36, no. 2 (February 1988): 27–30.

Tirrell, Norma. "The Archie Bray Legacy: Four Decades of American Ceramic Art." *Ceramics Monthly* 41, no. 10 (December 1993): 47–62.

"Two Locals Join in New York Exhibit of Live-in Ceramics." *The Independent Record,* July 5, 1985.

Updike, Robin. "The Power of Provocation." *Seattle Times,* March 18, 1999.

van Eeden-Kriek, Bibi. "In Gesprek met Akio Takamori." *KLEI* (November 1996): 4–7.

Vanesian, Kathleen. "Sexpots." *New Times* (Phoenix), April 18–24, 1996, p. 69.

Wagonfeld, Judy. "Head Games." *Seattle Post-Intelligencer,* March 18, 2002.

Winters, Mary. "Het gaat om het process, niet om het product." *Brabants Dagblad,* August 25, 1996.

Wolf, John-Paul. "Show of Architectural Ceramics." *West End Word,* April 18, 1985.

Zhou, Guangzhen "Po." "Akio Takamori and 'His Outside and Inside' Erotic Vessels." *Artist Magazine* (Taiwan) (November 1997): 436–38.

## Videos

**1986** *Akio.* Videocassette. Directed by Martin Holt. Helena, Mont.: Montana Art Works. 8 minutes.

**1991** *Akio Takamori Workshop at the Archie Bray Foundation.* Videocassette. Directed by Martin Holt. Helena, Mont.: Montana Art Works. 140 minutes.

# Lenders to the Exhibition

Gretchen Adkins
Dale & Doug Anderson
Arizona State University Art Museum
Devra Breslow
Joanne Bussutil
Garth Clark and Mark Del Vecchio
Garth Clark Gallery, New York
Mark R. Clark
Nancy and Jean Paul Coupal
Anne and Sam Davis
Judith Davis and Michael Mickaliger
Ken Ferguson
Stéphane Janssen
Jim and Marilyn Jonassen
Fay Jones
Sonny and Gloria Kamm
Maurice and Margery Katz
Kenneth and Nancy Kranzberg
Dr. Michael and Audrey Landy
Sara and David Lieberman
Vicente Lim and Robert Tooey
Patricia and Michael Marcus
Mint Museum of Craft + Design
Private Collection
Racine Art Museum
Barbara S. Rosenthal
Linda and Donald Schlenger
Paul Schneider and Lauren Eulau
Akio and Vicky Takamori
Jim and Carol Young

# ASU Administration, Staff, and Membership

## Arizona State University Administration

Michael M. Crow, President

Milton D. Glick, Executive Vice President and Provost of the University

Christine K. Wilkinson, Senior Vice President and Secretary of the University

Richard Stanley, Senior Vice President and University Planner

Jonathan Fink, Vice President for Research and Economic Affairs

Eugene E. Garcia, Vice President for University-School Partnerships and Dean, College of Education

Juan Gonzalez, Vice President for Student Affairs

Mernoy Harrison, Jr., Vice President and Provost, Capital Center Campus

Ira A. Jackson, President/CEO ASU Foundation

Gerald Jakubowski, Vice President and Provost, ASU East

Virgil Renzulli, Vice President for Public Affairs

James Rund, Vice President for University Undergraduate Initiatives

Mark Searle, Vice President and Provost, ASU West

Paul Ward, Vice President for University Administration and General Counsel

David Young, Vice President and Dean, College of Liberal Arts and Sciences

## Arizona State University Art Museum 2004–2005 Advisory Board of Directors

Lance Ross, Chair
Mikki Weithorn, Vice Chair
Beverly Adams
Jack Black
Joel Corman
Steve Davis
Gretchen Freeman
Debbe Goldstein
John C. Hill
Linda Hirshman
Karen Jilly
Carol Nunzio
Roger Robinson
Melanie Sainz
Eddie Shea
Peter Shikany
Ridge Smidt
Michelle Stuhl
Marilyn A. Zeitlin, *Ex-officio*
Mark Anderson, *Ex-officio* (Community Docents)
Ted Decker, *Ex-officio*
LaReal Eyring, *Ex-officio* (Store Volunteers)
Ron McCoy, *Ex-officio*
Janet M. Pinhorn, *Ex-officio* (Student Member)
John Risseeuw, *Ex-officio* (Arizona Print Forum)
Laura Stewart, *Ex-officio*
Susan Ables, Staff Liaison

*Honorary Member*
Richard Whitney

## Herberger College of Fine Arts

J. Robert Wills, Dean
Margaret Knapp, Associate Dean of Research
Gina Stephens, Assistant Dean of Student Affairs
Marty Wyas, Senior Business Operations Manager
Catherine Conover, Director of Development
Stacey Shaw, Director of Communications
Tanya Amos, Website Coordinator
Shannon E. Ecke, Graphic Design Senior
Megan Krause, Information Specialist Coordinator
Mica Matsoff, Information Specialist
Denise Tanguay, Information Specialist

## Arizona State University Art Museum Ceramics Research Center 2004–2005 Artists Advisory Committee

Patricia Sannit, President
Sharon Armann, Secretary
Luis Baiz
Joan Baron
Jeremy Briddell
Esmeralda DeLaney
Julius Forzano
Kaori Fujitani
Billie Jo Harned
Bridget Cherie Harper, Treasurer
Peter Held, Curator of Ceramics
Sam Hodges
Jane Kelsey-Mapel, Vice President
Sandra Luehrsen
Seth Rainville
Jon Read, Graduate Student Representative
Betsy Rosenmiller
Nina Solomon

## Arizona State University Art Museum Staff

Marilyn A. Zeitlin, Director/Chief Curator
Susan Ables, Administrative Assistant
Michael Brennan, Security Officer
Mili Choi, Curatorial Assistant
Howard Chook, Security Officer
Deborah Deacon, Windgate Intern
Ted Decker, Manager, Special Museum Initiatives
Bruce Erno, Chief Security Officer
LaReal Eyring, Museum Store Manager
Tiffany A. Fairall, Curatorial Assistant/Assistant Registrar
Fausto Fernandez, Exhibition Specialist
Peter Held, Curator of Ceramics
Stephen Johnson, Chief Preparator
Kimberly Kendall, Lead Security Officer
Heather Sealy Lineberry, Senior Curator
Jean Makin, Print Curator
Rudy Navarro, Windgate Intern
Janet Pinhorn, Intern
Jason Ripper, Security Officer
John D. Spiak, Curatorial Museum Specialist
Laura Stewart, Curator of Education
Anne Sullivan, Registrar
Theodore Troxel, Exhibition Specialist
Kathleen T. Wacker, Business Manager
Dawne Walczak, Office Specialist

## Friends of the ASU Art Museum as of April 15, 2005

### *Patron Members*

Ardie and Steve Evans
Jean and Harold Grossman
Diane and Bruce Halle
Lori and Howard Hirsch
Karen and Gabor Jilly
Merle and Steve Rosskam
Paula and Jack Strickstein
Mikki and Stanley Weithorn
Joann and Louis Weschler

### *Contributing Members*

Judy Ackerman and Richard Epstein
Mark Anderson
Gerry Apker
Sandy Besser
Theodore Braun
Richard and Mary Holland
Sara and David Lieberman
Susan Drescher-Mulzet and Mark Mulzet
Claire and John Radway
James and Joanne Rapp
Janet and Roger Robinson
Arlene and Mort Scult
Peter Shikany
Beth Ames Swartz

### *Supporting Members*

Audrey and Daniel Abrams
Beverly Adams
Caralee Allsworth
Gerry Apker
Alma and Gilbert Augenblick
Gary Avey
Sandra Baldwin
Sue Bass/Andora Gallery
Lynn and John Battenberg
Marlene and Ralph Bennett
Martha Benson
Carole and Joel Bernstein
Allison and Robert Bertrand
Carmen and Allan Bieber
Kathleen and Michael Bishop
Jack Black
Rachel and Jerry Blank
Dale and Marshall Block
Linda Blumel and Ron Finkel
Blaine and Brian Bolton
Carol and Bill Bombeck
Sara Brandt
William Bruder
Deanna and Robert Burger
Garth Clark and Mark Del Vecchio
Elaine and Sidney Cohen
Jane and Bruce Cole
Ruth Comstock
Joyce Cooper
Paula Cooperrider

Paula and Joel Corman
Mary Grant-Coster and Chris Coster
Barbara Balkin Cottle
Jane and Nick Couvdos
Catherine Conover Covert and Christopher Covert
Marcia and Lance Cypert
Sandy and Steve Davis
Denise and Dave Decker and Family
Ted G. Decker
Janet Deever
Liz and Phil Douglis
Sue and Frank Eyrand
LaReal and LeRoy Eyring
Debbie and Richard Felder
Gretchen Freeman and Alan Silverman
Ruth Garrison
Louisa Gerking
Peggy and Milton Glick
Karla and Walter Goldschmidt
Susan and Richard Goldsmith
Debbe Goldstein and David Pliskin
Midge and Jerry Golner
Mary Grant-Coster and Chris Coster
Thomasena and Eugene Grigsby
Trent Guerin/g² Gallery
Anne and Anthony Gully
Wendy Haas
William Hardin
Billie Jo Harned and Jack Rudel
Diane Harrison and Sherman Avel, MD
John Hill and Linda Sheppard
Linda Hirshman and David Forkosh
Camille and Skip Holt
Bill Howard
Richard Jemison
Ruth Jones
Jane Jozoff
Eric Jungermann
Kevin Keogh
Maureen and John Kricki
Mr. and Mrs. Norwin Landay
Carolyn Lavender and Brian Hughes
Sally and Richard Lehmann
Rene and Norman Levy
Marcia and James Lowman
John Lujan
Lesley and Marshall Lustgarten
William Lykins
Elizabeth and Paul Manera
Mary Ann Marcus
Jane Metzger
Bonita and Russell Nelson
Farraday Newsome and Jeff Reich
Peggy Jane and Francis Nickerson
Carol and Pat Nunzio
Doris Ong
Audrey and Leonard Oppenheimer
Craig Pearson
Dan Pote
Joan Prior and John Armstrong
Brian Quinn
Karen and Don Randolph
Don Reitz
Joan and Norton Remes
Louise Roman
Laura and Herb Roskind
Lance Ross
Barbara Rousso
Star and Seymour Sacks
Mindy Sand
Linda and Sherman Saperstein
Adrienne and Charles Schiffner
Lillian Schneider
Rana and Joseph Schwartz
Joseph Segura
Sue and Bud Selig
Lisa Sette
Ellyce and Eddie Shea
Sandra Sheinbein
Tana and Ridge Smidt and Family
Dorothy and Harvey Smith
Mary Statzer and Gene Kadish
Mary Stevens and Mack Jones
Michelle Stuhl and Howard Werner
Tom Sunderland
Faith Sussman and Richard Corton
Selma and Jerome Targovnik
Kathy and Fritz Thomas
Kathleen and Richard Vanesian
Annie Waters and Bob Ryan
Sandi Whyman and James Tanner
Karen and Glenn Williamson
Richard Winkelmann
Pamela Wood
Sybil and Shelby Yastrow
Judy and Sidney Zuber

## ASU Art Museum Supporters

**$500,000+**
Stéphane Janssen

**$100,000–$499,999**
Edward "Bud" Jacobson

**$50,000–$99,999**
Sara and David Lieberman

**$25,000–$49,999**
Linda Hirshman and David Forkosh
Joan and David Lincoln

**$10,000–$24,999**
E. Rhodes and Leona B. Carpenter Foundation
HBB Foundation
Institute of Museum and Library Services
Mikki and Stanley Weithorn
Windgate Charitable Foundation

**$5,000–$9,999**
Arizona Commission on the Arts
Arnold Horwitch Family Charitable Foundation
The Blakemore Foundation
Friends of Contemporary Ceramics
Jack and Grace Pruzan Faculty Fellowship
Karen and Gabor Jilly
Lila Wallace Foundation

**$1,000–$4,999**
Artists Advisory Committee, Ceramics Research Center
Rea Bennett and Jim Kaufman
City of Tempe Municipal Arts Commission
Ardie and Steve Evans
Evelyn Smith Family Exhibition Fund
Friends of Mexican Art
Midge and Jerry Golner
Ellie and Mark Lainer
Michael S. Ovitz
Janet and Roger Robinson
Lance Ross
Lisa Sette/Lisa Sette Gallery
Ellyce and Eddie Shea

Linda Sheppard and John Hill
Peter Shikany/PS Studios
Tana and Ridge Smidt
Michelle Stuhl and Howard Werner
Lawrence Van Egeren
The Zaltec Familian and Lillian Levinson Family Foundation

**$500–$999**
Elaine and Sid Cohen
Paula and Joel Corman
Monroe Klein, MD
Joanne and James Rapp
Merle and Steve Rosskam
Joan and Ron Yagoda

**$25–$499**
Anonymous
Charlotte and Michael Applen
Sandy Besser
Blechmann Asset Management Group
Janet and Martin Blinder
Dale and Marshall Block
Rena Bransten
Desiree and Franklin Brewer
Wendy J. Brewer
Gloria and Anthony Conyers
Paula Cooperrider
Elizabeth Carrie Decker
Theodore Joseph Decker
Diane DeGraff
James F. Fuhs
Wendy Haas/Cervini Haas Gallery —Gallery Materia
Diane Harrison and Sherman Avel, MD
Honeywell Engines
Debbie and Scott Jarson
Dr. Eric Jungermann
Orme Lewis, Jr.
Muriel Magenta
Maxine and Jonathan Marshall
Rosalyn and Morton Munk
Anned Muse
Hermine and Roy Olson
The Ronald and Maxine Linde Foundation
Edith Rosskam
Barbara Osif Rousso
Armena Schmidt
Jean Schroeter
Orinda and Douglas Seitz
Lorraine and Mark Shwer
Grace Anthony Smidt
Harrison Gallo Smidt
Remy James Smidt
Mary Stevens and Mack Jones
Faith Sussman and Richard Corton
Agnese Udinotti/Udinotti Gallery
Sarah Wentworth

## Ceramics Leaders of ASU (CLĀ) Members as of April 15, 2005

*Patron*
Judy Ackerman and Richard Epstein
Mark Anderson
Jane and Larry Ash
Becki and Scott Currey
Jean Grossman
Edward and Carol Hall
Billie Jo Harned and Jack Rudel
Leah Kaplan and The Kaplan Family Foundation
Sara and David Lieberman
Joan and David Lincoln
Doris Ong
David and Josefine Perry
James and Joanne Rapp
Janet and Roger Robinson
Edith Rosskam
Merle and Steve Rosskam
Judith and Robert Rothschild
Arlene and Mort Scult
Paula and Jack Strickstein
Barbara and Donald Tober
Mikki and Stanley Weithorn
Migs Woodside

*Regular*
Ted Adler
Jennifer Allen
Wesley Anderegg
Dan Anderson
Sharon and Neil Armann
Alma and Gilbert Augenblick
Darcy Badiali
Clayton Bailey
Luis Baiz
Joan Baron
Sue Bass and Erica Kern
Martha Benson
Sandra Blain
Linda Blumel and Ron Finkel
David Bradley
Sara Brandt
Lucy Breslin
Jeremy Briddell
Deanna and Robert Burger
Gail Busch
Rose Cabat and June Cabat
Jane and William Canby
Annetta and Robert Chester
Garth Clark and Mark Del Vecchio
Larry Clark
Tom Coleman
Jeanne Collins and Paul Brooker
Joyce Cooper
Catherine Conover Covert and Christopher Covert
Val Cushing
Esmeralda DeLaney
Stephen DeStaebler
Josh DeWeese
Barbara Dow
Leatrice and Mel Eagle
Lyndall Eddy and Phillip Wagoner
Sanam Emami
Janet and Jerry Etshokin
LaReal and LeRoy Eyring
Betsy Fahlman-Ball and Dan Ball
Ken Ferguson
Anita Fields
Robert "Irish" Flynn
Julius Forzano
Gretchen Freeman and Alan Silverman
Kaori Fujitani
David Furman
Julia Galloway
Joe Gans
Beverly Goldfine
Midge and Jerry Golner
Marc Grainer and Diane Grainer
Harold and Jean Grossman
Maurice Grossman
Fred and Emily Gurtman
Wendy Haas
Roberta and Bruce Hammer
Bridget Cherie Harper
Jason Hess
John Hill and Linda Sheppard
Halldor Hjalmarson
Sam Hodges
Richard and Judith Jacobs
Sarah Jaeger
Amanda Jaffe

Stéphane Janssen
Mark Johnson
Jun Kaneko and Ree Schonlau
Karen Karnes
Ann and Keith Kelly
Jane Kelsey-Mapel
Tom Kerrigan
Meagan Kieffer
Michelle Korf
John Kotelly
Les Lawrence
Rene and Norman Levy
Judy and Samuel Linhart
Frank Lloyd
Sandra Luehrsen
Luo Xiaoping
Marilyn Lysohir
Alvin and Nancy Malmon
Mary Ann Marcus
Maxine Marshall
Brad Miller
Herbert and Susan Miller
Clara Moore
Ric Moriarity
Nora Naranjo Morse
Farraday Newsome and Jeff Reich
Nobuhito Nishigawara
Jeff Oestreich
Georgette Ore
Jeanne Otis
Jess Parker
Jan Peterson
Susan Peterson
Michael Prepsky
Ken and Happy Price
Helme Prinzen
Seth Rainville
Jon Read
Alison Reintjes
Don Reitz
Mary Roehm
Louise Roman
Jim Romberg and Lynette Jennings
Betsy Rosenmiller
Kathy Royster
Star and Seymour Sacks
Patricia Sannit
Linda and Sherman Saperstein
Darlene Schaumburg
Katie and Randall Schmidt
Rana and Joseph Schwartz
Nancy Selvin
Junya Shao
Sherri Sheldon
Charles Sherman
Lorraine and Mark Shwer
Linda Sikora
Nina Solomon
Linda Speranza
Chris Staley
Phyllis and Stuart Steckler
Deanna Stulgaitis
Faith Sussman and Richard Corton
Richard Swanson
Akio Takamori
Nancy Tieken
Jack Troy
Sandra Trujillo
Rudy and Wanda Turk
Agnese Udinotti
Eric Van Eimeren
Patti Warashina
Kurt Weiser and Christy Lasaler Weiser
Neil Williams
J. Robert and Jeanne Wills
Tara Wilson
Suzanne Wolfe
Rosalie Wynkoop
Evans and John Wyro
Sherrie Zeitlin

## ASU Art Museum Community Partners

ASU Public Events/Beyond Broadway
Ben Franklin Press
Sandy Besser
Devra Breslow
Wann Caron
The Caterwauls
China Mist Tea Company
City of Tempe Fire Department
City of Tempe Public Works Department
Garth Clark and Mark Del Vecchio
Elizabeth Carrie Decker
Ted G. Decker
Theodore Joseph Decker
Geny Dignac
Tom Eckert
Frank Lloyd Gallery
Judie and Howard Ganek
Marylou George
Christine and Lawrence Gipe
William Hardin
Tatiana Hensley
Interlingua
Stéphane Janssen
KAET Channel 8
Mark Klett
Sara and David Lieberman
Maxine and Jonathan Marshall
Max Edward Martínez
Carol and John McAfee
Mesa Fire Rangers
MJ Bread
Ramone Muñoz
Richard Notkin
Susan Harnly Peterson
Phoenix Family Museum
Phoenix YMCA Teen Center Program
The Phoenix Zoo
Rayn Dance Theatre
Susan and Scott Robertson
Darlene Schaumburg
Ellyce and Eddie Shea
Charles Sherman
Star Video Duplicating
Summer Winds Nursery
SuperSigns
Richard Swanson
Tammie Coe Cakes
Robin and John Trick
Scott Walker
Kurt Weiser
Mikki and Stanley Weithorn
J. Robert Wills
Dr. R. K. Winkelmann
Marilyn A. Zeitlin

# Contributors

**Garth Clark** is a leading authority on international ceramics and has authored more than thirty books and some one hundred catalogue essays and articles on ceramic art. His titles include *American Ceramics: 1876 to the Present* (1986); *The Mad Potter of Biloxi* (1989), which earned the Art Book of the Year Award from the American Art Libraries Society of North America; *The Potter's Art: A Complete History of British Pottery* (1995); and *Shards: Garth Clark on Ceramic Art* (2003). He has received numerous awards, including two honorary doctorates, and in 1996 was made a Fellow of the Royal College of Art, London. He is the recipient of the 2005 Frank Jewett Mather Award from the College Art Association for distinguished art criticism, which was first given in 1963 to Dore Ashton and Lewis Mumford; recipients have included Clement Greenberg, Robert Hughes, Roberta Smith, and Ada Louise Huxtable. Clark currently directs the Ceramic Arts Foundation, New York, and together with Mark Del Vecchio operates two galleries for modern and contemporary ceramic art in New York City and Long Island City, New York.

**Peter Held** is the Curator of Ceramics for the Ceramics Research Center, Arizona State University Art Museum, Tempe. He was formerly the Director and Curator for the Holter Museum of Art, Helena, Montana. A past resident artist at the Archie Bray Foundation for the Ceramic Arts, he has curated more than fifty exhibitions since 1989, including *Ashen Beauty: Woodfired Ceramics* (1990); *David Shaner: A Potter's Work, 1963–1993* (1993); *Sisters of the Earth: Native American Ceramics* (1994); and *A Ceramic Continuum: Fifty Years of the Archie Bray Influence* (2001), for which he edited the book of the same title. He serves as a Board Trustee for the American Craft Council.

**Toyojiro Hida** has been an influential craft curator and writer since 1979. The former Curator of the Craft Gallery at the National Museum of Modern Art, Tokyo, he is currently Associate Professor at the Kyoto Institute of Technology. A graduate in art history from Tokyo National University of Fine Arts and Music, he has curated many groundbreaking exhibitions, including *Modernism and Craftsmen* (1983); *A New Century in European Design* (1994), *The Domain of the Medium* (1994); and *Tradition in Japanese Crafts* (2000). He has also authored numerous books, including *Takamura Toyochika* (1980); *The Works of Sasaki Shodo* (1989); *The Domain of Craft* (2003); and *Craftsmen: The Producer of the Tradition* (2004), among others. He was awarded the Ringa Prize in 1994.

**Edward Lebow** is an award-winning author of museum catalogues and articles published in numerous national and international journals, including *American Craft, Studio Potter,* and *Ceramics: Art and Perception.* He curated the 1995 retrospective of ceramics by Ken Ferguson for the Nelson-Atkins Museum of Art in Kansas City and wrote the catalogue essay for the 1992 survey of Kenneth Price's ceramics presented at the Menil Collection in Houston and the Walker Art Center in Minneapolis. More recent contributions have appeared in the catalogues accompanying *Miró: Playing with Fire* at the George R. Gardiner Museum of Ceramic Arts in Toronto and *Robert Archambeau: Artist, Teacher, Collector* at the Winnipeg Art Gallery.

# Index

Boldface page numbers refer to illustrations and color plates. Endnotes are indicated with a letter "n" followed by the endnote number.

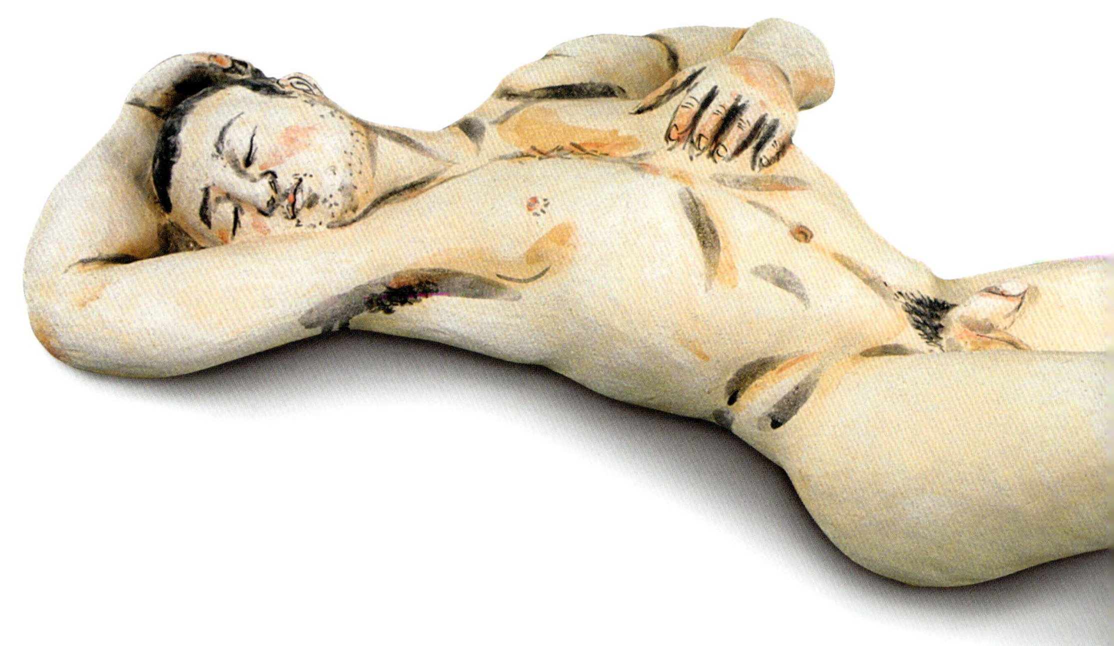